D1158070

More About Jane Austen

By the Same Authors

SPEAKING OF JANE AUSTEN

More About
JANE AUSTEN

By

Sheila Kaye-Smith

and

G. B. Stern

Harper & Brothers *Publishers*
New York *and* London

MORE ABOUT JANE AUSTEN

FIRST EDITION

G-Y

Table of Contents

More About Jane Austen

CHAPTER I

"What Is It About Jane Austen?"

G. B. STERN

BARBARA had asked if she could see me alone, because it was "madly important." Barbara is seventeen and a half, and we are not related, just good friends without any need for continual suppressed references in her mind to: "You are old, Father William," or in mine: "Honestly, I know it's difficult to believe, but you *will* feel differently when you're my age." Perhaps there is nothing more to say about her that would be relevant to my theme, except that her brain is potentially good, her mind and speech honest, her courage high, and her taste in nearly everything (according to my maturer values) fairly horrid. I like the child, and am always glad to see her; she has a sort of innocence which recalls the delightful naïveté of Catherine Morland; but that had to remain my private joke against her; a girl of her period, she had of course never read *Northanger Abbey*, otherwise it might have been fun to have heard her amazed and indignant rejection of such a charming prototype.

You may imagine, then, the quiet happiness which stole over me, my mills-of-God-grind-slowly reaction, when she flopped into the other big armchair and told me (getting it over with a rush) that deeply and finally she had fallen in love, and he was a distinguished soldier with a tough war record and all the manly virtues, but terribly old—I'd be surprised how old (" 'A woman of seven-and-twenty,' said Marianne . . . 'Can never hope to feel or inspire affection again!' ")—I received an impression of the middle thirties and hair greying at the temples . . . "though of course that couldn't matter less, if only silly people wouldn't keep on giving me kindergarten sums—'Don't forget, dear, when *you're* forty-one *he*'ll be a hundred-and-two.' . . ." Barbara paused for breath.

"Where's the real snag?" I asked.

For the first time she hesitated. Then: "It couldn't be more ghastly, and of course it *would* happen to me—he's simply bats on your Jane Austen."

I received the tremendous tidings in silence.

"It's his thing." And Barbara added, being a tolerant girl: "Nobody can help their thing."

"So if he's perfect in every other way, you can find it in your heart to overlook it?"

She was not too stupid to see through me. "Now you're being sarcastic, like the most Popular Mistress in the School. . . . The girls always fall for it; it's the masochistic streak in them. Yes, well, it was a shock, I don't deny it, when I first found out they were his bedside books and that he always took a couple of Janes with him when he went away—even to the Burmese jungle in the war. And d'you know," very earnestly, "I should have thought in anyone else that was a bit wanting, because she's only written six books, so he must have read them over and over and over again."

"The aged," I informed her, "do find quite a lot of pleasure in rereading."

"Oh, look here, he's not aged in that way; he doesn't read her because he's doddering and decrepit and can't read anyone else. I told you—he's got a brilliant intellect; he could *think* us all under the table whenever he wanted to."

"Come to the point, Barbara. You're serious about this man, I gather?"

"You've gathered right. I'm never likely to be so serious again."

"Then what do you want me to do? Talk him out of Jane Austen?"

"You couldn't."

"Talk you into her, then?"

Barbara drew a long breath and let herself in for it: "It amounts to that. I can't let him find me below standard in any way that's important to him. It might have been worse—it might have been Bach—or golf; if he were mad keen on golf, for instance, I'd have to take up golf and chuck my sailing."

"So as his vice happens to be Jane Austen—my poor baby, have you read nothing of hers?"

Out came the usual confession: she *had* read *Pride and Prejudice* because she had been taken to see the film, and it was marvellous; the book was not quite as good, but it made her laugh in places: where Mr. Bennet ticked off Mrs. Bennet. . . .

And they had been set *Emma* to read at school, but one of the girls had told her that Emma was a most ghastly snob, so she had decided not to be bothered with her.

I tried to stifle my invariable impatience at thus hearing Jane Austen pressed upon schoolgirls as a "classic." I would have her eliminated by law from every school curriculum. The stormier Brontës are not deemed so "suitable," not so prone to be labelled "just the right prize for Gillian or Rosemary or Jennifer"; and for that reason are usually preferred by the girls themselves. Fielding's *Tom Jones* is never pressed upon schoolboys because he is too sophisticated; yet Jane Austen is equally sophisticated (and mature, which is not to be confused with precocious); equally not meat for very young people. When we are young we read literally and miss the irony; we take it all as just "happening" in a drawing-room or in a village; if, missing out the irony, we take it as "happening" that Emma is a snob, naturally at that age we set up a resistance which may last for life; it never occurs to us that the author knows as well as we do, perhaps even better, that Emma is a snob.

So let us leave Jane Austen unread upon the shelves till we are ready for her. I wondered aloud at what age Barbara's man was drawn under the spell?

"Oh, I've never asked him; I'm avoiding the subject. I run like a hare when it crops up. I'll be all right, though, once I can get a line on what he can possibly see in her. What *is* it about Jane Austen? At least you can tell me that."

"Briefly?" I asked, again being like the most Popular Mistress in the School. But she was too intent on her own bewilderment to check my sarcasm, as she usually did.

"If it had been Nigel Balchin, for instance, or Nevil Shute, or Evelyn Waugh"—she tumbled out some more contemporary names, weighted by a few titles of biography and political economy. "But I really did imagine that Jane Austen was only read by maiden aunts in drawing-rooms, or by sissy men." . . . And once more, lest there should be any mistake, I had to hear the achievements of this splendid male at all times when he was *not* reading his favourite bedside books or packing his kitbag with superfluous Janes for the jungle.

"I could, of course, be strenuous about it; set my teeth and read the whole six about seven times each, and then pretend hard that they'd got themselves lodged in my system. I'd do more than that to please him, and to keep on being the one he's picked out from all the rest. But it wouldn't be honest, and I don't believe it would be convincing. You know when you see someone putting on an act, and it's all hollow, no solid rock behind it, you get it in one. And that's not good enough from me to him. How can I be sure that some accomplished woman with those sort of wide-apart Pallas-Athene grey eyes won't crop up in his life at any moment and know her Jane Austen backwards. And then I'm sunk."

I argued a discrepancy between Pallas Athene's eyes and a passion for Jane Austen; the intruder, I remarked, would be more likely to have dancing hazel eyes; I could see them as she entered with elastic step, certain of her welcome, with *Emma* or *Northanger Abbey* under her arm.

"What a *beast!*" exclaimed Barbara. Then sanity overtook her, and she laughed; but insisted nevertheless that whatever her eyes, wise, wide apart or dancing, that woman with her elastic-sided boots was a potential rival and a menace; and she, Barbara, should lose no time in arming herself against her.

"What you and he have found together doesn't entirely hinge on that, does it?" I suggested mildly.

"No. No, of course not. But I'm so far gone that I'm plain afraid of how I'd feel or behave if she *did* come along; like Othello, I expect."

Her predicament was genuine; and indeed she was sorely puzzled, this true child of 1949, at what had so undeservedly befallen her. I thought that the moment had come to be helpful.

"I remember a long time ago, in the early days of American tourists to England, being told of a lady who informed the guide: 'Now say, we've only half an hour in this spot, and what we want you to give us is the broad elemental Canterbury proposition.' "

Barbara got my point and laughed. "Yes, please, that's what I meant."

What is it about Jane Austen?

I could talk about this author for hours, but it must be to one of my peers in the realm; enthusiasm and quotation would be useless in conveying to Barbara that curious deep browsing satisfaction that no other writer in the world could give us; that lovely escape from reality—not into fantasy, but into a different kind of reality; that bewildering blend of sense and good manners, irony and gaiety, sophistication by grace and not by experience, that rose up from every page; and the more familiar the page, the stronger the flavour which rushed to meet you at once without first having to "get into it"; unfailing as one's intimate and endless conversation with the friend one sees every day, with whom one lives in the same house, meeting the same people, doing the same work; and still twenty-four hours is not long enough for all the daily discoveries to be shared between you. . . . And still six books would not be long enough, and indeed we could do with sixty or more of the same delight; except that the six never stop yielding up treasure—

"Wait a minute," Barbara broke in crossly; "you're just using *words*. Anybody can say 'treasure.'"

I gave her right (though inwardly, for discipline's sake). And changed "treasure" for "detail."

"There are two sorts of exploring, aren't there? Over a wide range, in broad sweeps; or the fascination of getting to recognise every minute detail about a group of people, all their absurd psychological processes—"

"Psychological processes? In Jane Austen?"

"Certainly. It's old-fashioned to believe because a girl wears high-waisted dresses and a feathered bonnet when she goes out, that she's got no psychological processes."

Barbara scored by informing me (with apparent meekness) that feathered bonnets were exactly what girls wore now. But then, really anxious for the information that might make her free of the kingdom, she once more became gentle, attentive and diffident. As though to her man she were saying, standing before him with bent head, her hands humble and empty:

> You see me, Lord Bassanio, where I stand,
> Such as I am: though for myself alone
> I would not be ambitious in my wish,
> To wish myself much better; yet for you
> I would be trebled twenty times myself;
> A thousand times more fair, ten thousand times
> More rich;
> That only to stand high in your account,
> I might in virtues, beauties, livings, friends,
> Exceed account: but the full sum of me
> Is sum of nothing; which to term in gross,
> Is an unlesson'd girl, unschool'd, unpractis'd;
> Happy in this, she is not yet so old
> But she may learn; happier than this,
> She is not bred so dull but she can learn.

So I went on trying to explain the inexplicable: "There's no such thing as a Jane Austen prescription; if one could write it out and hand it to another author, and they could write a story exactly according to the lines laid down, it would be a flat failure."

"You mean, we have to take for granted there's magic to start with, or there'd be thousands of Jane Austens instead of only one?"

"Yes, and the magic-to-start-with is— Oh, *dear*, Barbara, it feels awfully like work, to enlighten your darkness. And I never did like work out of working hours."

Barbara, who was quite well off as well off goes in these days, promised me a bottle of Calvados (from her father's cellar).

Thus bribed, I went on: "The initial magic, or call it her peculiar genius, is to create three-dimensional characters, character in the round, living, speaking, faulty human beings whom you remember and enjoy for ever, like Falstaff or Micawber or Mrs. Proudie or Countess de Soldar or Alan Breck or—"

"Swot that visiting-list. And go on with your Jane Austen."

"She's neither bitter nor boisterous about her people; instead, she has irony, tenderness, clear vision, and most of all a gorgeous sense of their absurdity which is never really exaggerated into more than life-size. You're absurd, I'm absurd, and so in some way or other are most of the people we meet. She does not have to distort or magnify what they're like; she just recognises them, delights in them herself, and then recreates them for our benefit without illusion or grandiloquence, and without any array of special circumstance, of drama, for instance, or horror, or even topical events of the day: luckily for her and for us, to leave them out was natural and not forced at her period, unless you were a gentleman actively involved in war and politics and religion and the struggle for existence; at her period you could be one of an isolated group living in the same country neighbourhood in England, without in any way meriting the reproach of escapism. Escape need have no 'ism' when we escape into Jane Austen; and when we have to return there's no wrench, no jolt, no descent from the aeroplane, no bump back to life with a shock, no subsequent daze and resentment; it's escape from our reality into her reality, and we can fuse our world with hers which is curiously and essentially 'unrubbishy.' So there they are, her characters, concentrated for our benefit into a small circle of time and space, deliciously giving themselves away not only in action but by the smallest working of their motives and preoccupations, absolutely unaware, of course, that anyone is catching them out at it. It's no crime to be a lover of Jane Austen; but if you aren't, you can't understand why we find her so restful because you're much too inclined to translate 'restful' into 'soporific'; if we just wanted an author who would send us nicely to sleep, we should *not* go to Jane Austen; she's restful from exactly the opposite reason: we're alert all the time when we're reading and rereading and re-rereading Jane, otherwise we might miss something, some tiny exquisite detail, an almost imperceptible movement in the mind of one of her characters. Her poise is unassailable; you can trust it, and that's restful in itself. The same with her judgments; you can trust them and relax; mind you, to be able to relax with an author, again isn't the same thing as to say she's relaxing; the air of Bath is relaxing, but the air of Jane Austen isn't; she's pungent, she's bracing; you're breathing good air while you read Jane, and so you feel well. Apart from her gorgeous sense of humour, her vision is so fairly and evenly adjusted that you don't have to get distracted all the time by the author's own prejudices and neuroses subconsciously creeping in and distorting the whole thing, and having to make allowances for environment—"

"Darling, do you think you could stop talking like a handbook on psychoanalysis? Because if it's just to please me—"

"Dear little girl, I'd forgotten for the moment that you were there; I was too absorbed in trying to work out for myself this broad elemental Jane Austen proposition. When you come along with a simple straightforward question, I always try to give you a simple straightforward answer, but 'What is it about Jane Austen?' is a real teaser."

"I'm sorry," Barbara murmured, a little subdued by the memory of how vital it was to her happiness that I should mysteriously whip out of my pocket the key which apparently no locksmith could procure. "Jane Austen's witty, isn't she? *He* says so, and I've seen him quietly smiling at her. But is she really *funny,* ever? Not like those ghastly clowns in Shakespeare, but funny for nowadays?"

"Irresistibly funny, and you really can take that from me. You see, she knows so much about her characters which they don't begin to know about themselves, that we can get together with her; and like froth-blowers, the more we get together, the merrier we can be. It's rather a lonely thing to be a Janeite on one's own. Now if another Janeite were here, we could compare you with Marianne Dashwood and get enormous satisfaction out of it, he and I and Jane Austen herself."

It was plain that Barbara noticed my pronoun for "another Janeite": "Thanks, that's a perfectly grand idea!" And I could see her registering silent determination that "he" and I should never meet.

"Marianne," I went on dreamily, "marries a man miles older than herself."

"Happy with him?" asked Barbara in an offhand way. One did not have to have a water-diviner's rod stirring and lifting in one's hand to register that directly she got home, Barbara would rummage about until she found this Marianne Dashwood, and start in on *Sense and Sensibility* at once.

"Gloriously happy. Everybody prophecied he was too old, but age doesn't make much difference really when you're in a certain condition of heavenly accord. . . . That's what I was trying to say just now about lovers of Jane Austen: that outside people exist and move about and talk and have their being and make asses of themselves all the time for your special entertainment."

" 'Lord, what fools these mortals be!' " Barbara quoted, right on the nail's head. "But Oberon wouldn't do froth-blowers with Puck; he always kept him a bit snubbed and remember-your-place, even about those four idiots wandering through the wood."

"Oberon had no sense of humour," I agreed.

Reassured on the subject of Jane Austen's humour, Barbara now required reassurance at the other extreme:

"One doesn't always want to be laughing," she remarked severely; "I mean, doesn't she ever get down to serious subjects? Can she think deeply *at all*?"

"Fine weather is true weather just as much as stormy weather, Barbara. She's not a Brontë, if that's what you're after, but her philosophy is water-tight, her wisdom lucid, and her principles incorruptible. Must authors be obscure before you can respect them? As for Jane Austen's emotional capacity, Rebecca West says— Bring me *The Strange Necessity,* will you? It's in my room, on one of the shelves next to my bed. Oh, and while we're about it, David Cecil's monograph on Jane Austen, and the first volume of *The Common Reader* by Virginia Woolf."

Barbara brought them, despising me that I had not these passages by heart. She did not know she was in for quite a long session. I found the page in *The Strange Necessity* and read aloud:

> It is dangerous to feel much unless one is great enough to feel much; and wise and charming as she is, her glance would be the pinprick to many an inflated emotion, though to many real ones she would be blind. . . . There are those who are deluded by the decorousness of her manner, by the fact that her virgins are so virginal that she is ignorant of passion. But look through the lattice-work of her neat sentences, joined together with the bright nails of craftsmanship, painted with the gay varnish of wit, and you will see women haggard with desire or triumphant with love, whose

delicate reactions to men make the heroines of all our later novelists seem merely to turn signs, "Stop" or "Go" toward the advancing male. And the still sillier reproach, that Jane Austen has no sense of the fundamental things in life, springs from a misapprehension of her place in time. She came at the end of the eighteenth century, when the class to which she belonged was perhaps more intelligent than it has ever been before or since, when it had dipped more deeply than comfortable folk have ever done into philosophical inquiry. Her determination not to be confused by emotion, and to examine each phenomenon of the day briskly and on its merits, was never a sign of limitation. It was a sign that she lived in the world of Hume and Gibbon. Her cool silence on the wherefore of the why is a million times more evidential of an interest in the fundamental things of life than " 'Brother, brother, how shall I know God?' sobbed Alyosha, who by this time was exceedingly drunk," or any such sentence from those Russians.

David Cecil came next:

> . . . the power to create living characters. It is true that she only draws them in their private aspects. But this is not a superficial aspect. A man's relation to his wife and children is at least as important a part of his life as his relation to his beliefs and career; and reveals him as fundamentally. Indeed it reveals his moral side more fundamentally. . . . For it is a profound vision. There are other views of life both higher and wider; concerned as it is exclusively with personal relationships, it leaves out several of the most important aspects of experience. But on her own ground, Jane Austen gets to the heart of the matter; her graceful unpretentious philosophy, founded as it is on an unwavering recognition of fact, directed by an unerring perception of moral quality, is as impressive as those of the most majestic novelists. Myself I find it more impressive. If I were in doubt as to the wisdom of one of my actions I should not

consult Flaubert or Dostoievsky. The opinions of Balzac or Dickens would carry little weight with me: were Stendhal to rebuke me, it would only convince me I had done right: even in the judgment of Tolstoy I should not put complete confidence. But I should be seriously upset, I should worry for weeks and weeks, if I incurred the disapproval of Jane Austen.

And lastly, Virginia Woolf:

. . . nothing is more obvious than that this girl of fifteen, sitting in her private corner of the common parlour, was writing not to draw a laugh from brother and sisters, and not for home consumption. She was writing for everybody, for nobody, for our age, for her own; in other words, even at that early age Jane Austen was writing. One hears it in the rhythm and shapeliness and severity of the sentences.

The girl of fifteen is laughing in her corner, at the world. Girls of fifteen are always laughing. They laugh when Mr. Binney helps himself to salt instead of sugar. They almost die of laughing when old Mrs. Tomkins sits down upon the cat. But they are crying the moment after. They have no fixed abode from which they see that there is something eternally laughable in human nature, some quality in men and women that for ever excites our satire. . . . But Jane Austen knew it from her birth upwards. One of those fairies who perch upon cradles must have taken her on a flight through the world directly she was born. When she was laid in the cradle again she knew not only what the world looked like, but had already chosen her kingdom. She had agreed that if she might rule over that territory, she would covet no other. Thus at fifteen she had few illusions about other people and none about herself. Whatever she writes is finished and turned and set in its relation, not to the parsonage, but to the universe.

Sometimes it seems as if her creatures were born merely to give Jane Austen the supreme delight of slicing their heads off. She is satisfied; she is content; she would not alter a hair on anybody's head or move one brick or one blade of grass in a world which provides her with such exquisite delight.

Nor, indeed, would we. For even if the pangs of outraged vanity, or the heat of moral wrath, urged us to improve away a world so full of spite, pettiness, and folly, the task is beyond our powers. People are like that—the girl of fifteen knew it; the mature woman proves it. . . . The discrimination is so perfect, the satire so just, that, consistent though it is, it almost escapes our notice. No touch of pettiness, no hint of spite, rouse us from our contemplation. Delight strangely mingles with our amusement. Beauty illumines these fools.

"*Well!*" Barbara exclaimed. I could see she was impressed by the champions I had chosen for the summing-up, and their unassailable reputations; she could hardly contend that Virginia Woolf, Rebecca West or David Cecil were likely to have spent their adult lives tatting and tattling in drawing-rooms. "Well, is it fair, when Youth comes to you questing for information, just to pick up a book and read aloud, instead of thinking it out for yourself?"

"And what do you suppose I've been doing for the last hour? Talking in my sleep? Anyway, surely it's a waste of time to think it all out for myself when I'm wholly in agreement with what has been thought out for me. And lately there's 'Harvey'—"

Barbara stared at this inclusion among my authorities. "I haven't seen it, but—"

"Pulitzer Prize play. The curtain of Act I, Scene I. Dowd is waiting for his sister, and to pass the time pleasantly, offers to read to his friend Harvey. He selects *Pride and Prejudice*: 'You liked *Sense and Sensibility*? Same author.' And begins to read as the stage gradually darkens: 'It is a truth universally acknowledged that a single man in possession of a good fortune must be in want of a wife.' And Harvey listened, fascinated."

"But—but Harvey's a large white rabbit."

I laughed. "Run along home, Barbara. And don't fall on your Jane Austen and start gulping them all down at once, and then come back to me and complain of indigestion. Take it easy. Rid your mind of all preconceived notions and prejudices, with 'maiden aunt' cut out, and 'drawing-rooms' and 'we did one of them at school.' Jane Austen is simply part of pleasure, that's the easiest way to think of her. I can't give you any other formula."

"Can you give me a cocktail instead?" Barbara suggested hopefully, "and then I'll go."

Over our cocktails she asked: "In what order shall I tackle them?"

"Damn it, don't you listen to a single word I say? You don't have to 'tackle' them at all. Who do you think you're obliging?"

She grinned happily at having teased a rise out of me, which indeed is never difficult where my special authors are concerned.

"Please, in what reach of this delectable stream shall I first dip and bathe and wallow in the sunshine?"

As I knew perfectly well she was going to begin with *Sense and Sensibility* because of Marianne's excellent taste in marrying Colonel Brandon in the sere and yellow (at the age of thirty-six), I advised her to leave that one to the last, because on the whole it was the least popular. ("Then of course I shall begin with it" was plainly evident in Barbara's mutinous silence.)

"Start with *Emma*"—("I'll *end* with *Emma*," reflected Barbara). "It's my own favourite, but it would be rather perverse of me for that reason not to push it forward; like the headmaster who treats all the other boys in the school more instead of less leniently than his own son."

"I never saw much sense in that, either; it proves that he

dared not trust himself really to treat them all alike. Must I forget that Emma was a ghastly snob? Was my girl friend wrong?"

"My darling, Emma at the age of twenty was the direst snob ever exposed on the pages of any novel. The fun of it is that that's the whole point of the book: Jane Austen knew it herself; so did Mr. Knightley, the man Emma worshipped . . . he was a great many years older than she was—"

"For the love of Mike, stop telling me about all these Elders; I'm beginning to feel like Susannah." Barbara blushed very easily; a habit which belongs to no period of history and ceases at no period of civilisation. When she cooled down: "Did Jane Austen herself—?"

"Nobody knows. Her elder sister burnt any letters that might have enlightened us."

"Good wench!"

This was perhaps the first time that Cassandra had been so heartily commended, and in those terms.

"Anyhow, Emma in the end finds out for herself what an awful Miss Know-All she's been, and how wrong every time. And all the minor comedy characters (not that you could ever call Mr. Woodhouse minor) are sheer heaven. After *Emma,* read *Northanger Abbey*—no, *Mansfield Park,* and for the same reason: the stage is rich with comedy and all the characters give themselves away. And it's really a good exciting story too; things happening all the time; not improbable things, but real-life things; only you must remember in *Mansfield Park* that the so-called hero and heroine, Fanny and Edmund, are both super-prigs; and this time I'm afraid without exonerating circumstances, because Jane was *not* aware of it herself; she was tenderly fond of Fanny; fonder even than of Elizabeth Bennet, the world's sweetheart; maybe because Fanny couldn't look after herself, and Elizabeth could. Besides, Elizabeth was obviously Jane Austen and authors are not usually narcissistic in their affections."

"Yes, you said all that in *Speaking of Jane Austen.*"

"D'you mean to tell me that you've read *Speaking of Jane Austen*?"

"Yes. Of course. Don't lose your temper. You're flattered really."

"In that case, may I ask why you've been squandering my time and energy this evening?"

"Not squandering." Barbara finished her cocktail and looked round for her handbag. "And I'm very grateful. The book was awfully good, though it wasn't my subject, I just read it in the spirit of pure investigation, whereas now—"

"Now, investigation has ceased to be pure?"

"It *has* become a bit personal, I'm afraid. 'Bye, darling. I'll ring you up when the spell's begun to work."

Left alone, I reflected that if the spell worked too well, and if irony took command of the situation, Barbara's man might become the Man Who Never Read Jane Austen Now. . .

CHAPTER II

"The Age in Which We Live"

SHEILA KAYE-SMITH

THAT atrocious thing, the eighteenth century," wrote Baron von Hugwl at the beginning of the twentieth. Also: "What a wretched affair the eighteenth century." Then again: "How vulgar the eighteenth century: a purely this-world affair." No doubt his strictures were based on his view of eighteenth-century philosophy, which he held to have taken a downward path towards intellectual chaos, and to which he attributed most of the heresies and miseries of nineteenth-century materialism.

It is not a popular view today, when many people look back nostalgically on a period when civilisation was not mainly a matter of plumbing nor did culture consist, as Miss Edith Sitwell so aptly says, in "reading all the wrong books." But my point here is that one does not have to think either with or against the Baron in order to be happy in Jane Austen's own time, for never did any time more lightly enclose its field of space.

It is true that all the novels were written at the fusion of the eighteenth and nineteenth centuries. They belong to the period of the French Revolution and the Napoleonic wars, to Hume's history and Kant's philosophy; but whether we think ill or well, much or little, of these things, they need not concern us, for Jane Austen ignores them entirely.

It is a commonplace that she ignores the big historical events of her day, but it is not so often realised how little she stresses its particular manners and tastes. We may feel tantalised by her habit of never describing any clothes in detail—

giving us only perhaps the name of a material or the hint of a sprig or a spot—of bringing us into rooms only vaguely furnished or sitting us down to meals without a menu. But such a procedure gives a much better sense of timelessness than minute illustration—which perhaps is why so many illustrated editions make us feel less intimate with the characters than before we saw them depicted.

Of course there are references here and there to passing fads and fancies, but it is remarkable how little of the really transient has a place in the novels. The poets and writers she mentions are mainly those that we too know and admire—Pope, Scott, Cowper, Byron, Fanny Burney . . . even Mrs. Radcliffe is not unknown to us, though perhaps unread. Possibly we should not have heard of "Lovers' Vows" if it had never been rehearsed at Mansfield Park, but we have heard of and possibly seen all its proposed alternatives, while in her pages Shakespeare has entirely escaped from earlier misprisions and receives the same honours as in our own day.

Her world is small, and it is possible that we might receive more shocks in a larger one—for instance, cock-fighting and bear-baiting would almost certainly have cropped up among the amusements of a less restricted society. But Jane Austen's men—for the most part leisured country gentlemen—indulge in no sports more bloodthirsty than such as survive in the countryside today. Nor are we given a hint of the savage criminal laws which were a part of "that atrocious thing." Only our own knowledge informs us that Mr. Rushworth's boasted "zeal after poachers" might involve their transportation for life. It is true that in *Sense and Sensibility* there is mention of a "sponging house," but it is only a glancing reference and has no real place in the story.

Indeed, in order to give Jane Austen's times their full importance in the substance and texture of her stories it is necessary, at least in my case, to make a deliberate act of evocation. The sense of reality while reading the novels is so complete that her times as it were become ours and we accept any discrepancies with the present day from her side of the interval rather than our own.

For instance, how tranquilly we pass into the atmosphere of Hartfield in that first scene of *Emma,* when she and her father are sitting alone after Miss Taylor's wedding to Mr. Weston. "The wedding over, and the bride-people gone, her father and herself were left to dine together, with no prospect of a third to cheer a long evening." We know, however, that a third, and a very acceptable third, was soon with them in the person of Mr. Knightley, who "had returned to a late dinner after some days' absence" with the John Knightleys in London. It was not till I had read this scene many, many times that it struck me as odd that neither Mr. Knightley nor his former hosts had attended Miss Taylor's wedding. She was his very old friend and Isabella Knightley had been her pupil. Surely they should both have been present on such an occasion. But they were not, and no explanation, no apology, is made for their absence. It apparently does not require one.

So strange did this omission seem to me that I noted it in our earlier book, *Speaking of Jane Austen,* and the note brought me some very interesting correspondence, with glimpses of letters and family records, which showed that most weddings at this time were celebrated almost privately. This was no doubt in reaction against the riotous celebrations of an earlier date, which had frequently passed the bounds of decorum, if not of decency. (It is hard to believe that less than thirty years divide Miss Taylor's wedding from the cat with walnut shells tied to its feet which so disturbed the new-found bliss of Humphrey Clinker.) Only near relations would be present, and doubtless none would be expected to come from a distance, which excuses the Knightleys.

A certain amount of finery is sanctioned at weddings, for does not Mrs. Elton comment on the absence of it at Emma's? "Very little white satin, very few lace veils; a most pitiful business. Selina would stare when she heard of it." Sir Thomas Bertram gives each of his daughter's bridesmaids a new gown, and it was also considered right to start married life with a new carriage, for the absence of this in Maria Bertram's case is considered exceptional. But other times seem underlined more strongly than usual in the absence of Mrs. Rushworth, who before her son's wedding had retired with "true dowager propriety to Bath." It seems strange to us today that the bridegroom's mother should not have been present, yet there is a reason for that too to be found in the period. Owing no doubt to the difficulties and expenses of travel, honeymoons were not the general rule and did not start on the wedding day. Later on, we know, Mr. Rushworth took Maria to Brighton, but her first removal was to his and her own house, where perhaps it was just as well not to find a mother-in-law in residence.

2

Emma also has a wedding-trip, which gives her at last her longed-for glimpse of the sea. But she would not have had it if the John Knightleys had not been able to keep Mr. Woodhouse company while she was away. He is the reason why Emma, in spite of her wealth, is the least mobile of the heroines. In the other novels there are frequent changes of residence—even Fanny Price spends some months at Portsmouth —but in *Emma* the scene never varies, because the principal character is never away from home.

Leaving home was then a much more serious matter than it is now, for it generally involved an absence of several weeks. The Miss Steeles apparently stayed for months at Barton Park and again for months with their cousins in Bartlett's Buildings. Elizabeth Bennet and Maria Lucas disappointed Lady Catherine de Bourgh by staying only six weeks with Mr. and Mrs. Collins, while Catherine Morland had been a month at Northanger Abbey before suggesting she should go home. Which made Eleanor Tilney ask why she was in such a hurry to leave them—" 'Oh, because she had been there so long'—'Nay, if you can use such a word I can urge you no further. If you think it long—' 'Oh, no, I do not indeed. For my own pleasure I could stay with you as long again.' And it was directly settled that, till she had, her leaving them was not even to be thought of."

When we consider this hospitality we realise how not only the time but the *tempo* has changed. Life, though shorter—Mrs. Dashwood at forty was not thought likely to live another fifteen years—was very much slower and less crowded with single events. People had more leisure—more time to spend in one another's houses. Of course such visits necessarily involved the incorporation of the guest in the normal life of the family, for it would have been impossible to suspend it for so long by any special treatment or entertainment. It is true that Mr. Collins drove out Sir William Lucas in his gig, "showing him the country," but then Sir William had come, exceptionally, only for a week, and when he went away "the whole family returned to their usual employments."

One reason for these long visits is to be found in the difficulties of travel. Jane Austen does not emphasise these as some of her contemporaries have done, but a visit of only a few days could not be worth the expense and discomforts of a journey lasting for the whole of one of them or even longer. Catherine Morland's journey from Northanger to Fullerton was only seventy miles, but it took her all day, even with an early start, while though Darcy might think Mrs. Collins settled within an easy distance of her family—"What is fifty miles of good road? Little more than half a day's journey"—Elizabeth insists that "My friend would not call herself *near* her family under less than *half* the present distance."

In her case the journey from Longbourne to Hunsford was broken in London, where she stayed with the Gardiners and Jane, but where there were no friends with houses on the road, accommodation must be found at inns if the journey was a long one. Mrs. Jennings and the Miss Dashwoods spent two nights on the road to London from Devonshire, and Mrs. Churchill, travelling from Yorkshire "with her own sheets," did the same. Even the Tilneys' journey of no more than thirty miles from Bath to Northanger Abbey involved the "tediousness of a two hours' bait at Petty France."

No wonder such expeditions were not made frequently, though "You would be amazed" says Mrs. Elton "to hear how my brother, Mr. Suckling, sometimes flies about. You will hardly believe me, but twice in one week he and Mr. Bragge went to London and back again with four horses."

As Maple Grove was a hundred and twenty-five miles from town, I am reluctantly compelled to agree with Mrs. Elton that this was a considerable exploit, to be equalled only by Willoughby's dash in the opposite direction to Cleveland in Somerset. We are not told what impelled the activity of Mr. Suckling and Mr. Bragge, but Willoughby had all the incentive of Marianne's illness and his desire for her pardon. He arrived some time after dark, for Eleanor saw "the flaring lamps of a carriage," but he had "left London this morning at eight o'clock, and the only ten minutes I have spent out of my chaise since that time procured me a luncheon at Marlborough."

Another reason for paying long visits, besides the time spent on the road, was the fact that such visits often took the place of that change of air and scene which most of us now find in an annual summer holiday. In Jane Austen's time the removal of a family from home to rooms at an inn or lodging-house was still exceptional. What a fuss is made about the John Knightleys' visit to South End!

Visits to the sea, as to inland watering places, were still made ostensibly for reasons of health—"A little sea-bathing would set me up for ever," says Mrs. Bennet when she wants to follow the regiment to Brighton. There is only one instance in the novels of a real honest-to-goodness holiday trip on modern lines and that is Elizabeth Bennet's "tour of pleasure" with her uncle and aunt. Change the horses for horsepower and we have something very like a modern motoring holiday.

3

Going to South End had prevented the John Knightleys' coming to Hartfield for the summer, which was apparently their usual custom. So it was arranged that they should spend the whole of "the Christmas" with Mr. Woodhouse instead of giving a share to Mr. Knightley. This visit emphasises another difference between the reigns of the sixth and the third Georges, and gives us a very different Christmas from our own. It was still in essence a religious festival, though on this occasion—after what had happened on the way home from the Westons' dinner party—Emma is relieved to find the snow too thick for her to go to church. At home there is no Christmas tree, no Christmas cards, no Christmas presents, even for the little Knightleys. All these things have to wait for Dickens and Queen Victoria. At the turn of the eighteenth century Christmas was mainly kept with family reunions, school holidays, "a roaring Christmas fire," and a certain amount of junketing.

In *Sense and Sensibility* Sir John Middleton characteristically looks forward to "that festival which requires more than an ordinary share of private balls and large dinners to proclaim its importance." Yet, returning to *Emma,* we find her considering anxiously "one complete dinner engagement," which there was "no avoiding, though at Christmas." There seems a little inconsistency here, which makes us wonder what Christmas really was like. Mr. Woodhouse welcomed his daughter and her family to Hartfield as a matter of course, but Edmund Bertram's absence at Christmas from his family at Mansfield Park is equally taken for granted when it occurs. Miss Crawford's remarks on his absence are not based on the time of year, indeed she suggests that Christmas may be the reason for his being away longer than he originally intended—"Is it Christmas gaieties he is staying for?"

Christmas at Mansfield Park seems indeed to have been a very subdued affair, with everyone away—Edmund gone to stay with the Owens at Peterborough, William returned to Portsmouth and Crawford in London. No one thinks it at all strange that they should be away at such a time. "We miss our young men," says Sir Thomas—incidentally Tom has not come home for Christmas—but makes no comment on the season. Indeed I sometimes wonder if the old-fashioned Christmas of the Christmas numbers and Christmas cards had any real existence after the Middle Ages. It lingered on into the seventeenth century, when it was officially suppressed by the Commonwealth, but though revived in a measure at the Restoration it was soon to become—if we judge by Jane Austen's novels—a poor shadow both of its own self and of our present commercial adaptation.

4

In most of the county towns of England may still be seen the houses that were once the town houses of the neighbouring country gentry. Into Lewes, for instance, every winter moved families from the neighbouring parishes, anxious to escape the dreariness that would be their fate if they were cut off from society by bad weather and bad roads. Their houses, now mostly sliced up for democratic use, still stand on either side of the High Street, from the Cliffe up to St. Anne's, survivals of the days when no one would live in the country in winter who had sufficient wealth to escape to the nearest town.

In Jane Austen's time conditions had so far improved that this exodus from the countryside was no longer general. We frequently meet in the novels even well-to-do families—the Woodhouses, for instance, and the Bertrams—who stay in the country all the year round. But though it is no longer the rule, there is a smaller movement of a smaller circle to such centres as London and Bath.

In all the novels except *Emma* we encounter this migration, and in no less than three of them it plays an important part in the story. In *Northanger Abbey,* of course, it *is* the story—the story of Catherine Morland's visit to Bath, with the friends that she made there and the visit that she consequently paid to those friends. All her adventures stem from that invitation from Mr. and Mrs. Allen—"probably aware that, if adventures will not befall a young lady in her own village, she must seek them abroad"—and though the title of the book is *Northanger Abbey* only eight chapters are actually staged there as against eighteen in Bath.

Bath is again important in *Persuasion,* though not to the same extent. We note that till he was forced to economise, Sir Walter Elliot had always wintered in London. "But Mr. Shepherd felt he could not be trusted in London, and had been skilful enough to dissuade him from it, and make Bath preferred. It was a much safer place for a gentleman in his predicament: he might there be important at comparatively little expense."

Jane Austen herself had spent some years in Bath, and perhaps that is why in her novels it seems, at least to me, more clear and more alive than London. But this may also be because in the centuries between her day and ours it has changed less. We can still shop in the streets where Anne and Catherine and Isabella bought their hats and ribbons and changed their library books, we can stay at the hotel which used to be smaller as the White Hart, we can use the same Warm Bath as Mrs. Smith, and frequent the same pumproom as that wherein Catherine yawned and Isabella flirted. We can walk up to Belmont through those very streets where Anne's "musings of high-wrought love and eternal constancy" were "almost enough to spread purification and perfume all the way."

But in London the streets have changed. We should search Gracechurch Street in vain for the home of a family like the Gardiners, and if we had to find lodgings for a modern Willoughby we should not look for them in Bond Street. Wimpole Street and Harley Street, where the Middletons and Palmers had their town houses, have declined—if it be a decline

—from fashion to medicine, and we should not expect to see Mrs. Jennings' carriage waiting in Berkeley Street, unless she was visiting a shop.

Sense and Sensibility is Jane Austen's only "London" novel. It was the first of them to be written in its original form, and possibly for this reason the move from the country into the town is much more general than in the later books. Only Mrs. Dashwood and Margaret are left at home. But this may also be a device (and Jane Austen in her earlier work is not above devices) to keep all the characters together—which suggests yet another reason why London is chosen rather than Bath. I cannot convince myself that Bath would not have been a more likely winter resort for the Middletons, Steeles, and Palmers, for Willoughby and Colonel Brandon, all of whom lived in Devon or Somerset. London was nearly two hundred miles away, Bath only about fifty. But it was essential that the Ferrars and John Dashwood families should also be in town, and it is not likely that they would have crossed half England from Sussex to the smaller resort when London was so much nearer.

So everybody had to go to London, but I do not think that we gain thereby any remarkable insight into the life of the capital at this period. The setting is entirely social—shopping, visits, and evening parties—and but for the different names of streets, London might be Bath. It might also—again but for the different names of streets—be the London of the present day instead of the London where Fielding had only just ceased to be magistrate . . . which brings us back to the point from which we started.

5

While reading the novels of Jane Austen's immediate forerunners we are nearly always aware of another time than ours. This is not due only to a wider canvas, on which more differences are bound to appear, but to a conviction which she did not share that a novel to be worth reading must be several sizes larger than life. We do not find a fantastic and ridiculous plot only in the sensational works of Mrs. Radcliffe, but in the works of a presumably "straight" novelist like Maria Edgeworth. The plot of *Belinda,* for example, brings us up at every twist and turn against a totally different way of fiction from ours. There is also to be reckoned with the clumsiness of an earlier technique, further hampered by a grandiose and artificial style in which the purple patch is assiduously cultivated.

We know what Jane Austen thought of the monstrosities of the circulating library, and it is not only the open parody of *Northanger Abbey* that brings them into ridicule, though here only is she explicit. "A heroine returning at the close of her career, to her native village, in all the triumph of recovered reputation, and all the dignity of a countess, with a long train of noble relations in their several phaetons, and three waiting maids in a travelling chaise-and-four behind her, is an event on which the pen of the contriver may well delight to dwell; it gives credit to every conclusion, and the author must share in the glory she so liberally bestows. But my affair is widely different . . . and no sweet elation of spirits can lead me into minuteness. A heroine in a hack post-chaise is such a blow upon sentiment as no attempt at grandeur or pathos can withstand."

"A heroine in a hack post-chaise . . ." thus she takes her aim at realism and makes her claim to sobriety. And since a novel dates less by its incidents than by its fantasies, we are less conscious in that hack post-chaise of the march of time than we should be did we travel in "several phaetons."

This sense of ease and familiarity is still further encouraged by the style. Here if we compare Jane Austen with other novelists of her day we can plainly see what we have escaped in the way of "grandeur and pathos." I have already noted the prevalence of the purple patch, but apart from this the ordinary narrative style of the period was highly artificial, though the worst infections of "Johnsonese" were on the wane. It was still considered necessary for books to be written in a different language from that commonly spoken, and Jane Austen's easy, colloquial, yet incomparably vivid style must have been something new to her readers. I doubt if at the time it did her much credit with a public debauched by *Rasselas* and kindred works, but we in this age may well be thankful. She is entirely without those digressions and asides which make us so time-conscious with Fielding, or indeed later with his ungrateful disciple Thackeray, nor—though no doubt her dialogue is sometimes more formal than common speech—do we get those interminable, monologuing, artificial conversations that Maria Edgeworth delights in.

Certain words and phrases, it is true, have changed their meaning. A candid criticism is now the reverse of kindly, and "I daresay" expresses doubt rather than conviction. But the number is small. Jane Austen is one of the easiest authors to read, and though she never tries us with a conscious aim at a literary style, she constantly achieves it by vividness of presentation and an unfailing instinct for the right word.

But the circumstance which I think most makes for our ease in that hack post-chaise is a psychological one. I cannot explain myself better than by sending the reader to the scene in *Pride and Prejudice* where Elizabeth, sitting down for want of a partner, overhears Darcy's remarks about her. "She is tolerable: but not sufficiently handsome to tempt me; and I am in no humour at present to give consequence to young ladies who are slighted by other men." What girl could ever forget that? And though Elizabeth "told the story with great spirit among her friends," it helps us to understand all her subsequent prejudices. I suspect, too, that it had its share in the motives that induced her change of heart, since Darcy's proposal—in spite of its deficiencies—might pass very well as an expiation.

Any girl in any period who has ever overheard a disparaging remark about herself—and which of us, however good or beautiful, has not?—will feel like a sister to Elizabeth Bennet here. And if a sister, then a contemporary, and not in *Pride and Prejudice* only, for all the novels are made up of these intimate touches of fellow-feeling . . . that scene at another ball when Harriet Smith is suddenly raised from abasement to exaltation by Mr. Knightley's invitation to dance—"Such a change! In one moment such a change! From perfect misery to perfect happiness." Or Anne Elliot's first meeting with Captain Wentworth after all the years—" 'It is over! it is over!' she repeated to herself again and again in nervous gratitude, 'the worst is over' "—And then the worse that followed, when he rose from the music-stool and said "with studied politeness: 'I beg your pardon, madam, this is your seat.' His cold politeness, his ceremonious grace were worse than anything" . . .

Even Fanny Price, who seems less like ourselves than any other heroine, has moments of sisterhood—chiefly, I think, moments that involve the discomfiture of Aunt Norris. Which of us does not triumph with her—or rather for her, for Fanny was incapable of triumphing over anyone, even Aunt Norris, and we are told "had feelings almost of a criminal" towards her on this occasion—when, after she has done all she can to spoil her niece's pleasure at being asked to dinner at the Parsonage ("and if it should rain, which I think exceedingly likely, you must not be expecting the carriage to be sent for you") Sir Thomas puts his head in at the door and asks: "Fanny, at what time would you like the carriage to come round?" . . .

But we could go on multiplying these instances indefinitely, for they are of the very stuff and texture of the novels. They make us forget that dinner is at four o'clock, that we work by candlelight, drop curtsies, travel in a post-chaise, dance country dances, and go on two-month visits to our friends. They are the common exchanges of everyday life, ordinary human reactions to humble events and small contingencies.

"That young lady," said Sir Walter Scott, "had a talent for describing the involvements, feelings and characters of ordinary life which to me is the most wonderful I have ever met with." Such involvements, feelings and characters do not change even with the centuries. And this I think is the chief reason why we have to perform a deliberate act of evocation before we consciously realise that Jane Austen writes of a different time from ours.

CHAPTER III

"Her Fine Eyes . . . Were Brightened by the Exercise"

G. B. STERN

IN JANE AUSTEN'S mind, good looks are invariably associated with good health. "Sickly" is her most contemptuous adjective to signify a girl's lack of allure for the male; sickly, not ugly, Elizabeth Bennet perceives this undesirable quality in Miss de Bourgh; and in her antagonistic mood to proud Mr. Darcy, rejoices at it. " 'I like her appearance,' said Elizabeth. . . . 'She looks sickly and cross. Yes, she will do for him very well. She will make him a very proper wife.' "

Freckles also were unattractive; and again naughty Elizabeth notices, in glee, that the rich Mary King suffers from freckles, glee because Wickham the Fortune-hunter has usefully attached himself to Mary King. Mrs. Clay too is apparently a martyr to freckles; and Anne Elliot marvels that her father, usually so lofty and fastidious in his estimate of a woman's looks, should yet in the case of Mrs. Clay show himself increasingly oblivious: "You cannot do better than well; or I should recommend Gowland, the constant use of Gowland, during the spring months. Mrs. Clay has been using it at my recommendation, and you see what it has done for her. You see how it has carried away her freckles." Gowland must have been a contemporary equivalent to Cleopatra's bath in asses' milk. Mrs. Clay, that clever adventuress, had to combat another blemish in the eyes of Sir Walter: a clumsy wrist; she was able (in our modern idiom) to rise above it.

A true hero in Jane Austen must first be tall; that is essential. After that, he must conform to her version of our modern slogan that handsome men are slightly sunburnt; for "open" and "glowing" are her favourite adjectives. When Anne meets Captain Wentworth again after eight years, "the years which had destroyed her youth and bloom had only given him a more glowing, manly, open look, in no respect lessening his personal advantages"; glowing can hardly mean anything but a healthy complexion—(remember that Wentworth was a sailor), yet what exactly did she visualise by "open"? Perhaps "straightforward" would be our nearest approach; the opposite to furtive; we would have had little success in offering her a hero with one of those mysterious subtle enigmatic faces; not open; not glowing.

Nevertheless, height came first in her estimation. Mr. Darcy towered above his fellow men; so did Mr. Knightley. "Underhung," an adjective constantly recurring in Jane Austen, like "open" and "glowing" has passed out of currency; it refers, no doubt, to the lower jaw projecting beyond the upper; lantern-jawed. Mr. Elliot was underhung, besides being not nearly tall enough to have a chance with the heroine; but Henry Crawford, who according to the jealous Mr. Rushworth is "such an undersized, little, mean-looking man," nevertheless succeeds in being fascinating to us as well as to both the Bertram girls and to the whole of London society. And when I say that he succeeds, and not that Jane Austen succeeds in making him so, it is because I firmly believe that he was originally intended by her as a candidate for Fanny's hand; and it was only near the end of *Mansfield Park* that she perversely exerted her authority to reduce his status—and who knows, also to correct his height? Henry Crawford may have begun as a tall man, tall as Mr. Darcy, tall as Mr. Knightley. Jane Fairfax, roused suddenly from abstraction to take an interest in Mr. Elton, whom she had never seen, can think of nothing else to ask but: "Is he—is he a tall man?" She had been dreaming, of course, of Frank Churchill, but the company thought it a perfectly natural question to come first.

As in real life, the characters in Jane Austen are chary of

using the actual word "beauty," and only bestow it where definitely recognised as an asset. Lady Bertram goes so far as to resent Mrs. Grant's achieving a tolerably good match without enough obvious beauty to merit her luck, a characteristic example of Miss Austen's delicious gift of irony. "She had been a beauty, and a prosperous beauty, all her life; and beauty and wealth were all that excited her respect. To know Fanny to be sought in marriage by a man of fortune, raised her, therefore, very much in her opinion. By convincing her that Fanny *was* very pretty, which she had been doubting about before, and that she would be advantageously married, it made her feel a sort of credit in calling her niece.

" 'Well, Fanny, I have had a very agreeable surprise this morning. . . . I give you joy, my dear niece.' And looking at her complacently, she added, 'Humph, we certainly are a handsome family!' " Take the parcelling-out of the Bennet family of girls: Lydia, the youngest, her mother's favourite, is the bouncing dairymaid type, with "good-humour" her only asset, by which we are trusted to understand that she will rapidly grow blowsy. But Jane, the eldest, really is a beauty: "Oh my dear, dear Jane. . . . I was sure you could not be so beautiful for nothing! . . . Oh, he is the handsomest young man that ever was seen!" Mrs. Bennet simply cannot open her mouth except to utter an injudicious sentiment better left unsaid; fortunately Jane's disposition was too sweet to be ruined. Even Mr. Fitzwilliam Darcy, walking about clothed in haughtiness at his friend Bingley's ball, asking no girl to dance, even Darcy acknowledges the beauty of the eldest Miss Bennet. "Tolerable" is another semiscornful adjective now fallen into disuse; Elizabeth was tolerable, but the great Mr. Darcy needed more than that. "She is tolerable, but not handsome enough to tempt me." How extraordinary that nevertheless and in spite of his own intolerable behaviour, Darcy does not wholly damn himself in our eyes. What can be his glamour, his glowing attraction? Even before Elizabeth falls for him, we begin to wish that she would; we desire to hasten on her forgiveness, and we fear that Wickham with his more agreeable manner may succeed in keeping her blind too long to Mr. Darcy's real quality. Of course, we may argue, he has breeding; and no doubt Wickham's good looks were cheap and flashy; certainly he cannot have been as tall as Mr. Darcy. And then suddenly in one simple sentence Darcy becomes physically attractive to Elizabeth, and we may breathe a sigh of relief: "Elizabeth walked on in quest of the only face whose features would be known to her. At last it arrested her; and she beheld a striking resemblance of Mr. Darcy, with such a smile over the face as she remembered to have sometimes seen when he looked at her. She stood several minutes before the picture in earnest contemplation." Curious, the skill of the born writer to achieve magic that can never be analysed; magic which here rises up from the page as though with a three-dimensional value. We are safe from Wickham now; for Elizabeth will never again think of her haughty wooer except as he appeared in that portrait; and when she confesses to Jane in her lively way, "but I believe I must date it from my first seeing his beautiful grounds at Pemberley," she is not very far from the truth. Elizabeth herself, as he remarked, was no beauty; nevertheless, she had fine eyes; Jane Austen admires Elizabeth's eyes excessively; and employs them as Darcy's Nemesis, a speedy revenge on him for his insufferable "She is not handsome enough to please *me*." And Nemesis moves quickly; Miss Bingley remarks, barely disguising her jealousy: "I am afraid, Mr. Darcy . . . that this adventure has rather affected your admiration of her fine eyes." "Not at all," he replied, "they were brightened by the exercise."

Undoubtedly vivacious and sparkling, Elizabeth can therefore be placed in the same category with Jane Austen's other brunettes, Mary Crawford and Marianne Dashwood, even though I cannot find confirmation that she was as gypsyish as either of these. Nevertheless, the blondes excel here as in all periods, all fable, all literature, deferentially acknowledged as the Show Girls.

I wish I may not be wrong (how one catches here and there the infection of her phrases!) in seeming to detect in Jane Austen that while submitting to this universal habit of tribute to the golden girls, she involuntarily betrays a slight personal penchant towards the dark vivacious type nearer her own looks. Indeed, her descriptions of Princess Goldilocks have a flavour of wistfulness, though every now and then she is irresistibly and most humanly impelled to create a really horrid character with that colouring; not only Isabella Thorpe and Maria Bertram, but Lucy Steele and Elizabeth Elliot. While all her dark girls were darlings. Yes, all; I repeat it defiantly, for I can hear her trying to argue with me that Mary Crawford was far from being any sort of a darling.

It was specifically stated that the fair Miss Bertrams could well afford not to be jealous of Mary Crawford's intrusion into their neighbourhood ("She was most allowably a sweet pretty girl, while they were the two finest young women in the county"). Anne Elliot had "delicate features and mild dark eyes"; Fanny Price and Elinor Dashwood were fair, and that adorable little chump, Harriet Smith, whose looks Emma so loyally overestimates. Indeed, and long before Anita Loos lifted her voice, I have always found brunettes are wont to overestimate blondes, while blondes can afford to be gracious and encouraging to their sister brunettes. . . . Naturally they emerge a little self-satisfied from being thus hymned and lauded; Troy's Helen so far surpassing Jason's Medea. In vain to remind us of Shakespeare's Cleopatra in her black-browed glory; has it not fairly recently become known that Cleopatra was a redhead?

"Bloom" appears to be an Austen essential to match "glowing" in the male; the loss of bloom weighs as a serious matter; especially when it overtakes a heroine before she is twenty. At twenty-seven, of course, bloom will have flown for ever; except in Anne Elliot's case, where a miracle of love restores it. We may smile indulgently nowadays at the idea that a second blooming at twenty-seven should be such a matter for incredulous thanksgiving; but before we ejaculate "how ridiculous!" we should take into account that probably young women of the nineteenth century *did* begin to lose their bloom halfway through their twenties. Anne Elliot is a character so free from personal vanity, so unselfish, so steeped in wisdom's own good sense, that we cannot but love her the more for her little lapse into normal gratification that the sailor hero who had thought her faded past all recognition, should turn to gaze at her with new eyes only because a personable stranger had apparently found her looks worth a backward glance:

> She was looking remarkably well; her very regular, very pretty features, having the bloom and freshness of youth restored by the fine wind which had been blowing on her complexion, and by the animation of eye which it had also produced. It was evident that the gentleman (completely a gentleman in manner) admired her exceedingly. Captain Wentworth looked round at her instantly in a way which shewed his noticing of it. He gave her a momentary glance, a glance of brightness, which seemed to say, "That man is struck with you, and even I, at this moment, see something like Anne Elliot again."

Although a gypsy, Marianne Dashwood must have been more than pretty; really beautiful; the author pauses in the narrative to allow us details instead of a mild summing-up. But later, ravaged by grief, she gives occasion for her half-brother to sound the familiar Dirge to a Young Woman Who Has Been a Beauty. Yet it is stated on the last page of *Sense and Sensibility* that she recovered her bloom after its premature decay; for Willoughby, mourning that she had become "Another's"—though he himself had previously also become Another's—always openly toasted young Mrs. Brandon and "made her his secret standard of perfection."

Unaware that her beauty is soon to fade, Marianne holds forth over the question of men's looks in a fashion intolerant and exacting as only seventeen can be; criticising her sister's choice of the amiable Edward Ferrars as "the kind of young man—there is something wanting, his figure is not striking—it has none of that grace which I should expect in the man who could seriously attach my sister. His eyes want all that spirit, that fire, which at once announce virtue and intelligence."

Catherine Morland, that ingenuous child, with far prettier manners than Marianne—(Marianne had none at all, so there can be no comparison)—was to make the same type of discovery over Henry Tilney, as Marianne over Willoughby: "of all manly dresses a shooting jacket was the most becoming"; while of Tilney: "His hat sat so well, and the innumerable capes of his great coat looked so becomingly important." All her partiality for his capes, however, cannot make of Henry as striking a hero as Darcy, nor as fetching a villain as Willoughby. He was only "rather tall"; and were not Catherine bewitchingly modest in her estimate of what she could ever hope to attract, "rather tall" must have had little chance with her. Yet—"his address was good"; Henry used wit and satire without cruelty; with that in his favour, he might well remain not quite a handsome man. Catherine herself had only just learnt with astonishment that she had any pretensions at all to be admired; we are told she was: "for many years of her life, as plain as any. She had a thin, awkward figure, a sallow skin without colour, dark, lank hair, and strong features." Moreover, we first meet her as a healthy young tomboy, kind to her nice little brothers and sisters, noisy and wild, hating lessons and even cleanliness, and with a strong predilection for rolling down the green slope at the back of the house. At fifteen came the dawn of hope: "appearances were mending; she began to curl her hair and long for balls, her complexion improved, her features were softened by plumpness and colour, her eyes gained more animation and her figure more consequence." An odd phrase; I cannot at any moment of her girlhood visualise Catherine Morland's figure with such a label, for "consequence" in the Austen vocabulary means importance. Perhaps "poise" is nearer to how we should describe her accession to a little more dignity than a schoolgirl carries. " 'Catherine grows quite a good-looking girl; she is almost pretty today,' were the words which caught her ears now and then; and how welcome were the sounds! To look almost pretty is an acquisition of higher delight to a girl who has been looking plain the first fifteen years of her life than a beauty from her cradle can ever receive." If we marvel that the heroine of this particular book is deliberately described in such moderate terms, it must be remembered that Jane Austen is here exercising her satirical talent to guy those more splendiferous creatures of Mrs. Radcliffe's popular romances, and her joy is in pricking the balloon by deliberate understatement. Let us follow Catherine to her first ballroom in Bath, chaperoned by Mrs. Allen, and see how she fares with only such strictly rationed charms: "She was now seen by many young men who had not been near her before. Not one, however, started with rapturous wonder on beholding her, no whisper of eager enquiry ran round the room, nor was she once called a divinity by anyone. Yet Catherine was in very good looks and, had the company only seen her three years before, they would now have thought her exceedingly handsome."

While we are quoting phrases, I must recall being "in looks," where today we would be more inclined to say "looking her best"; and we must not forget either the frequent tribute of "elegance." Emma says of Mr. Elton: "He was reckoned very handsome, his person much admired in general, though not by her, there being a want of elegance of feature which she could not dispense with." "Elegant" is still in vogue, but rarely if ever when we speak of young unmarried girls. "She knows how to wear her clothes" would be more in accord with the sort of phrase likely to be heard in the 1940's. But we hear of Eleanor Tilney that: "a good figure, a pretty face, and a very agreeable countenance; and her air, though it had not all the decided pretension, the resolute stylishness, of Miss Thorpe's, had more real elegance." I have an idea, while we are still discussing the Tilneys, that Jane Austen despises elderly men, or at all events fathers of a grown-up family, who preen themselves on their good looks. General Tilney was "a very handsome man," etc. and of Sir Walter Elliot in *Persuasion*: "He had been remarkably handsome in his youth, and at fifty-four was still a very fine man. Few women could think more of their personal appearance than he did . . . he considered the blessing of beauty as inferior only to the blessing of a baronetcy"; both these gentlemen are presented to us so warmly wrapped in greatcoats of their own conceit as to be entirely detestable. Forever complacently thinking and speaking of appearance, Sir Walter refers to his own with immense approbation, and to others with an air of deploring their unfitness to be coupled in the same street with himself, metaphorically and actually: "Sir Walter, without hesitation, declared the Admiral to be the best-looking sailor he had ever met with, and went so far as to say, that if his own man might have had the arrangement of his hair, he should not be ashamed of being seen with him anywhere. . . . 'How is Mary looking?' said Sir Walter, in the height of his good humour. 'The last time I saw her she had a red nose, but I hope that may not happen every day.' 'Oh! no, that must have been quite accidental. In general she has been in very good health and very good looks since Michaelmas.' "

But we must reread *Emma*—a task from which I am never averse—to learn how two dark young beauties respectively subjugate a tall hero with a decided manner and a handsome though somewhat rattle-pated young sub-hero; while the golden-haired Harriet, falling in love three times with amazing rapidity, finally finds her level with a plain sensible young farmer, who shocked Emma by being totally "without air." Yet when the young of our own period sternly criticise Emma Woodhouse for her snobbery, they are a little inclined to forget that it is at least offset by her disarming lack of conceit, forever fancying that the eligible men of the neighbourhood, Mr. Elton, Mr. Churchill, Mr. Knightley, are in love with

Harriet and not herself. She swaggers about her judgment, which proves always wrong (but that is the whole point of the book), and is childishly eager to exact full respect as mistress of her father's house; but when it comes to proposals, Emma gets taken by surprise every time; she is incredulous and can hardly find speech to express her indignation with Mr. Elton for not finding Harriet fair enough to transcend all other considerations: "She was a very pretty girl, and her beauty happened to be of a sort which Emma particularly admired. She was short, plump, and fair, with a fine bloom, blue eyes, light hair, regular features and a look of great sweetness."

When Emma paints Harriet's portrait, she has no scruples in recommending her little friend's beauty by adding to her stature (could Harriet have been dumpy?), and by touching up her eyebrows and eyelashes ("It is the fault of her face that she has them not," remarked Mrs. Weston.) Nor is it envy of the beauty of Jane Fairfax which causes Emma to dislike her until nearly the last chapter; but that she has been fatally bored by Miss Bates's injudiciously thrusting down her throat this niece's many perfections; it was natural that perverse human nature should strongly react in the opposite direction. Apart from this, Emma admired Jane, admitting her elegance:

> After a two years' interval, she was particularly struck with the very appearance and manners which for those two whole years she had been depreciating. Jane Fairfax was very elegant—remarkably elegant; and she had herself the highest value for elegance. Her height was pretty, just such as almost everybody would think tall, and nobody could think very tall; her figure particularly graceful; her size a most becoming medium, between fat and thin, though a slight appearance of ill-health seemed to point out the likeliest evil of the two. Emma could not but feel all this. And then her face—her features—there was more beauty in them all together than she had remembered; it was not regular, but

> it had a pleasing beauty. Her eyes, a deep grey, with dark eyelashes and eyebrows, had never been denied their praise; but the skin, which she had been used to cavil at as wanting colour, had a clearness and delicacy which really needed no fuller bloom. It was a style of beauty of which elegance was the reigning character, and as such she must in honour, by all her principles, admire it; elegance which, whether of person or of mind, she saw so little in Highbury.

"Elegance" recurs six times in a page; rarely can we trip up Miss Austen for such redundance; can it be that she herself once overheard someone accuse her, or worse still, her sister Cassandra, of a lack of elegance, to account for that indefinable quality having taken up a permanent lodging in her system?

Nowhere else in Jane Austen's novels do we meet with so much discussion on looks versus health as in *Emma.* Indeed, Frank Churchill gravely links the two, as we are presently to link them, though I trust in greater honesty, for Frank is here using all his dissembling talents to try and make dupes of Emma and Mrs. Weston; they must not suspect the secret engagement between him and sweet Jane Fairfax, nor his infatuation over every dark hair of her head, till circumstances force him to recant and reveal his love:

> "Did you ever see such a skin—such smoothness, such delicacy, and yet without being actually fair? One cannot call her fair. It is a most uncommon complexion, with her dark eyelashes and hair, a most distinguishing complexion! So peculiarly the lady in it. Just colour enough for beauty." "I have always admired her complexion," replied Emma archly; "but do I not remember the time when you found fault with her for being so pale?" . . . "You will be glad to hear," inclining his head, and whispering seriously, "that my uncle means to give her all my aunt's jewels. They are to be new set. I am resolved to have some in an ornament for the head. Will not it be beautiful in her dark hair?"

> "Very beautiful indeed," replied Emma; and she spoke so kindly that he gratefully burst out, "How delighted I am to see you again, and to see you in such excellent looks!"

But this is to anticipate; within the sequence of fiction, Emma is prevented from skipping (as we have just done), and Frank's duplicity arouses her generous defence of Miss Fairfax and her complexion: " 'Miss Fairfax is naturally so pale as almost always to give the appearance of ill health—a most deplorable want of complexion.' " Emma would not agree to this, and began a warm defence of Miss Fairfax's complexion. " 'It was certainly never brilliant, but she would not allow it to have a sickly hue in general; and there was a softness and delicacy in her skin which gave peculiar elegance to the character of her face.' " He listened with all due deference, acknowledged that he had heard many people say the same; but yet he must confess that to him nothing could make amends for the want of the fine glow of health. Where features were indifferent, a fine complexion gave beauty to them all; and where they were good, the effect was—fortunately he need not attempt to describe what the effect was. " 'Well,' said Emma, 'there is no disputing about taste. At least you admire her except her complexion.' He shook his head and laughed. 'I cannot separate Miss Fairfax and her complexion.' "

It would here seem that Jane Austen identifies her own opinion with Frank Churchill's falsehood; she quaintly associates a want of glow and colour with a lack of candour and integrity. It is no news to us that she builds her books on a structure of right principles, right sense and right taste; and that the name over the door of the building is "Proportion." Granted that Emma talks nonsense to Harriet—and what nonsense!—yet note the author's perfect command of fine shades: Emma's nonsense, and even Marianne Dashwood's wild inflated stuff, cocksure and over-youthful, is only just enough exaggerated—while still remaining credible to the characters and solution—for us to be sure that Jane Austen is herself delightedly aware of it *as* nonsense. (How sad that when Fanny Price sometimes talks or thinks *her* solemn humourless nonsense, we have no such reassurance passed to us from within.)

The theme of *Emma* and *Sense and Sensibility* is common to both girls: they will have to be chastened in the end; "have the nonsense knocked out of them," as fathers say when they send their high-spirited sons to school. Elinor Dashwood and Anne Elliot never talk nonsense; they are not like the other two girls, subjects for auto-intoxication, a sort of wilful headiness which Jane Fairfax owns to adoring in her Frank: " 'I did not make the allowances which I ought to have done for his temper and spirits—his delightful spirits—and that gaiety, that playfulness of disposition, which under any other circumstances, would, I am sure, have been as constantly bewitching to me as they were at first.' " Elizabeth Bennet and Mary Crawford do talk nonsense; but usually to divert not only others, but themselves; they can quite well stop whenever they please, because their nonsense is under control. Jane Austen's two most simple ingenuous characters, Catherine Morland and Harriet Smith, do *not* talk nonsense (except when Catherine is influenced by her friend Isabella and the romances of Mrs. Radcliffe); they are too honest and too gullible, listeners to nonsense, but not makers; directly Henry Tilney interprets Catherine's hyper-romantic outlook into terms of gay teasing nonsense, she is immediately ready to abandon it.

Emma's responsibility in planting Harriet's receptive mind —if we can call it a mind?—with snobbery and false nonsense may not be so heavy as would appear on the surface. Below the blame attaching to an older richer girl dominating the opinions of a protégée who so obligingly has none of her own, lies a very real admiration for Harriet's naive and unpretentious nature. It is significant as well as touching how Emma's subconscious humility is apt to deify these qualities, from a fundamental sense of what is lacking in herself, but to translate them, for current usage, into terms of fair and dark. Harriet is fair, and Emma only dark; but Harriet is also fair in making no claims; and Emma's passionate diatribe to Mr. Knightley on what Harriet may have a right to expect in the worldly line is perhaps not such headstrong nonsense as Mr. Knightley would have us believe, though her youth may have led her to word it foolishly, and we must grant him a wiser notion of what would or would not eventually make Harriet happier. Far indeed removed from snobbery was Emma's democratic assertion that Harriet had claims in her own right; of Harriet's bringing modesty and a good disposition as a more valuable dowry than Mrs. Elton's fortune of "as near £10,000 as makes no difference." And again, the anger lurking behind Emma's playful defiance—may it not be the conflict between her Jekyll and her Hyde? Because undoubtedly one side of her is for worldly status, social suitability and importance; a side which later, in secret anguish rejecting Harriet's suddenly incredible idea of marrying Mr. Knightley, goes back on its earlier recognition. We have a glimpse of Hyde there.

Nevertheless, much may be forgiven Emma; she is in love with Knightley; fears herself in danger of losing him; the same emotion working underground could account for her perpetual stress on Harriet's beauty . . . Emma would so gladly have shown fair for Mr. Knightley! She might have been at rest had she heard Mrs. Weston and Knightley in conference on that very subject; Mrs. Weston in affectionate praise and Mr. Knightley so offhand as immediately to fall under our darkest suspicion:

> "How well she looked last night!" "Oh, you would rather talk of her person than of her mind, would you? Very well; I shall not attempt to deny Emma's being pretty." "Pretty! Say beautiful, rather. Can you imagine anything nearer perfect beauty than Emma altogether—face and figure?" "I do not know what I could imagine, but I confess that I have seldom seen a face or figure more pleasing to me than hers. But I am a partial old friend." "Such an eye!—

the true hazel eye—and so brilliant! regular features, open countenance, with a complexion—oh, what a bloom of full health, and such a pretty height and size—and such a firm and upright figure! . . . She is loveliness itself, Mr. Knightley, is not she?" "I have not a fault to find in her person," he replied, "I think her all you describe. I love to look at her; and I will add this praise, that I do not think her personally vain. Considering how very handsome she is, she appears to be little occupied with it."

Emma and Harriet are the only two of Jane Austen's heroines who pair off with their equals: Emma with Mr. Knightley, Harriet with Mr. Martin. Pondering on this, I began to suspect a preoccupation with the Cinderella legend. All the rest of these young women (not only heroines in its traditional meaning) illustrate and restate the theme, though without sentimentality: they marry above their station, and achieve it on beauty and virtue in equal parts. Wise and prudent men like Mr. Bennet and Sir Thomas Bertram and Mr. Palmer married beautiful fools infinitely below them in wit and understanding as well as in wealth, rank and connections. Jane Bennet, we are told, had "her mind improved"; so had her sister Elizabeth, and Fanny Price, and Jane Fairfax; yet their beauty was what we may call a strong contributing factor; and it is doubtful whether Bingley or Frank Churchill, for instance, would ever have been sufficiently drawn to them by compassion alone; or even Edmund Bertram by his timid dowerless little cousin Fanny. Cinderellas all, they married the prince; they married a man who stooped to conquer. So did Catherine Morland; so did Elinor and Marianne Dashwood. I cannot recall a single instance in Jane Austen's books of the situation reversed. Anne Elliot? But she does not raise her Frederick while he is still poor and undistinguished; it was he who on the contrary raised his Anne from being a Cinderella in her father's household, when he has at last proved to Lady Russell, Anne's mentor, that he could offer

Sir Walter Elliot's daughter what he had previously lacked: distinction in his career, and prize-money.

We certainly hear more of Elizabeth Bennet's wit than of her looks, which except for her fine eyes, took such a second place compared with her elder sister's. Though her ability to spring over puddles, jump stiles, and, crossing field after field, walk three miles at a quick pace before breakfast, are of service in captivating Mr. Darcy, who "was divided between admiration of the brilliancy which exercise had given to her complexion and doubt as to the occasion's justifying her coming so far alone."

Jane Austen herself has often insisted that beauty is not wholly a matter of features, breeding and elegance, though these must all contribute, but that male admiration every now and then springs into flame from noticing the glow and sparkle of good health. To such an extent would her own conviction seem to be animating her heroes, that much of what she says might well be taken from its context and used today for advertising patent remedies. Captain Wentworth manages to keep his heart aloof from his early love, Anne Elliot, when he meets her in a second incarnation, faded by age and sorrow; then suddenly he catches sight of her at Lyme Regis when her looks have had the benefit of fresh sea air—"Her very regular, very pretty features, having the bloom and freshness of youth restored by the fine wind which had been blowing on her complexion, and by the animation of eye which it had also produced. It was evident that the gentleman (completely a gentleman in manner) admired her exceedingly."

Mens sana in corpore sano; the instant stimulating effect of a rival and a stranger on his indifference, must have given Jane Austen a happy moment when she first hit upon the device; her sense of irony could never flag while the little world about her consented so readily to nourish it.

Fanny Price alone is allowed by her creator to indulge in frail health without loss of feminine appeal: "My dear little creature, do not stay at Portsmouth to lose your pretty looks.

Those vile sea-breezes are the ruin of beauty and health." True indeed that Mary Crawford's opinion of the sea air contradicts our previous estimate of its effect upon Anne Elliot's pretty looks; but as Jane Austen persistently set up what we should nowadays call a "sales resistance" to every idea put forward by Mary Crawford, one need attach little importance to this.

What exactly could have been Fanny's ailment? We cannot but wonder, hearing so often of her indifferent health. She cannot, for instance, bear fatigue of any sort; perpetually she is advised to lie down, sent to bed before the ball is over, bidden walk in the shrubbery for some fresh air; she suffers from too much confinement in the house, yet droops all too visibly when Aunt Norris (who does not hold with fussing over the young, especially over the indigent young) despatches her twice across the Park on redundant errands after she had already been picking roses in the hot sun—

> "I dare say it will be well tomorrow. Suppose you let her have your aromatic vinegar; I always forget to have mine filled." "She has got it," said Lady Bertram; "she has had it ever since she came back from your house the second time." . . . "I cannot think I was unreasonable to ask it. How often do I pace it three times a day, early and late, ay, and in all weathers too, and say nothing about it?" "I wish Fanny had half your strength, ma'am." "If Fanny would be more regular in her exercise she would not be knocked up so soon. She has not been out on horseback now this long while, and I am persuaded, that when she does not ride, she ought to walk."

Her cousin Edmund not unnaturally feels guilt at her headache; for he had especially provided a ladylike horse to bear her, and then snooped it away again to let Mary Crawford ride it and show herself off as a natural horsewoman—a contrast tactfully underlined by the old coachman lest Fanny should have missed any of it: " 'She did not seem to have a thought of fear. Very different from you, Miss, when you first began, six years ago come next Easter. Lord bless you! how you did tremble when Sir Thomas first had you put on!' " Quietly Edmund brought a glass of Madeira to the sofa where Fanny lay, choked with tears. Lavender drops or a glass of wine were remedies frequently administered to the ladies, irrespective of whether their pain were of the heart or of the head. When poor passionate little Marianne Dashwood has been jilted by that scoundrel Willoughby, Mrs. Jennings in her good-natured way begs Elinor to take the invalid a glass of the finest old Constantia wine, prescribed to her late husband for his cholicky gout—"He said it did him more good than anything else in the world." Elinor compromises by drinking the wine herself; cynicism, somewhat beyond her age, reminded her that its "healing powers on a disappointed heart might be as reasonably tried on herself as on her sister." I am, however, darkly inclined to suspect that the doctor's enjoyable prescription had been invented by the late Mr. Jennings all out of his own head; surely a fine old wine would have been crossed off his diet sheet in double-quick time after a diagnosis of cholicky gout?

Returning to our own diagnosis of Fanny's chronic limpness, I should set it down physically to anaemia and low blood pressure; morally, to an inferiority complex and a touch of exhibitionism. . . . She had a talent for earning pity by saying sweetly and patiently that nothing was the matter with her and that she would be better presently. Again and again I am puzzled to account for never being similarly irritated by Anne Elliot, though she too was easily fatigued, probably from the same causes, anaemia and low blood pressure; yet she never exploits it either by positive or negative means; and if Fanny's champions (though I know of none except Fanny's author) should argue that the poor girl had been brought up in circumstances of poverty and overcrowding, I should and do reply that Anne may have been reared in all the spacious advantages of Kellynch Hall, but oppressed by unkindness and a lack of sympathy from her family; *she* had no affectionate brother William with whom to jump about when the hand-organ was in the street.

Jane Fairfax could make a trio with Fanny Price and Anne Elliot in struggling against "a great tendency to lowness"; she too caused her good aunt much anxiety by headaches and loss of appetite. We have already noticed her pallor; the reader is not in the least uneasy; remembering that while staying with her relatives at Highbury, Jane was enduring severe nervous strain; and that directly her irresponsible young man, Frank Churchill, released her from having to dwell on close daily terms with falsehood and prevarication, a trial contrary to her nature though not to his, she was likely to recover her full health as well as her spirits; though living against the grain might not altogether have accounted for the delicate throat which roused Mr. Knightley to expostulate with Miss Bates (in the indignant short sharp barks of a jealous watchdog), for permitting all those duets with a ghastly bounder who thought of nothing but showing off his own voice—(needless to say, "ghastly bounder" is not in the text).

Jane Bennet had the misfortune to get soaked to the skin when her matchmaking mother, in pursuit of Mr. Bingley as a son-in-law, insisted she should ride over on horseback to Netherfield Park. The apothecary was summoned; he kept her in bed with a violent cold, and dosed her with draughts of medicine unspecified; to Mrs. Bennet's delight, her daughter was so feverish and hoarse she had to continue an invalid in a strange house for nearly a week, nursed by her sister Elizabeth, while Mr. Bingley's acid sisters "convinced that no country advice could be of any service, recommended an express to town for one of the most eminent physicians." However, Jane Bennet's sweet and unselfish disposition had no need of any salutary discipline from a serious illness, and her author allowed her soon to recover; Mrs. Bennet, deeply disappointed, tried her utmost to delay sending the carriage to fetch them home; she had "calculated on her daughters remaining at

Netherfield Park till the following Tuesday, which would exactly finish Jane's week."

Feverish colds apparently needed continual care, then as now. Harriet Smith, usually a blooming little creature, causes the greatest alarm in the Rev. Mr. Elton when she is prevented from coming to the Weston party by a "putrid" throat. "Putrid"—would that be what we understand by septic? Mr. Elton's chivalry, however, turns out disconcertingly to be on behalf of the rich Miss Woodhouse, not the poor Miss Smith —" 'So scrupulous for others and yet so careless for herself. She wanted me to nurse my cold by staying at home today, and yet will not promise to avoid the danger of catching an ulcerated sore throat herself.' " Putrid—ulcerated—infectious —Harriet probably had influenza. She, too, is restored without complications to her normal health; but when lovesick Marianne Dashwood picks up a similar sore throat by miserably roaming at twilight in the wet, wild grass, it does not as obligingly depart, but develops into a "putrid fever." The Oxford dictionary defines "putrid" as decomposed, rotten, foul, noxious, corrupt; a putrid fever as typhus, and a putrid sore throat as gangrenous pharyngitis, diphtheria. The term would seem to have deteriorated not a little, though I have heard young ladies discuss "a perfectly putrid party." The chapter of *Sense and Sensibility* dealing with Marianne's illness gives us more detailed symptoms than any other in Jane Austen; it was important from the point of view of the story, in which the wilful headstrong girl, who always knew better than her elders, was obliged to suffer a complete change of heart. Any illness which was to bring her from lamenting Willoughby to accepting Colonel Brandon, had to be dangerous indeed. "Prescriptions poured in from all quarters and as usual were all declined." She spent two restless feverish nights, and was weary and languid by day, shivering on the sofa. By that time, (in my first reading of *Sense and Sensibility*) I shared the melancholy apprehensions of Colonel Brandon; I too was astonished at Elinor's calmness, and had almost reached the stage of wishing I could have been there myself to prod the elder sister to greater exertions. Only on the second day did they send for the apothecary, Mr. Harris. (Mr. Jones attended Jane Bennet, Mr. Perry, lord and king of apothecaries, the Woodhouses. Romeo's apothecary, however, is never inserted.)

Mr. Harris pronounced Marianne's disorder to have (of course) a putrid tendency; and by using the word "infection," he rapidly cleared the house; for Mrs. Palmer had recently had a baby; so they all departed except Mrs. Jennings. Bad marks against poor Marianne, the world's nuisance wherever she was invited as a guest. On the third day of illness, she was declared materially better, her pulse stronger, and every symptom more favourable. Scarcely had Elinor cheered up on this verdict than Marianne sank into delirium, and Colonel Brandon had to hurry off posthaste at dead of night to fetch her mother. With the apothecary's early morning call, my curiosity was again aroused, for he "talked of the relief which a fresh mode of treatment must procure." On this, Marianne grew visibly worse; and Mrs. Jennings, helping Elinor nurse her, grieved (aloud, I think) over "the rapid decay, the early death of a girl so young, so lovely as Marianne."

Punctually, as promised, the apothecary revisited his dying patient; all medicines had failed; the fever was unabated; Marianne remained in a heavy stupor—"He had still something more to try, some fresh application, of whose success he was almost as confident as the last"—A miraculous "application," for slowly, very slowly, she began to mend, and fixed her eyes on Elinor "with a rational though languid gaze" (difficult to reproduce on the stage). Illness had played its necessary part: exit Bad Willoughby for good; enter Good Colonel Brandon to receive his reward. Had Jane Austen been that inaccurate type of author who throughout the nineteenth century treated us to harrowing scenes of "brain-fever," a picturesque disease which, I have been assured by the medical profession, simply does not exist, no doubt but that brain-fever would have been Marianne's lot, instead of the neglected cold which developed by quick stages into influenza with threatening pleurisy and pneumonia. But was the actual word "pneumonia" not in circulation then? We can answer for an influenza epidemic being mentioned by name, for Mrs. John Knightley's apothecary, Mr. Wingfield, speaks of it as general and heavy; and her father, Mr. Woodhouse, counters with the opinion of his own Mr. Perry on whose word he fondly dotes: "Perry says that colds have been very general, but not so heavy as he has very often known them in November. Perry does not call it altogether a sickly season."

And with little Bella's throat, we enter upon a saga which to my mind has not its equal in all Jane Austen: the saga of Mr. Woodhouse at war with Mr. Wingfield. True, it cannot be said that this is exactly the leading theme in *Emma,* but we feel a little deprived when mere lovers occupy the scene. The saga begins offstage, during the previous autumn, when Mr. John Knightley, a man of strenuous and independent will, took his family to South End instead of to healthy bracing Hartfield. An awkward business, says Mr. Woodhouse, dwelling on this gravely in retrospect; and further remarks that (like Mary Crawford) he never had much opinion of the sea air.

> Mr. Wingfield most strenuously recommended it, sir, or we should not have gone. He recommended it for all the children, but particularly for the weakness in little Bella's throat—both sea air and bathing.
>
> Ah, my dear, but Perry had many doubts about the sea doing her any good; and as to myself, I have been long perfectly convinced, though perhaps I never told you so before, that the sea is very rarely of use to anybody. I am sure it almost killed me once.

At once the atmosphere crackled with the peril of this subject; and in vain Emma and the elder Mr. Knightley rushed in with futile attempts to divert attention; their cause is lost before the battle even begins. When Emma fatally suggests that

Isabella has not yet inquired after Mr. Perry, Mr. Woodhouse informs her that Perry is bilious (a fascinating item which we docket for later reference) and then in an offhand manner, a little dreamily, goes on to suggest that Mr. Perry had better look at little Bella's throat. The *casus belli* almost immediately shifts from little Bella's throat to the air of London. Mr. Woodhouse surprises us by his asserting that *nobody* is healthy in London, where the air is "notoriously bad." A brave man, old Mr. Woodhouse; a brave, rash man. Even Isabella, mildest and most yielding of daughters, flares up and retorts that their own part of London is superior to most others—"You must not confound us with London in general, my dear sir."

Nobody can accuse dear old Mr. Woodhouse of tact, but at least we can honour his intrepidity when, after telling them they had all arrived at Hartfield looking very ill, he makes a special reference to his son-in-law. "I think Mr. John Knightley very far from looking well." And then, as Jane Austen might have said a hundred years later, then the balloon went up . . . or would have gone up but for Emma's hasty intervention once again. It went up ten minutes later—"if you must go to the sea, it had better not have been to South End. South End is an unhealthy place. Perry was surprised to hear you had fixed upon South End." "I know there is such an idea with many people, but indeed it is quite a mistake, sir. We had our health perfectly well there, never found the least inconvenience from the mud, and Mr. Wingfield says it is entirely a mistake to suppose the place unhealthy." "You should have gone to Cromer, my dear, if you went anywhere. Perry was a week at Cromer once, and he holds it to be the best of all the sea-bathing places." After this, he has only time to quote Mr. Perry thrice more, when Mr. John Knightley, breaking in and breaking out, loses his temper in a big way. Metaphorically, he gets dragged from off his opponent by his brother George, leaving Mr. Woodhouse "rather agitated by such harsh reflections on his friend Perry."

Rarely can any family doctor, surgeon, specialist, physician, have been so highly esteemed by a patient as Perry the Apothecary of Hartfield; more than esteemed, saddled with a whole-hearted faith that must at times have been extremely embarrassing.

> Poor little Emma! You were very bad with the measles—that is, you would have been very bad but for Perry's great attention. He came four times a day for a week. He said from the first it was a very good sort, which was our great comfort; but the measles are a dreadful complaint. I hope whenever poor Isabella's little ones have the measles, she will send for Perry.

No hot-blooded young lover flinging down the gauntlet to all who dare assert that their lady falls by one fraction short of perfection, is more on the *qui vive* than Mr. Woodhouse where Perry is concerned. Psychoanalysis might discover, after prolonged search, how this Perry-fixation came into existence, or whether the life of Mr. Woodhouse ever knew a pre-Perry period? Nevertheless, we would heartily wish him not to be cured of it. And we would like to have been shown Mr. Perry professionally in action, to get an idea of his overwhelming personality; because setting aside his effect on Mr. Woodhouse, I might have been tempted to sum him up as a nice conscientious little man going his busy rounds on a trotting cob (for we have it on Miss Bates's authority that nothing came of the project for setting him up with a carriage). Yet in the course of this book we could hardly have seen him in action, for Mr. Woodhouse, though undisputed President of the Worshipful Society of Hypochondriacs, is in point of fact never ill at all; I should even add, after prolonged study, that unlike really tiresome hypochondriacs, he does not even desire to be ill, pretend to be ill, trade on being ill, unless for such minor exploitations as not going to the Coles's dinner-party or not taking the head of the table when he and his daughter themselves entertain a party for dinner. He is quite happy to be tolerably well, and yet a hypochondriac. Is this a contradiction in terms? I think not. Absorbed in making infinitesimal scratches on his own imaginary health-chart, he certainly at one instant felt the fire rather too much, but moves back his chair a little, a very little and all was well . . . but cares far more about the health of others than his own; and that keeps him entirely happy. He is, in short, a vicarious hypochondriac: a somewhat rare variety. Mary Musgrove—we shall come to her in a moment—can stand for a very fair example of the ordinary kind; she amuses us but we dislike her, and I should hazard a guess that she is as exasperating to her creator as to her husband, her family and her readers; for Mary concentrates entirely upon herself, and there, in contrast with our tender, affectionate Mr. Woodhouse, lies the whole difference. Solicitude for others, let us not deny it, is not quite as bad as anxiety on one's own behalf; the jagged edges of alarm are pleasantly blunted. Looking outwards instead of inwards, Mr. Woodhouse not only wins all hearts, but dwells in a constant state of romantic excitement, like a serendipidist who never knows from day to day what small treasure may be acquired. He worries over "poor Miss Taylor," Emma's governess, when she marries Mr. Weston and goes to live in a house of her own; he worries over James the coachman who does not like to put out two horses for a short way (nor for a long way); he worries over Mr. Knightley catching cold when he walks over to see them on an evening when it had been wet for half an hour in the morning; over Frank Churchill having to cross the road in Highbury where there might be a puddle, in order to get to the other side; over Jane Fairfax not instantly changing her stockings after she had been to the post-office in the rain; over the effect on old Mrs. Bates's digestion, of a fricassee of asparagus and sweetbreads; and over the digestion of everybody who refuses to include a nice smooth basin of gruel in their principal diet. He worries over the colds they will catch from a draught in the passage of The Crown where the Westons give their ball; and whether the rooms will be thoroughly aired—"rooms in inns are always draughty"—And as for dancing with open windows, never in a hundred years could Mr. Woodhouse have possibly imagined young people being allowed by Providence to do such a dreadfully dangerous thing. By every latitude and longitude, his is a thrilling, an enviable universe, with these continual hazards to counter by unselfish precautions on behalf of those who would very much rather that he left them alone to take an occasional risk, and with his perpetual championship of Mr. Perry where he grows fierce as a lion and unmerciful as a tigress whose cub is threatened. One can truly say Mr. Woodhouse never has a dull moment.

Mary Musgrove, we have already observed, is a hypochondriac of a vastly different colour, wretched not only in her imaginary sufferings but in the imaginary neglect of others towards these same sufferings. I have no conception how Mary would have diagnosed her complaints. A desire for importance appeared to be at the root of it all; and her hope to attract such importance by an account of her symptoms worked out as unsuccessfully as any clamour for consequence usually does, that cannot be left to spontaneous solicitude. . . . "I made the best of it; I always do; but I was very far from well at the time; and I do not think I ever was so ill in my life as I have been all this morning; very unfit to be left alone, I am sure. Suppose I were to be seized of a sudden in some dreadful way, and not able to ring the bell!" In the subsequent interview, even Anne, who handles Mary better than most other people, seeks in vain to discover what exactly was the matter? The list of symptoms is not particularly revealing: Mary's husband went out although she told him how ill she was; she could not bear the noise of her little boys; her in-laws talk and laugh a great deal too much for her, yet she complains of their neglect; at a dinner-party the day before, her mother-in-law took up all the room in the carriage and crowded Mary into the back seat—"I think it very likely that my illness to-day may be owing to it." The rest of Mary's hypochondria is merely repetition; she is a bore; and unlike Miss Bates or Mr.

Rushworth, not even an enchanting bore, terrible to their associates but ever glorious to us. Her uselessness when her own little son meets with an accident and hurts his back, her selfish hysteria when Louisa Musgrove dramatically falls from the Cobb at Lyme Regis, sets her in the class of those who are more to be despised than pitied.

The livelier of the two Musgrove sisters, Louisa, did not figure as a truly important character in *Persuasion*; yet even those who have only read the books of Jane Austen once "for the story," and remember little about them, will usually bring forth a vivid impression of wilful Louisa's accident; probably because it is a really dramatic scene with action and suspense; Henrietta Musgrove swoons at the sight of her sister lying apparently lifeless, and a stage crowd rushes along to enjoy the sight of a dead young lady "nay, two dead young ladies, for it proved twice as fine as the first report." Thrillingly conceived, the episode was probably invented originally for the purpose of character, not plot; for Jane Austen was aware that character should take precedence of incident as the horse should precede the cart; and Frederick Wentworth had somehow to be made aware that a determined disposition in a future bride was not perhaps as desirable as he defiantly believed; the defiance a fling-back at Anne's gentle surrender in her early youth to Lady Russell's persuasion that young Wentworth was no fitting match for a daughter of Sir Walter Elliot. But Louisa always knew her own mind, always acted on impulse, was always convinced that to heed any proffered advice could only be a sign of contemptible weakness; yet Louisa, after all, might have fared better and given less agony all round, had she not insisted on being jumped down the steep flight of steps from the high to the lower Cobb. Wentworth was unwilling, but no, she smiled and would not listen; too precipitate by half a second, she fell before he could put out his hands to catch her.

In a state of despair, Captain Wentworth knelt with her in his arms. Henrietta, as we have already noticed, swooned.

Mary not only had hysterics, but caught hold of her husband's arm to prevent him too from being of any use to his sisters (why nobody thought of knocking Mary unconscious as well, remains a riddle). Only Anne remained calm with no thought of herself; only Anne suggested everything that could be of practical service in this terrible emergency. It may be, not at once but in the course of the next few days, that Wentworth realised how not only in her returning beauty was Anne lifted supreme over any other girl he had met or was ever likely to meet. Reviewing the scene of Louisa's accident, I myself was struck by another excellent reason for loving Anne and rejecting Fanny Price; try to imagine how Fanny, instead of Anne, would have behaved in the crisis . . . . There would have been *three* dead young ladies, nor two; and no one left with presence of mind to suggest on the spur of the moment that it should be Captain Benwick and not Captain Wentworth to rush for a surgeon, as the former already knew the neighbourhood and would not lose time in searching (A "surgeon"; apparently for this particular case, not an apothecary? Our own cry would be for a doctor unspecified, in all cases of emergency; the separate functions of surgeon, apothecary and doctor appear to have changed since the early nineteenth century; indeed, I doubt if Jane Austen ever uses the word "doctor" at all). The surgeon came along to relieve their horror and suspense: Louisa had suffered a severe concussion, but her limbs had escaped and she had a chance of recovery, especially with the experienced nursing that kind Mrs. Harville was willing to give her. And very slowly she did recover, so that Frederick's brother-in-law, Admiral Croft, was able to exclaim without showing himself too heartless: " 'A new sort of way this, for a young fellow to be asking love, by breaking his mistress's head, is it not, Miss Elliot? This is breaking a head and giving a plaster, truly!' "

Anne had been for many weeks removed to Bath and out of touch with what was happening to her friends at Uppercross, before we receive final news of Louisa's state of health; a laughable and somewhat ridiculous outcome of her tragic misadventure: she was engaged to Captain Benwick, the quiet, melancholy young sailor who had come among them supposed to be inconsolable for the death of Captain Harville's sister, yet of whom it had been rumoured that he had lifted his head and was turning towards Anne for refreshment. But Louisa is altered, Charles Musgrove tells Anne: "there is no running or jumping about, no laughing or dancing; it is quite different. If one happens only to shut the door a little hard, she starts and wriggles like a young dab-chick in the water; and Benwick sits at her elbow, reading verses, or whispering to her, all day long." Since I read this, I never see a dab-chick without immediately thinking of Louisa Musgrove.

Another accident by which Jane Austen cleverly contrived to change the whole course of events happened in Mansfield Park: Tom Bertram, the dissipated elder son, had a fall when rioting with a party of young men at Newmarket; subsequently a good deal of drinking brought on a fever, and poor Tom (like Louisa Musgrove, a minor character) became for a few pages the centre of attention while his life was in danger. The departure of the fever left him with some "strong hectic symptoms; they were apprehensive for his lungs"—which seemed a bit odd, as the result of a fall. Tom was a rake, thoughtless but not wicked, so as with Louisa and to a much greater degree Marianne, he therefore had to suffer and undergo reformation by trial and error. Through Fanny we hear that "there was not only the debility of recent illness to assist; there was also nerves much affected, spirits much depressed to calm and raise, and her own imagination added"—(Fanny's would!)—"that there must be a mind to be properly guided."

Marianne Dashwood fell and sprained her ankle in the first chapter of *Sense and Sensibility,* long before she was ready for the salutary effects of a serious illness or accident; and Jane Austen was still half mocking at the romantic tradition of Mrs. Radcliffe, which she had burlesqued more openly in *Northanger Abbey*: beautiful young ladies should be rescued by handsome young cavaliers for a first meeting, not tamely introduced to them at a party. So Marianne runs swiftly downhill to their cottage, rejoicing in the fleetness and the exercise and buffeting winds, and a few moments later is carried home in a young man's arms (her blushes concealed, no doubt, against his most becoming shooting-jacket). Her younger sister named Willoughby "Marianne's preserver"; and having served its purpose, the ankle healed more rapidly than one could have believed possible. We need not censure her good fortune, however; a severer chastisement is in store before she too becomes good and sweet and gentle, ready to overlook Colonel Brandon's twinges of rheumatism, and conceal her blushes against his elderly flannel waistcoat.

Even Jane Austen, then, conforms to sentimental tradition when she allows illness to work these miracles in character.

Tom Bertram's illness has an equally beneficial effect on his mother. Until confronted with it, nothing has disturbed her placid existence in a corner of the sofa, Pug beside her and Fanny to wait on her. But now Lady Bertram suddenly becomes a real woman. Lady Bertram is ever my delight, second only to Mr. Woodhouse; but nobody can pretend from a domestic point of view that she pulls her weight; to say that she leads a sheltered existence is an understatement in terms. She is no *malade imaginaire,* and does not, like Mrs. Bennet, claim her household's undivided attention when there is bad news, retiring to her dressing-room and thus giving, as Mr. Bennet bitterly remarked, "a parade to impart elegance to misfortune." Lady Bertram's crime is no more than that she "stays put" till the shock of Tom's illness works a transformation touchingly revealed in her letter to Fanny, which begins by a sort of playing at being frightened in long phrases, and ends by her writing as she speaks, in simple sincere platitudes of maternal alarm.

Of what we may call ordinary illnesses, as for instance Emma's measles, little is to be found in Jane Austen. Dr. Grant died of apoplexy by eating three great institutional dinners in one week, but three great institutional dinners can hardly be called an illness. Undoubtedly, however, his condition would nowadays be attributed to stupendously high blood pressure. Mrs. Smith, Anne Elliot's lowly friend at Bath, was a victim of rheumatoid arthritis; she had to be carried to and from the hot baths, and it is to be hoped they did her good, for we do not wish her ill, though we are not disposed to like her very much.

Then there are two or three pregnancies lightly sketched in, though not with such hyperdelicacy as to irritate us; Mrs. Weston has a child in *Emma;* Charlotte Palmer in *Sense and Sensibility*. The beautiful Mrs. Wallace, object of Sir Walter Elliot's complacent speculation, never makes a personal appearance in *Persuasion,* for she too is a Lady in an Interesting Condition.

Mrs. Tilney might well have died merely of being General Tilney's wife, were we not told by her son that the malady from which she passed away (long before the book opens) was a "constitutional" bilious fever. It was necessary for Henry to place the facts of her death clearly and carefully before Catherine, for he discovered that that darling little goose had conceived the pleasing notion of Mrs. Tilney's having been secretly murdered (or walled up) by the General. We are never told the cause of Lady Elliot's death, Anne's mother; though I am ready and willing to believe that she did indeed die of Sir Walter, if not actually by his hand.

Mothers and wives in Jane Austen apparently never took air and exercise; though where her heroines are in need of both, the evils of too great confinement to the house are so repeatedly laid before our notice that I should not be at all surprised to learn that Jane Austen herself, or maybe Jane and Cassandra, were recognised in the neighbourhood as "very odd indeed" for their independent behaviour and views in that very matter. Fanny, after a weeping fit, is sent by Sir Thomas to take a few turns in the shrubbery as being the driest place to recover poise and self-control; and Emma, after a more than usually trying day patiently spent in keeping her father amused, goes to walk in the shrubbery towards evening to try and freshen her spirits and relieve her melancholy at the thought of having lost Mr. Knightley to Harriet. We have already seen that Marianne walked enthusiastically on the downs against the gales of a high southwesterly wind; she would gladly have accepted Willoughby's present of a horse that she might gallop at will over these same downs, had not her more prudent sister Elinor pointed out that the gift must lead to buying another horse for a servant to ride with her, and then engaging another manservant and building a stable, all of which might put their mother to some trifling extra expense, for it was still not considered right for a young girl to ride alone. Jane Bennet also rode, and Elizabeth was a tireless walker. No doubt Emma, from what we have learnt of her, would have been almost a female Centaur; but though the scene where she asks her father if he would "mind" unfortunately must have taken place before the book opens, we cannot for a moment doubt the flood of nervous objections that his imagination would have summoned up to dissuade his darling from such a mettlesome project. . . . Oh, the dangers that would have beset his Emma, even with an attendant groom, once she put herself voluntarily in the power of even the most ambling horse! On second thought, and knowing Mr. Woodhouse, Emma probably did not even try to persuade him, but worked off some of her boundless energy on foot; we are told that she dreaded her more confined prospects when Miss Taylor, married to Mr. Weston, could no longer be her companion on these walks, and how she welcomed Harriet as an answer to the problem. Catherine Morland probably enjoyed walking; General Tilney had succeeded in putting her into a flutter of pleasure, before she began to dislike and suspect him, by congratulating her upon the "elasticity" of her walk . . . so we may be sure she set off for her walk with Henry and Eleanor to the top of Beechen Cliff with even more than her usual elasticity. Then that unbearable rattle,

John Thorpe, tricked her out of her walk with the Tilneys and into driving with him in an open carriage (which mysteriously made it worse in the eyes of authority); she was glad when her host, Mr. Allen, said it was not at all the thing. A favourite expression in Jane Austen; Mr. Woodhouse solemnly remarks to Mrs. Weston that her stepson Frank is not at all the thing—he threw windows open without being requested to do so!

We are treated to no actual deathbed scenes in any of Jane Austen's books, unless perhaps in retrospect where Mrs. Price tells Fanny of the death of her little sister Mary; which might easily have been in the vein of the Death of Little Nell or of Little Paul had Dickens been given the handling of it, but is here rendered slightly ludicrous by the previous quarrel between Betsy and Susan over a silver knife—"Poor little soul! she could but just speak to be heard, and she said so prettily, 'Let sister Susan have my knife, mamma, when I am dead and buried.' " An odd phrase, by the way, for a dying child to use, or even for a dying adult; "burying" is more generally brandished as a threat when in a state of robust health: "You'll be sorry for this when I'm dead and buried!"

We did not assist at the actual deathbed of Mrs. Churchill, but news of it was produced with such solemnity as to assure us that here, if never again, readers were supposed to join the rest of Highbury in pulling a long face: "A sudden seizure, of a different nature from anything foreboded by her general state, had carried her off after a short struggle. The great Mrs. Churchill was no more." "After a short struggle" was obviously not meant to be humourous. Until the event, Mrs. Churchill had suffered from nerves, and an iron determination that her nerves should be duly considered by those dependent on her; it is interesting to note, however, that a little while before, the Churchills have detained Frank (from his strawberry-party at Donwell) "by a temporary increase of illness in her—a nervous seizure, which had lasted some hours," so that it was really inaccurate to state that the seizure which ended her days was entirely a surprise.

There are exceptions. On the whole, the death rate in Jane Austen is low and not encouraged for its own sake. Her interest is in life, not in death.

CHAPTER IV

"Towards Perfect Felicity"

SHEILA KAYE-SMITH

THOSE whose coarse pleasure it is to breathe on the glass of perfection have accused Jane Austen of concentrating her ideas exclusively on the business of getting married. Her heroines, they say, have no other interest and almost no other occupation. That being so, it is remarkable that in our earlier dissections of the six novels my collaborator and I should have ignored the subject entirely. We have investigated the food eaten and the clothes worn, we have examined in detail the daily lives of the characters and conjectured freely on their education, recreation and religion. But we have entirely passed over their main obsession. How did this come about?

In the first place, I think, because to both of us the novels are not so much six separate histories as a single society—a world in which we take much the same sort of interest as we take in our own. We discuss the inhabitants as we discuss our neighbours, but with this difference—that their love affairs cannot be so absorbing as those of the world we are escaping from, because they are as it were Given, settled from above, without flux or uncertainty. We can conjecture indefinitely as to what Elizabeth Bennet wore at the Netherfield ball, but after the first reading of *Pride and Prejudice*—indeed at the first—there can be no conjecture as to whether she will or will not marry Mr. Darcy. The thing is fixed and decided for us.

This may explain why we have hitherto ignored what might reasonably be called the mainstream of each novel while exploring so many subsidiary currents. But if it explains it does not quite excuse, and here am I already embarked on reparation. The love stories of the six novels shall be examined and we shall see if there is anything more in them than their detractors allow.

I had better begin by facing the fact that, engrossing as modern readers may find the details of the heroines' daily lives, their author's main object in creating them was to marry them to attractive and eligible young men. Nor can I deny that the stress on husband-finding—I will not say hunting, for that would be unfair and untrue—is greater than will be met with in the average novel today. I do not put this down to the changes in our mode of life—for, humbug apart, pretty girls and even those not so pretty are as interested now in their matrimonial chances as ever a Catherine Morland or a Fanny Price—so much as to the changes in our mode of fiction. We have, perhaps temporarily, perhaps finally, abandoned the Boy-Meets-Girl type of story to the films and their more uncritical frequenters. The sophisticated reader prefers to study love in its post- and extra-matrimonial manifestations, which indeed the present age has enlarged beyond all the conceptions of our ancestors.

In Jane Austen's time there was not much that one could do with even the unhappiest marriage save grin and bear it. Divorce was only for the wealthy and influential, and so devastating in its consequences that even by them it was seldom resorted to. It certainly had no place in the life of a heroine, and Jane's solitary and reluctant venture into its shadows in *Mansfield Park*—"let other pens dwell on guilt and misery" —is typical not only of her own attitude but that of her generation.

For sheer lack of other material, the early novelist was forced to confine himself to the approaches of the married state. Not for him the disillusions, partings, reconciliations, readjustments and reassortments of modern life. If Miss Brown married Mr. Jones she had to stick to him or lose her character entirely. There could be no second Spring of happiness with Mr. Robinson. So the acquisition of Mr. Jones becomes the main interest of her love life, with all the added incentive of a final choice.

Note that it is a choice. The free choosing of each other by the married partners was not taken for granted in Jane Austen's day as it is in ours, so the coming together of an Elizabeth Bennet and a Fitzwilliam Darcy, of a Catherine Morland and a Henry Tilney, of a Fanny Price and an Edmund Bertram would have a freshness and originality for contemporary readers that repetition and social custom since have dulled.

At the turn of the eighteenth century this freedom was something new. There had always been solitary instances of it—the classic love stories of poetry and history—but these could serve only to emphasise the accepted rule. Now it was becoming widespread and a matter of public interest. Whether the Romantic Revival had started the movement or merely given it expression would be hard to decide. But those were days of change and a certain social disruption, and the old-fashioned way of arranging a marriage through the parents was passing away with hoops and powdered periwigs.

It is notable that most of the early stories of free romance end tragically—Tristan and Isolde, Abelard and Eloise, Romeo and Juliet know nothing of "happy ever after." They are in a sense rebels and society is avenged in their frustration. But now society has accepted romance and the acceptance must be justified. The fairy-tale ending where there is really no end but a beginning is the direct consequence of this new approach. While marriage was conditioned by family requirements, the personal happiness of the young couple was taken for granted. Women accepted their husbands as they accepted their fathers and mothers and children, and weighed them in the same balance as they weighed the rest of the family. But now romance has taken command and must be vindicated by a bliss surpassing all other blisses. "The anxiety which must be the portion of Henry and Catherine can hardly extend to the bosom of my readers, who will see in the tell-tale compression of the pages before them that we are all hastening together to perfect felicity"—so writes Jane Austen in the last chapter of *Northanger Abbey,* endearing herself to us with the suggestion that she is the first to see through her own devices.

Indeed to form any just idea of her attitude towards the whole subject we must stand back beside her and view it as far as possible through her eyes and without our modern prejudices. Not only was the question of finding the right husband more novel in her day but it was also more urgent. Apart from the new romantic outlook on marriage there were considerations which made the failure to achieve it an actual disaster.

We have grown so used to the idea of single women and their honourable function in the world that we may find it hard to picture their very different lot a hundred and fifty years ago. Then the unmarried woman was just an Old Maid, "the proper sport of boys and girls," with no real place in society, and unless she had her own private fortune, doomed to a life of poverty and dependence. The only profession open to an educated woman was that of governess, and though a governess might be a Miss Taylor and marry a Mr. Weston, she was far more likely to find herself a desolate anomaly in another woman's house, shut up in a sort of no-man's land between the drawing-room and the servants' hall, at the mercy alike of her superiors and her inferiors. Even in the Brontës' time, fifty years later, the position had not much improved, if we are to judge by the united evidence of *Jane Eyre, Agnes Grey* and *The Tenant of Wildfell Hall.*

Yet it was the only alternative to marriage for the portionless, who were by the same token the least likely to get married. For the new romantic outlook had not entirely done away with the need for a "fortune," and Jane Austen uses this fact to lengthen the odds against her heroines and heighten the interest of their stories. None of them except Emma has a dowery worthy to appear on the marriage-announcements page of the *Gentleman's Magazine*. Anne Elliot, it is true, has ten thousand pounds, but that, though it might do very well in some quarters, is mean for a baronet's daughter. Catherine Morland has only three; and Elizabeth Bennet, as Mr. Collins is urgent to remind her, no more than "one thousand pounds in the four per cents." A thousand pounds is equally the portion of Elinor and Marianne Dashwood. Fanny Price has nothing.

But even with this handicap, Jane Austen obviously regards real, bloodthirsty husband-hunting with the same disapproval as the most enlightened of her critics. My own opinion is that, considering the circumstances, Mrs. Bennet might be forgiven for making it "the business of her life to get her daughters married." What would become of them if they remained single? The most ordinary maternal affection might well seek to provide them with husbands as an alternative to a life of indigence. But Jane Austen has no mercy on Mrs. Bennet. Nor is she particularly kind to Charlotte Lucas, who marries Mr. Collins "solely from the pure and disinterested desire of an establishment." She is degraded equally with the reader and with her friend—"Elizabeth felt persuaded that no real confidence could ever exist between them again."

So if husband-hunting is to be found in *Pride and Prejudice* it is a blood-sport that is not approved of, and in none of the other novels do we find it at all. Marianne Dashwood's lack of calculation in her affection for Willoughby is equalled only by her lack of concealment, while her sister for most of the book loves Edward Ferrars faithfully and hopelessly through his engagement to another woman. Catherine Morland, though caressing Henry Tilney with the innocent flattery of her adoration, has no thought of marriage till his father puts it into her head. Fanny Price, most destitute of all the heroines, is shocked and disgusted when a rich man lays his heart at her feet. There is no design or even hope in Anne Elliot's love of Captain Wentworth, while Emma, rich and independent enough to play with the notion of a single life, pictures Frank Churchill's addresses only with a view to declining them, and does not realise her own love for Mr. Knightley until her imagination has made him over to another woman.

No, they are not a husband-hunting set, and if the thought of marriage looms more largely in their lives than in those of other heroines of fiction, that is because Jane Austen deliberately confines herself within the boundaries of a woman's world, which in her day was a very small world indeed. It was all very well for Fielding and Smollett to crowd their pages with picaresque adventure, or Sir Walter Scott to enlarge some rather thin human emotions with history. Jane Austen knew the limitations not only of her world but of her powers. The comparison of her work with that of a miniature painter is her own. She deliberately refused to write a Gothic romance, distrusting her imagination to take her beyond the reach of her experience.

But within her own world she is as stark a realist as either of her two male predecessors and far more uncompromising. For both Fielding and Smollett are capable of sentimental jaunts and romantic surrenders, whereas though Jane Austen was sufficiently of her date to give romance an occasional break against probability, she will have no truck with sentiment whatever.

This lack of sentiment, or rather of sentimentality, lifts the stress from love and marriage and allows the novels to be read without that sense of suffocation which accompanies the more aggressively feminine novels of Richardson. The astringent quality which informs all her observation of society, informs equally her observation of the more treacherous and misleading passion of love. Indeed that astringency may sometimes be said to have shown the defect of its own virtue in drying up springs which should have been emotionally deep.

For the question arises—does this writer whose main subject is the approach to marriage give us any of the classic, unforgettable love scenes of fiction? And the answer comes uncompromisingly—no. Indeed, I should say that with one exception the love scenes in the six novels are inferior to the rest. The exception of course is in *Persuasion*—the scene in which Captain Wentworth writes his letter of love and penitence while listening to Anne's conversation with Captain Harville. . . . "All the privilege I claim for my own sex (it is not a very enviable one, you need not covet it) is that of loving longest, when existence or when hope is gone."

These are moving words. They move the reader as doubtless they moved the author. But nothing else moves, and *Persuasion* remains—with some scenes of a different nature in *Sense and Sensibility*—the only indication that Jane Austen herself was ever in love.

One must remember of course the conventions of the day. There could be at that period and in that society no actual love-making. A kiss would be unthinkable, and in the six novels there are no kisses, at least between lovers. Mr. Knightley once nearly kissed Emma's hand—"He took her hand, pressed it, and was on the point of carrying it to his lips when, from some fancy or other, he suddenly let it go." But that was before, not after their betrothal, and "the affectionate farewell of a brother" which Edmund gave Fanny on her departure for Portsmouth belonged to his cousinship and not to any amorous impulse. It was a bad blunder in a recent dramatization of *Pride and Prejudice* to let Jane build her hopes of Bingley on a kiss. To have kissed a girl he was not engaged to would have been an unspeakable outrage; even in the course of a proposal it would not have been allowed. Hands might be "pressed" or even "seized," but that was the limit of demonstration. The eighteenth century was a time of incredible formality and even Christian names were used with care by engaged couples—" 'Jane' indeed!" writes Frank Churchill to Mrs. Weston after his engagement to Jane Fairfax has been made public, "You will observe that I have not yet indulged myself in calling her by that name even to you."

2

Jane Austen's only outlet for the passion attending pursuit is in the proposal, which, as was natural in such a formal society, amounted in her day to very much more than it does in ours. It would still at some time have to be made to the parents of the young lady, but the new freedom allowed it to be made to her first, and this is what happens in every case. There is a passage in *Pride and Prejudice* where Elizabeth, misled by Mr. Bennet's raillery, imagines he has received a proposal for her hand from Mr. Darcy and "was undetermined whether most to be pleased that he had explained himself at last or offended that his letter was not rather addressed to herself." But of course the letter turns out to be only from Mr. Collins and Elizabeth soon afterwards receives his addresses in person, though when she has accepted them he must, as with Mr. Bingley in the case of Jane, make a formal application to her father.

Pride and Prejudice is unique among the novels in containing two proposals of marriage to the same woman from the same man. Captain Wentworth, in *Persuasion,* must of course have proposed twice, but his first offer is not recorded, while in the earlier novel we are given an opportunity of comparing the two.

The first opens with more fire than the second: "In vain have I struggled. It will not do. My feelings will not be repressed. You must allow me to tell you how ardently I admire and love you." But the second, though tamer—"If your feelings are still what they were last April tell me so at once. My affections and wishes remain unchanged"—is more convincing. Indeed I find it difficult to believe in the first proposal at all. Surely an intelligent and well-bred man like Darcy would never have spoken in such a manner to the lady he hoped to win. "His sense of her inferiority, of its being a degradation, of the family obstacles which judgment had always opposed to inclination, were dwelt on with a warmth which seemed due to the consequence he was wounding, but very unlikely to recommend his suit." Do I believe that he himself would not have been aware of this? I do not. Whatever his private thoughts, he would not have expressed them in such a way at such a moment. Nor can I quite believe in Elizabeth's later scruples at the violence with which she rejected him. Indeed the ding-dong row into which the proposal degenerates gives it its best claim to actuality.

It also makes it altogether a livelier affair than the second proposal, where the author almost immediately takes the situation into her own hands, with results that are curiously flat.

> Elizabeth, feeling all the more that common awkwardness and anxiety of his situation now forced herself to speak; and immediately, though not very fluently, gave him to understand that her sentiments had undergone so material a change since the period to which he alluded, as to make her receive with gratitude and pleasure his present assurances. The happiness which this reply produced was such as he had never probably felt before; and he expressed himself on the occasion as sensibly and warmly as a man violently in love can be supposed to do.

This hardly conveys the passion of love, violent or otherwise. Indeed we have a feeling as if the author were hurrying over this part of the business, as if she disliked it. Is this idea imaginary? Some might say that having already devoted several pages to the earlier proposal she might well feel that the second should be disposed of more quickly, especially as the issue is never in doubt. But I have noticed elsewhere a tendency on Jane Austen's part to cut short her love scenes. Take, for instance, Mr. Knightley's proposal to Emma.

Here all is most promising until Emma really begins to understand him. At first, we know, she thought he was speaking of Harriet. Then—

> He stopped in his earnestness to look the question, and the expression of his eyes overpowered her.
>
> "My dearest Emma," said he, "for dearest you will always

be, whatever the event of this hour's conversation, my dearest, most beloved Emma—tell me at once. Say No if it is to be said." She could really say nothing. "You are silent," he cried, with great animation; "absolutely silent! at present I ask no more."

This could not be better, nor his next speech:

"I cannot make speeches, Emma. If I loved you less, I might be able to talk about it more. But you know what I am. You hear nothing but truth from me. I have blamed you, and lectured you, and you have borne it as no other woman in England would have borne it. Bear with the truth I would tell you now, dearest Emma, as well as you have borne with them. God knows I have been a very indifferent lover. But you understand me. . . ."

She does. While he has been speaking she had been thinking.

What did she say? *Just what she ought, of course. A lady always does.*

With these few words, in my italics, the author lets down the scene with a facetious crack unworthy of it. It recovers later, but by then there is nothing left but narrative and explanation. The voice of love no longer speaks.

Is Jane Austen shirking this part of her job?—the part one might expect to be the most congenial to a romantic novelist. I notice throughout the novels a tendency to contract or avoid proposals. There is none at all in *Sense and Sensibility*. Marianne does not receive hers till the book is finished, and of Edward's declaration to Elinor, after so many vicissitudes, all we hear is:

His errand at Barton was a simple one. It was only to ask Elinor to marry him . . . how soon an opportunity of exercising it occurred, in what manner he expressed himself, and how he was received need not particularly be told. This only need be said:—that when they all sat down to table at four o'clock, he had secured his lady, engaged her mother's consent, and was not only in the rapturous profession of the lover, but in the reality of reason and truth, one of the happiest of men.

If Jane Austen really enjoyed writing love scenes, this is self-denial indeed. But it is the same in *Northanger Abbey*. Mrs. Morland has left Catherine and Henry alone in the parlour, and instead of being left with them the reader must follow her upstairs and find, as she did, the whole thing settled on her return. And in *Mansfield Park*:

Scarcely had [Edmund] done regretting Mary Crawford, and observing to Fanny how impossible it was that he should ever meet with such another woman, before it began to strike him whether a very different kind of woman might not do just as well—or a great deal better. . . . I purposely abstain from dates on this occasion, that everyone may be at liberty to fix their own, aware that the cure of unconquerable passions, and the transfer of unchanging attachments, must vary very much as to time with different people. I only entreat everybody to believe that exactly at the time when it was quite natural that he should do so, and not a week earlier, Edmund did cease to care about Miss Crawford, and became as anxious to marry Fanny as Fanny herself could desire.

Fanny's earlier proposal from Henry Crawford is naturally lost in the mists of her own diffidence:

"Don't, Mr. Crawford, pray don't. I beg you would not. This is a sort of talking which is very unpleasant to me. I must go away. I cannot bear it. . . . No, no, no, this is all nonsense. Do not distress me. I can bear no more of this. . . . I do not want, I cannot bear, I must not listen to such —no, no, don't think of me. But you are *not* thinking of me. I know it is all nothing."

We are told that he "pressed for an answer," but not what he actually said, though I feel that, coming from Henry Crawford, it might have been something well worth our overhearing. Indeed we may ask if this romantic economy impoverishes the novels to any extent. The only proposal that is given us in detail, where the dialogue is not broken into or broken off by an author apparently anxious to bring it to an end, is the proposal to Elizabeth Bennet from Mr. Collins, and this belongs throughout to farce. Nearly as full is Mr. Elton's proposal to Emma, and here although we do not approach farce, there is a comic irony in the situation that has brought it about. In both cases the gentleman's regard is, as the lady realises, quite imaginary.

Are we by these tokens to see Jane Austen as a typical "blighted spinster," envious and uneasy in the presence of true love, and recording its expressions only when these are manifestly insincere? The answer of course is No. A hundred passages in the novels contradict such a notion. But the fact remains that in spite of all her detractors may have to say about her stress on marriage, she is not a romantic novelist. Her genius is primarily realistic and secondarily comic. She therefore avoids or curtails those scenes which romance might threaten to overbalance if given full play. A number of proposals given in detail might deserve for her the reproach that otherwise is made unjustly. There is also the question of variety. Professions of true love tend in their essence to be very much alike, so she constricts them in favour of others not quite so true. Only the romantically minded could quarrel with her on that account and the romantically minded should not read Jane Austen.

All of us, however, whether romantically minded or not, will conjecture as to how much autobiography there is in the various love stories. She was a spinster. She never married in an age when it was exceptional for a woman not to marry. Why did she remain single? It is hard to believe that so attractive a creature as she was by all accounts should never have had a chance. Her novels were not published till she was past what in her day was considered a marriageable age, so it was not those that frightened the men away. Her letters show her engaged in a number of flirtations, and though they show nothing more we know that the letters are not complete.

The legend runs that if her sister Cassandra had not unpardonably destroyed a number of them we should have known of a love affair approaching Anne Elliot's affair with Captain Wentworth, though without its happy ending. It is difficult to believe that certain passages in *Persuasion* have not been lived. The same applies with equal force to passages in *Sense and Sensibility*. The agonies of Marianne's love for Willoughby are in my opinion beyond imagination. Indeed I do not think that I have met anywhere in fiction more poignant scenes of suffering young love than we find in this novel. It is usual to look for the inspiration of *Persuasion* in the author's life, but I insist that if Jane Austen ever knew a Captain Wentworth she also knew a Willoughby.

Marianne and Anne are in their different ways most certainly in love, but of some of the other heroines I am not so sure. I can never quite bring myself to believe in Elizabeth Bennet's change of heart, linked as it is with another change of heart still more incredible. Nor do Jane's complacent reactions to Bingley's suit suggest the depths that we are told exist. Never could it be said of her as of Anne Elliot "their union, she believed, could not divide her more from other men than their final separation."

Catherine Morland's artless preference for Henry Tilney was doubtless to flower into true love in the course of marriage, but we are purposely shown it only in the bud. Emma on the other hand, when at last she realises her love for Mr. Knightley, plucks the flower of friendship in full bloom. That she has been blind to its earlier stages is only in keeping with her art of self-deception. No doubt hers is not love as Marianne Dashwood understood it, but though it makes no appeal to sensibility it has much that would be approved by sense.

This also is true of Fanny Price's love for Edmund Bertram. Indeed I would risk the statement that Fanny is the most completely in love of all the heroines. She is temperamentally saturated in her object. She *is* Edmund, even more consistently than he is himself. This explains many phases of her character that irritate us. Remember that she came under his influence at an early, impressionable age and that he bound her shrinking, grateful little heart to his by a really beautiful if simple act of kindness. When I read the account of this letter written to William from the sender, "My dear little cousin, what can be the matter?" to the final generosity of "half a guinea under the seal—" I can forgive Edmund much that happens later on.

It is easy to imagine the effect of this episode on Fanny. It was the first real kindness that had been shown her since her coming to Mansfield Park, and it was shown by a godlike being far above her, who continued moreover to offer her his interest and protection. "Edmund's friendship never failed her: his leaving Eton for Oxford made no change in his kind dispositions. . . . He was always true to her interests and considerate of her feelings . . . he recommended the books which charmed her leisure hours, he encouraged her taste, and corrected her judgment. . . . In return for such services she loved him better than anyone in the world except William: her heart was divided between the two."

It is interesting to conjecture how Fanny would have turned out if she could have seen more of William—enough to make him an influence in her life instead of an occasional relief. I am sure we should have escaped much that we dislike in her, and she would almost certainly have married Henry Crawford. But it was not to be. William appears only occasionally, whereas Edmund is there all the time, moulding her into his own image while in her heart childish gratitude and affection pass silently into love.

There is no sudden discovery of her love for Edmund as Emma discovers hers for Mr. Knightley. It is always there, growing from childhood to womanhood with the rest of her. Because she loves him she grows into a prig. He is a prig, so she becomes one too, though with more humility and more consistently than he can show. But I maintain that it is because she loves Edmund and not just because she is a prig that she refuses to marry Crawford and stands aloof from his sister. There are many expressions of censure and disapproval, but these are mere rationalisations of a situation that is primarily emotional. Jane Austen herself does more than suggest that Crawford would have won her in the end if her heart had been her own to give away.

There is a similar explanation of her coldness to Mary, whose friendship had been so often so practically expressed. She may criticise her by the paragraph, but the fundamental antagonism lies surely in the fact that they are rivals in love, between whom any true friendship is impossible and any semblance of it a mockery. Mary Crawford is not aware of this, but Fanny is aware and would, had she encouraged the intimacy, have followed Edmund in the last stages of his Prig's Progress and become a hypocrite.

3

But Fanny's love, like Emma's, like Elizabeth's, like Jane's, like Catherine's, like Elinor's, is love observed from without. I do not think there can ever have been an Edmund in Jane Austen's life. Only in the love affairs of Marianne Dashwood and Anne Elliot do we find those deep stresses which point to experience. But when from love we pass to flirtation, and a secondary column of young men steps forward—Wickham, Colonel Fitzwilliam, Frank Churchill, Captain Benwick—we seem once more to move inside the author's life. Apart from the revelations of her letters, it is plain that Jane Austen was an experienced flirt.

The word has become vulgarised of late and dragged into meanings remote from its true self. "Flirting" has been regarded as synonymous with the hideous Edwardian "spooning" or the scarcely less hideous "necking" of modern times. It bears but little relation to them. Anyone can spoon and anyone can neck, but we still speak of an "accomplished flirt." For flirting is an art—becoming, I fear, a lost art. It expressed an attitude lighter than love to which it bore the same relation as fencing would bear to serious combat. There must be play, skill, excitement, but no wounds.

Only three of Jane Austen's heroines flirt. Marianne is too ardent and Elinor too serious for flirtation, Catherine too ingenuous and Fanny too prim. Nor would we expect to see Jane Bennet engaged in a fencing bout—she would be afraid of causing some injury even with the foils. But her sister Elizabeth is of a very different temperament and we soon find her enjoying herself with George Wickham.

She understands perfectly the rules of the game, though in her case it must be noted that the impulse is not purely one of sport. Neither her heart is engaged nor his, but there is behind his attraction for her a serious motive. He is able to feed her dislike of Darcy. Their recorded conversation has none of the light exchanges of flirting—it could not be said of them as Emma acknowledges could have been said of herself and Frank Churchill: "Mr. Frank Churchill and Miss Woodhouse flirted together excessively." They meet rather on the ground of a common dislike and resentment.

But all their consciousness of each other belongs to flirtation. Before the ball at Netherfield Elizabeth "dressed with more than usual care, and prepared in the highest spirits for the conquest of all that remained unsubdued of his heart, trusting that it was not more than might be won in the course of the evening." Later on when her aunt warns her against what she sees to be a growing partiality she replies: "At present I am not in love with Mr. Wickham: no, I certainly am not. But he is beyond all comparison the most agreeable man I ever saw." Her immunity continues through his disaffection to Miss King—indeed she takes his part against this same aunt, who would "be sorry to think our friend mercenary." It is true that Mrs. Gardiner ends by saying, "Take care, Lizzy; that speech savours strongly of disappointment," but I do not believe that Elizabeth was disappointed—only a little affronted. She regarded Wickham as a few weeks later she was to regard Colonel Fitzwilliam—a delightful man, with whom, if he had not been poor and she been penniless, she might have been tempted to fall in love. But as things were she would get the best out of the situation by treating it lightly.

Elizabeth, as might have been expected, is the most accomplished practitioner of the art. Emma's flirtation with Frank Churchill has, like most of Emma's performances, too much self-delusion about it to be in the best form. Rather, she is playing at love, except of course in that lamentable scene on Box Hill when she "gave him all the friendly encouragement, the admission to be gallant, which she had ever given in the first and most animating period of their acquaintance; but which now in her own estimation meant nothing, though in the judgment of most people looking on, it must have had such an appearance as no English word but flirtation could very well describe."

Frank Churchill himself of course had been flirting with Emma from the start. He had no idea that she had ever taken him seriously, nor—which was less pardonable—that Jane Fairfax could seriously object to his behaviour. Like Wickham he is the typical male flirt, and though I can believe that he made a better husband than Wickham, I think that both Janes—his wife and his author—were inclined to forgive him too much.

When I read the latter's strictures on Henry Crawford I confess that I am a little bewildered by her sympathetic tolerance of a man who was far more stupid, reckless and unfeeling than he. Crawford had his faults—an irresistible tendency to flirt was one of them—but he also had qualities of strength and sense which Frank Churchill lacked entirely. Nevertheless Jane Austen never ceases to castigate him and the liking which most readers soon begin to feel for him grows in her despite.

It is true that he flirted shamelessly with the two Bertram sisters, one of whom was engaged to another man. But they should both have been better able to look after themselves, and Maria's engagement was not to be taken seriously from any but a worldly point of view. Nothing but good could have come of her breaking it off, and it was her own fault—the fault of her own worldliness and pride—that she did not do so. Crawford might have become her deliverer, even without marrying her himself.

As for his determination "to make Fanny Price in love with me," it was reprehensible, no doubt, for Fanny understood nothing of the art of flirting and would have been defenceless but for an armour he did not know of. But when he discovers that it is he and not she who has been caught, his behaviour is at once of the best and most honourable. Neither pride nor self-interest can deflect him from continuing the courtship seriously. I have the greatest admiration for the behaviour of both the Crawfords at this juncture, and a little resent their author's refusal to give them the credit due.

However, Henry Crawford is the only character whom Jane Austen will not allow to flirt, and I have already pointed out in an earlier book that there is some sort of a cloud over *Mansfield Park,* making its approach to life both darker and heavier than in the other novels. Certainly in its immediate successor she is back in the sunshine and prepared to forgive Frank Churchill almost anything. In *Persuasion* too the sunny mood prevails, though the atmosphere is not so conducive to flirting. Nevertheless we get a touch of it in Anne's relations with Captain Benwick. No doubt, properly speaking, this is not a flirtation at all, but it has this in common with flirtation, that it is an attraction short of love bringing interest and pleasure to both parties.

Captain Wentworth, too, is on terms similar to flirtation

with the two Musgrove sisters. Here the situation of Crawford with Maria and Julia Bertram repeats itself on a much lighter, more amiable note, though with the difference that in this case the man is passive and the woman active: "they both seemed so entirely occupied by him that nothing but the appearance of the most perfect good will between themselves could have made it credible that they were not decided rivals." Later on, we know, Louisa took the lead, and by his friends' misunderstanding of a situation that he himself had never taken seriously, Captain Wentworth felt himself committed. Flirtation could lead its unwary practitioners into matrimony, but nowhere in the novels do we find two flirts marrying each other. They all marry someone else—Wickham marries Lydia, not Elizabeth, Frank Churchill has never dreamed of marrying Emma when he marries Jane; Henry Crawford married somebody no doubt, but none of the three ladies he flirted with at Mansfield Park, while "that is the end of his being in love with Anne" says Mary Musgrove when Captain Benwick marries Louisa—and also, Anne might have said, to Louisa's being in love with Captain Wentworth.

4

This survey of love in the six novels would not be complete without a glance at the married couples that jostle the flirts and the lovers in their pages. The fact that Jane Austen will not allow the married life of her heroines to have any part in their stories does not mean that she is uninterested in those who are already married and therefore according to her time and technique beyond the reach of amorous complications. She is indeed a very shrewd observer of matrimony as an accomplished fact, and in spite of the "Happy-ever-afterwards" of her last chapters she has no illusions about it.

It is true that we never meet in her novels the tragically mismated—except of course for that brief excursion into "guilt and misery" which provides the moral of *Mansfield*

Park. Even the late Mrs. Tilney's woes existed mainly in Catherine Morland's imagination, and though we are given to understand that Anne Elliot's mother had never been valued as she ought by her silly husband, we have no evidence that he was ever untrue or deliberately unkind. But the couple who jog along just because they have to make the best of a bad job appear more than once.

The most closely observed are Mr. and Mrs. Bennet. Here a gifted, intelligent man, "captivated by youth and beauty and that appearance of good-humour which youth and beauty generally give, had married a woman whose weak understanding and illiberal mind had very early in their marriage put an end to all real affection for her." She herself was too silly to realise what had happened and doubtless considered herself a happily married woman till the end of her life. But "all his views of domestic happiness were overthrown," though he "was not of a disposition to seek comfort for the disappointment which his own imprudence had brought on in any of those pleasures which too often console the unfortunate for their folly or their vice. He was fond of the country and of books; and from these tastes had arisen his principal enjoyments. To his wife he was very little otherwise indebted than as her ignorance and folly contributed to his amusement."

The reader is in the same position, and some of our best moments in *Pride and Prejudice* undoubtedly arise from what his daughter Elizabeth recognised as "the impropriety of [his] behaviour as a husband . . . the continual breach of conjugal decorum which, in exposing his wife to the contempt of her own children, was so highly reprehensible"—and entertaining. Entertaining at least to us who are the gods, for we can imagine that Elizabeth had some very different reactions to his exchanges with her mother over the entail ("If it was not for the entail I should not mind it"—"What should not you mind?"—"I should not mind anything at all"—"Let us be thankful that you are preserved from a state of such insensibility") or over her offer of marriage from Mr. Collins. ("Your mother insists upon your accepting it. Is it not so, Mrs. Bennet?"—"Yes, or I will never see her again."—"An unhappy alternative is before you, Elizabeth. From this day you must be a stranger to one of your parents. Your mother will never see you again if you do *not* marry Mr. Collins and I will never see you again if you *do*.")

My own opinion is that if Mr. Bennet had married the right woman he would have made an excellent husband, for he had a good understanding and an affectionate heart. I find myself liking him more and more at every rereading of the book. But was he likely to have chosen right if another of his teasings had come true— "Let us flatter ourselves that *I* may be the survivor"? We will leave that question unanswered and turn to a couple whom I have always regarded as a rather amateurish preliminary sketch of Mr. and Mrs. Bennet.

Though both Mr. and Mrs. Palmer are improbable and overdrawn, we find here another intelligent man married to another very silly, pretty woman, and reacting to the situation in a way not unlike to Mr. Bennet's, though where the latter is often witty Mr. Palmer is invariably rude. But "Elinor was not inclined to give him credit for being so genuinely and unaffectedly ill-natured or ill-bred as he wished to appear. His temper might perhaps be a little soured by finding, like many others of his sex, that through some unaccountable bias in favour of beauty, he was the husband of a very silly woman—but she knew that this blunder was far too common for any sensible man to be lastingly hurt by it."

One feels that it must have been common in Jane Austen's own little world, for some form or other of the situation is to be found in most of the novels. Emma refuses to believe that Harriet's folly will protect a sensible, well-judging man like Mr. Knightley from the enchantment of her pretty face. She is wrong, of course—Emma is nearly always wrong—but she seems to speak for her author when she asks: "Was it a new circumstance for a man of first-rate abilities to be captured by very inferior powers?" Mrs. Allen again, in *Northanger Abbey* "was one of that numerous class of females whose society can raise no other emotion than surprise at there being any man in the world who could like them well enough to marry them." But in her case it was not beauty that made her the choice of "a sensible intelligent man like Mr. Allen," and this may have saved the situation, for we are never given any reason to suppose that she and her husband did not get on very well together. Equally harmonious was the life of the sensible, thoughtful Sir Thomas Bertram and his hen-brained lady, though with her again it was beauty that had baited the trap, for "her uncle, the attorney, himself allowed her to be at least three thousand pounds short of any equitable claim" to a baronet.

There is only one example of the opposite case in which a sensible woman marries a silly man. "My friend," says Elizabeth Bennet of Charlotte Collins, "has an excellent understanding—though I am not certain that I consider her marrying Mr. Collins the wisest thing she ever did." However, Charlotte has enough sense to make at least something tolerable of the situation— "Poor Charlotte! It was melancholy to leave her to such society! But she had chosen it with her eyes open; and though evidently regretting that her visitors were to go, she did not seem to ask for compassion."

Thus a divorceless society mended its marriages or rather kept them unbroken, and shall we say that the sum of married happiness was greater or less than it is now?

There are many other married couples who might be described as "average." Mrs. Grant must have had much to bear from the greedy and cantankerous Doctor, but her cheerful disposition carried her lightly through it all and she was happy enough to be continually recommending marriage to her young brother and sister. The John Dashwoods were a grim couple, but apparently got on with each other, and indeed were so matched in selfishness and insipidity that they would have had little to quarrel about. The same could not be said of the overgenteel Lady Middleton and her expansive vulgar husband, who was so fond of company that when Elinor and

Marianne came to town we are told "he rejoiced that two had been added to the inhabitants of London." However, Lady Middleton was too well bred to quarrel and Sir John too good-natured, so once again all was well. Mrs. Churchill must have been an even greater trial as a wife than she was as an aunt, but her husband was notably and commendably silent on the matter.

In *Emma* we find several marriages well observed and two at least that are really happy. Mr. Weston, of course, drew a prize in Miss Taylor, while Isabella's single-hearted devotion to John Knightley and their children blinded her to his uncertain temper. Mr. Woodhouse might shake his head and pity "poor Isabella" when the time came for her to leave Hartfield —"which poor Isabella, passing her life with those she doted on, full of their merits, blind to their faults and always innocently busy, might well have been a model of right feminine happiness."

The Eltons as a married pair were certainly not so attractive as the Knightleys, but they were not ill-matched, and there was truth as well as spite in Frank Churchill's outburst— "Happy couple! How well they suit one another! Very lucky—marrying as they did, upon an acquaintance formed only in a public place!" Apart from the love stories of the heroines, and Maria Bertram's tragedy, the Elton marriage is the only one in which we meet even one of the parties in the prenuptial state. All the other marriages spring up fully made and complete. Even Mrs. Weston has ceased to be Miss Taylor by a few hours.

When we come to *Persuasion* we are told that Charles and Mary Musgrove, in spite of occasional disagreements, "passed for a happy couple." Their marriage always seems to me particularly well observed; but it is an uncertain, teasing affair compared with the true devotion of the Crofts and the Harvilles. Evidently Jane Austen believed that sailors make the best husbands, probably because they attract the best type of woman as a wife. Mrs. Croft is the Admiral's true friend and companion, sharing all the dangers and discomforts of a sailor's life at sea:

> "I do assure you, ma'am, that nothing can exceed the accommodation of a man-of-war . . . and I can safely say, that the happiest part of my life has been spent on board a ship . . . the only time that I ever really suffered in body or mind was the winter I passed by myself at Deal, when the Admiral was in the North Sea . . . but as long as we could be together nothing ever ailed me."

It was to a marriage like hers that Anne Elliot came when she married Captain Wentworth, and for many reasons the happiness of her married life impresses me more than that of the heroines of the other books. To Elizabeth Bennet Jane Austen gives Pemberley and ten thousand a year, to Jane Bennet four thousand a year and another big estate, while Anne has specifically nothing more to boast of than "a very pretty landaulette." But her "spring of felicity" was in

> the warmth of her heart. Anne was tenderness itself and she had the full worth of it in Captain Wentworth's affection. His profession was all that could ever make her friends wish that tenderness less, the dread of a future war all that could dim her sunshine. She gloried in being a sailor's wife, but she must pay the tax of quick alarm for belonging to that profession which is, if possible, more distinguished in its domestic virtues than in its national importance.

Curiously enough I think it is these last words that bring the biggest conviction of happiness to my mind. This novel does not end on quite the fairy-tale note of the others. The sun is not in full shine—a cloud no bigger than a question mark has been allowed to drift across it. So we escape out of the glare of "perfect felicity" and see the married pair in the ordinary daylight of human happiness, "finely checkered à la mortal"—which most of us find more congenial as well as more convincing than the conventional "happy-ever-after."

CHAPTER V

"Always Be Contented, but Especially at Home"

G. B. STERN

I FIND I cannot set down my impressions of parents in Jane Austen (or grandparents or uncles and aunts), unless I make awards as though I had been asked to officiate with gracious airs at a prize-giving. Naturally this Order of Merit list is drawn up on my personal opinions, and therefore I am ready to defend them stubbornly against all argument. Probably most of you will agree with me in my awards for the Worst in each category; trouble is more likely to arise when I adjudicate according to my individual ideas of the Best.

Not at once, however; I am certain no one can dispute that as parents, Mr. and Mrs. Morland are without serious rivals; they are, in fact, the only important mother and father in Jane Austen where both emerge coupled in unselfishness and good sense; we find them disposed to indulge their large family where indulgence can do no harm, yet to check any tendency towards bad manners, sulking or affectation. We are not allowed to see much of the Rev. Richard Morland, though we are assured he was "a very respectable man" and not in the least addicted to locking up his daughters; our good opinion of him is chiefly based on the fact that when his wife acts sensibly (the word must recur often in any description of Mrs. Morland), she is apparently not in any fear of opposition from her husband. Most of us, as children, were told somewhat sententiously that people are likely to judge our parents according to the way we behave . . . to which we gave our shoulders an impatient shrug and muttered inaudibly: "Don't believe it." The older I grow, the more the truth of this comes home to me: Catherine Morland, the heroine of *Northanger Abbey,* displays so much honesty and spontaneous politeness in her conduct, as well as a genuinely modest measurement of her own claims to notice, no tiresome shrinking nor constant need of reassurance (can I *again* be thinking of Fanny Price?) that she reflects the greatest possible credit on her mother's upbringing and her father's judgment in the selection of a wife; in the latter respect he compares well with Mr. Bennet and Sir Thomas Bertram.

Mr. and Mrs. Morland must also be commended (like Mrs. Dashwood) for their willingness to allow their daughter to have a good time whenever a good time presents itself. She receives ready permission to accept Mr. and Mrs. Allen's invitation to Bath, and General Tilney's to Northanger Abbey. Nor has Catherine any doubts but that they will allow her to prolong the second visit directly she writes to ask. ". . . papa and mamma were in no hurry at all. As long as she was happy, they would always be satisfied."

In this respect, I am not sure whether Mr. Morland would not have done better, on receiving news of his son's engagement, to have made time to visit Bath himself to see this unknown Miss Isabella Thorpe, before announcing by letter his generous intentions:

> A living, of which Mr. Morland was himself patron and incumbent, of about four hundred pounds yearly value, was to be resigned to his son as soon as he should be old enough to take it; no trifling deduction from the family income, no niggardly assignment to one of ten children. An estate of at least equal value, moreover, was assured as his future inheritance.

It must have been evident that James Morland was still very young indeed, not only in years but in susceptibility. But his father may have trusted that the two or three years of waiting before marriage could take place, would reveal any drawbacks in the young lady; the Morland parents believed in the precept that time will show. My excellent opinion of Mrs. Morland is borne out by her lack of undue fuss when it transpired that Catherine (at the age of seventeen) had been packed off so cavalierly from Northanger Abbey and allowed to travel seventy miles by post-chaise, unattended. As she reached home without mishap, Mrs. Morland saw no point in making moan over the harm that might have happened. Normally indignant she certainly was, but expressed this with moderation, possibly that Catherine herself might not feel too heavily oppressed by General Tilney's unfeeling behaviour.

> Mr. and Mrs. Morland could not but feel that it might have been productive of much unpleasantness to her; that it was what they could never have voluntarily suffered.

(She displays the same brisk commonsense on the score of her son's disillusion with Miss Thorpe: "I dare say he will be a discreeter man all his life, for the foolishness of his first choice.")

I am forced to admit, however, that Mrs. Morland's psychology, or shall we say her imagination, was not equal to her practical kindness; it never once occurred to her that Catherine might have fallen in love, though they must have known there was an unmarried son at the Abbey.

> "Well, we must live and learn; and the next new friends you make I hope will be better worth keeping."
>
> Catherine coloured as she warmly answered, "No friend can be better worth keeping than Eleanor."
>
> "If so, my dear, I dare say you will meet again some time or other; do not be uneasy. It is ten to one but you are thrown together again in the course of a few years; and then, what a pleasure it will be."

Yet Mrs. Morland must once more be received back into favour, for her understatement to the Allens of Catherine's adventure:

> . . . no inflated representation, no studied appeal to their passions. "Catherine took us quite by surprize yesterday evening," said she. "She travelled all the way post by herself, and knew nothing of coming till Saturday night; for General Tilney, from some odd fancy or other, all of a sudden grew tired of having her there, and almost turned her out of the house. Very unfriendly, certainly; and he must be a very odd man; but we are so glad to have her amongst us again! And it is a great comfort to find that she is not a poor helpless creature, but can shift very well for herself."

How many mothers of that period, or of the present time, could have remained as well-balanced over an injury done to their child? Three days later she has again a lapse in imagination, and becomes "motherish": Catherine's loss of spirits, her listlessness, her sad and silent air, Mrs. Morland attributes to a hankering for gaieties:

> "You should never fret about trifles. . . . I hope, my Catherine, you are not getting out of humour with home, because it is not so grand as Northanger. That would be turning your visit into an evil, indeed!"

and the good lady trots upstairs to look for an essay in a book called *The Mirror* on the subject of "young girls who have been spoilt for home by great acquaintance." Really, Mrs. Morland, it might have penetrated your understanding that Catherine's was an ailment for which the cure was *not* a priggish essay in *The Mirror*.

I was delighted when she finally reinstated herself as an excellent parent by her instant welcome of Henry Tilney on his unexpected appearance, treating him with no resentment, and even conniving presently at his walk alone with Catherine to give him a chance to explain matters; and this, I am persuaded, without any worldly motive that a son of General Tilney, even the second son, would prove an advantageous match. When Henry asked their consent to an engagement,

Catherine's father and mother had not a single objection, and only one serious obstacle to be mentioned.

> That the General should come forward to solicit the alliance, or that he should even very heartily approve it, they were not refined enough to make any parading stipulation, but the decent appearance of consent must be yielded.

Had we had any doubt before as to the author's own very hearty approval of the Morlands, her astringent wording of this paragraph must have dispelled it, with its amused contempt of parents she must have known who *were* refined enough to make parading stipulations.

And now, one more bouquet for the Best Parents in Jane Austen, lenient without being fond and foolish: "And whenever Catherine received a letter, as at that time happened pretty often, *they always looked another way.*"

Mr. and Mrs. Musgrove, from *Persuasion,* I have selected as runners-up on the Morlands; equally good-natured, equally indulgent to their children, equally ready for Charles, Henrietta and Louisa to have a good time, and to make it easy for them to marry where desire led them, unencumbered by anxious consideration of ways and means, they were only less eligible than the Morlands in maybe a harmless deficiency of brains and breeding, somewhat more inclined to let their good-humoured spoiling of the young folk brim over into a lack of proper control. Louisa in particular, giddy, heedless, self-willed Louisa, would have been none the worse and probably very much better for the equivalent of a good spanking every now and then.

Our liking for Mr. and Mrs. Musgrove was warmed and increased whenever we caught sight of them as the centre of their happy family circle. We can leave their final eulogy to Anne Elliot; poor Anne, with no mother and a cold-hearted snobbish father, could yet rejoice without envy in the very different lot of the Musgrove daughters:

"Such excellent parents as Mr. and Mrs. Musgrove," exclaimed Anne, "should be happy in the children's marriages. They do everything to confer happiness, I am sure. What a blessing to young people to be in such hands! Your father and mother seem totally free from all those ambitious feelings which have led to so much misconduct and misery, both in young and old."

Nevertheless, Mrs. Musgrove as a mother becomes responsible for perhaps the one passage of Jane Austen that strikes us as heartless and in bad taste. Irritated herself by the poor woman's "large fat sighings" over the loss of a loutish only son Dick, who had been sent to sea because he was stupid and unmanageable on shore, she invites us to share her amusement and for once invites us in vain. I have read somewhere in defence of such a ruthless attitude, that Mrs. Musgrove had not cared at all for Dick while he had been alive, and that her later laments were the outcome of sentimentality, not of true grief. Quite simply, I do not concur; Mrs. Musgrove strikes me as an indiscriminate mother, as likely to dote (Jane Austen always spells it "doat") on an unsatisfactory son as on two fairly satisfactory daughters. She can, in fact, figure twice over in this chapter; I have room for her in my Dotage Department. We will see later on, as the specimens of mothers, fathers and aunts in their dotage swell the list, that Jane Austen must undoubtedly have encountered a good deal of it. We can be sure that had she been a mother herself, a corrective good sense would have been more in her line, and she is always ready to point out to us that doting parents, though luck may sometimes award them a good daughter (as Emma to Mr. Woodhouse), are more likely to produce an Isabella Thorpe, a Betsey Price, a Mr. Rushworth or a Lydia Bennet.

My award for being the Worst Father in Jane Austen goes to Sir Walter Elliot. I debated for some time whether he and General Tilney should not have been bracketed together, but came to the conclusion that though Henry and Eleanor suffered from their father's snobbery and his outbreaks of violent temper, he must yet have had some warmer quality unperceived by us: a childish ability, it may be, to be pleased by trifles, an affectionate dependence on his wife while she lived, that would place him only as runner-up to the baronet. Sir Walter was never childish and very rarely pleased; nothing pleased him except flattery to his person and deference to his rank. The General was unforgivably insulting to Eleanor's young friend who was a visitor in his house; unjust and over-credulous, he was perpetually putting his children to shame by his fulsome compliments and inconsistent partiality. Nevertheless, I can spare a few chips of forgiveness to fling in his direction every time I read, for example, of his delight in hearing about the superiority of his garden over Mr. Allen's:

> "How were Mr. Allen's succession-houses worked?" describing the nature of his own as they entered them.
>
> "Mr. Allen had only one small hot-house, which Mrs. Allen had the use of for her plants in winter, and there was a fire in it now and then."
>
> "He is a happy man!" said the General, with a look of very happy contempt.

A bad father, yes, but apparently quite a good husband. Catherine was a little more than wrong on facts when she supposed he had cruelly murdered his wife:

> "But your father," said Catherine, "was *he* afflicted?"
>
> "For a time, greatly so. You have erred in supposing him not attached to her. He loved her, I am persuaded, as well as it was possible for him to— We have not all, you know, the same tenderness of disposition; and I will not pretend to say that while she lived, she might not often have had much to bear; but though his temper injured her, his judgment never did. His value of her was sincere; and, if not permanently, he was truly afflicted by her death."

"I am very glad of it," said Catherine; "it would have been very shocking—"

I have, however, sought in vain for any such redeeming feature in Sir Walter Elliot's family life. Least of all could he appreciate his daughter Anne; she was so far superior in every attribute of mind and manners that I am convinced he really disliked her; his indifference to her well-being and happiness actually amounted to cruelty. So little did he consider her as a human being with any claims upon him, that General Tilney comes out well in comparison, for the General does at least, according to his own terribly inferior standards, concern himself to forward his children's interests, while Sir Walter is hardly even aware of Anne's existence. He is extravagant with money on his own behalf, but grudges the smallest outlay on a daughter:

"How is Mary looking?"—said Sir Walter. . . . "The last time I saw her she had a red nose, but I hope that may not happen every day. . . . If I thought it would not tempt her to go out in sharp winds and grow coarse, I would send her a new hat and pelisse."

Anne was considering whether she should venture to suggest that a gown, or a cap, would not be liable to any such misuse . . .

Imagine Anne's going to her father in any predicament, relying on his understanding, on his good offices on her behalf, on his wisdom and experience to advise her. Compare him with Sir Thomas Bertram, whose constant solicitude for his sons and daughters' welfare has won him an award which I am sure will surprise many into hot debate. For I declare him to be the Best Father in Jane Austen.

Here we may pause to define the adjective. By "best" I mean not necessarily wise in his guidance; far from it; one of the fundamental themes of *Mansfield Park,* revealed in its summing-up at the end, is that Sir Thomas lived to "acknowledge the advantages of early hardship and discipline, and the consciousness of being born to struggle and endure," or, in less stilted terms, that he owned up he had been wrong to hope his son Edmund might do better for himself than marrying his little cousin Fanny Price; owning up that Maria's marriage with the rich Mr. Rushworth had been a complete flop. No, by "best" I mean that he was constantly and affectionately preoccupied with the welfare of his offspring; their education mattered to him, their health and happiness; and he sought to procure them these blessings, not alone by spending money, but by much earnest endeavour and thought. Briefly, Sir Thomas was a "family man" with a sense of deep responsibility . . . and not a grain of humour to lighten his burden; there are moments when we might even have wished him a degree more feckless in his administration. Nevertheless, the man's integrity no less than his invariable courtesy, commands our respect.

And he was not altogether devoid of perception. When he returned from Antigua and had it well dinned into him by Maria's Aunt Norris how she had manoeuvred her favourite niece into a marvellous match, not all the extent of the Sotherton estate could blind his judgment to the fact that Mr. Rushworth was a very heavy, stupid young man, with whom there was a risk that Maria, in spite of being a socially ambitious young woman, might never be able to settle down to any sort of conjugal felicity. We are told how he tried to understand Maria's feelings, but it could not have been easy at that moment, for she was secretly trying to combine a sudden infatuation for Henry Crawford with the worldly prospects in a more advantageous, more definite alliance. Had Crawford openly spoken of *his* feelings in the matter—but on Sir Thomas' return, he seemed to relinquish any idea of wooing and winning her away from his rival. So she was in a mood to be impatient of the slightest parental restraint. Sir Thomas had not the right touch with daughters; poor man, he would gladly have received their confidence and helped them through their troubles, but Maria gave him no clue as to what these troubles could possibly be. We can imagine her saying to herself: "Oh, what's the use?—Daddy wouldn't *understand*"—as daughters have thought and will continue to think till the world rolls to an end. Sir Thomas could no more successfully be Maria's "daddy" than he could act Santa Claus dressed up in a white beard . . . but it was sweet of him to have made an attempt at daddying, and hard lines that his solemn manner should have frustrated such a genuine effort of imagination, which though it creaked stiffly when put into use, was at least not altogether absent:

> Sir Thomas addressed her; told her his fears, inquired into her wishes, entreated her to be open and sincere, and assured her that every inconvenience should be braved, and the connection entirely given up, if she felt herself unhappy in the prospect of it. He would act for her and release her.

Can we suppose Sir Walter Elliot would ever bring himself to offer escape to a daughter about to marry creditably? Sir Walter thought only of himself. Sir Thomas, as far as I can see, never considered himself at all through the whole of *Mansfield Park*. Therefore my award remains.

Nor did he stop short at being an excellent father. He was an excellent uncle as well; his own relations are never mentioned, but he concerned himself with the children of Lady Bertram's poor sister Price as though they were his own. Lady Bertram herself remained fairly tranquil when the desperate appeal arrived from Portsmouth, after eleven years of estrangement between the sisters. For Mrs. Norris with her inimitable talent had stirred up bitter feelings; and the bustle she now made about coming to the relief of her sister Fanny, "who could no longer afford to cherish pride or resentment," must undoubtedly have been from motives of self-consequence; and self-consequence, moreover, at Sir Thomas' expense. He, after his stately mental processes had been put into action, was ready to admit little Fanny Price into his household, to be brought up with his daughters; and to bestir himself with money and advice to get the eldest boy into the navy. With a certain not unlovable deliberation, he laid down his fears that either of his own sons might later on fall in love with little Fanny. That was fairly natural, especially in a father of the period; and we can forgive him for the sake of his explanation that "we must secure to the child, or consider ourselves engaged to secure to her hereafter, as circumstances may arise, the provision of a gentlewoman, if no such establishment should offer as you are so sanguine in expecting." To which Mrs. Norris might have replied, (but did not): "Well, you can't say fairer than that." To be impetuously kind and generous is always an easier matter than to engage oneself to provide for an indigent niece consistently for a lifetime, as Sir Thomas Bertram was prepared to do. Of course when the child arrived, he terrified her out of her wits by his "well-meant condescension"; but the stress should be on "well-meant." Besides, Fanny was an unusually timid little niece, and we have ample evidence that though her uncle could not put her at her ease, he did think out from time to time any scheme that might be for her delight: William, before he went to sea, was asked by him to spend a week at Mansfield Park. And when they are both grown-up, and William was invited again to stay at the Park, Sir Thomas bloomed into real sweetness of disposition—though we may still laugh at his pompous choice of phrase—when he determined to give a ball at Mansfield while his own daughters were away, simply to gratify William's carelessly expressed desire to see his sister dance. Mrs. Norris, whose notions of aunthood must have been taken from the tales of the bad old fairy who bounced in to spoil the christening, was furious at seeing William and Fanny so indulged; and I like to suppose that if ever Sir Thomas allowed himself a twinkle of amusement, it was in thwarting all her proposals and suggestions, by having the whole business prearranged: "a very complete outline," before he openly spoke a word about it. All his inclinations were against Aunt Norris' determined efforts to keep Fanny in her place, and a very lowly place too:

> "Fanny, at what time would you have the carriage come round?" . . .
>
> "My dear Sir Thomas!" cried Mrs. Norris, red with anger, "Fanny can walk."
>
> "Walk!" repeated Sir Thomas, in a tone of most unanswerable dignity, and coming farther into the room. "My niece walk to a dinner engagement at this time of the year! Will twenty minutes after four suit you?"
>
> "Yes, sir," was Fanny's humble answer, given with the feelings almost of a criminal towards Mrs. Norris.

And even when he was displeased with the young girl for throwing away such an opportunity of being honourably and suitably settled in life with Mr. Crawford, he does tell her to dry her tears (after a speech of a page and a half), and go out for an hour on the gravel in the shrubbery; he does remember to give orders to the housemaid that in future she is to have a fire in her own room every day, a comfort hitherto denied her. By whom? Need we ask! By her Aunt Norris.

It is not within our scope to talk of Mrs. Norris' shrill failure as an aunt; nor to give examples of the hundred and one ways in which she contrived to make Fanny's life a misery. Certainly she stands as a monument of the Worst Aunt in Jane Austen, with a long score of moral and physical cruelty to her discredit. We cannot even plead for her that she did not know what she was doing; she knew perfectly well; the Prices were objects of her repulsive looks for no better reason than that they were poor; William and Susan were nearly as unpopular as Fanny, or we might have supposed it was Fanny's creep-mouse ways that goaded an active aunt into irritable reaction. To her Portsmouth nieces and nephew, Aunt Norris displayed herself as a scold, a snob, a bully, a spoil-sport and a nagger; she flattered and indulged Maria and Julia, especially Maria, because they were the daughters of Sir Thomas Bertram. *Not* a nice character, our Aunt Norris. I cannot myself find any redeeming feature in her—(have I forgotten to mention she was also stingy and officious?)—so I must borrow one from Jane Austen—and disagree with it:

> Of her two sisters, Mrs. Price very much more resembled Lady Bertram than Mrs. Norris. She was a manager by necessity, without any of Mrs. Norris's inclination for it, or any of her activity. Her disposition was naturally easy and indolent, like Lady Bertram's; and a situation of similar affluence and do-nothingness would have been much more suited to her capacity than the exertions and self-denials of the one which her imprudent marriage had placed her in. She might have made just as good a woman of consequence as Lady Bertram, but Mrs. Norris would have been a more respectable mother of nine children on a small income.

No, and again no. Mrs. Norris would have been equally horrid as a mother of nine children on a small income; and I do not quite understand what Miss Austen means in this context by "respectable." Possibly that the home at Portsmouth would have been more orderly (and that the two maids would have given notice even oftener than they already did).

Nevertheless, we cannot maintain that Captain and Mrs. Price were good parents. Captain Price stands third on my list of Worst Fathers. He was proud enough of William, but Fanny and the rest of his noisy hallooing tribe meant nothing to him; and he made no sacrifices on their behalf; he was insensitive and coarse in grain. Opening the book at random, I find also "he swore and he drank, he was dirty and gross." Perhaps in placing him as third, I am overestimating him; perhaps he was a worse father than either Sir Walter Elliot or General Tilney. He should not have made Fanny "the object of a coarse joke" . . . and we ought to be ashamed of a slight stir of curiosity in our lower natures, to hear more details.

We have already had a verdict on Mrs. Price as a mother, but we must not forget that this emanated not so much from a detached Miss Austen, as from Miss Austen in protection of her dear Fanny. Fanny's home had been at Mansfield Park for the last nine years, and when she did return to Portsmouth she was a visitor; we cannot be surprised that "Mrs. Price's heart and time were already quite full." Her injudicious spoiling of little Betsey, the youngest of the Prices, reminds me to place her in our collection of Doting Parents, together with Mrs. Rushworth, who "saw nothing but her son."

Mostly they are fools who dote; and Lady Bertram proves once again that for all her indolence, she is no fool; for though fond of her children and of her nieces and nephew, she does not overindulge any of them, and is well content to let Sir Thomas preside over their lives. Nor can this be set down to her coldness of heart; the maternal instinct is there; we see it displayed when Tom Bertram is brought home seriously ill, and when she receives Fanny back at Mansfield Park after long absence. A natural effect of her Sister Norris' spreading and bouncing all over Mansfield Park, might easily have been to keep an unquarrelsome disposition quietly anchored on the sofa with Pug, doing fancy work. An interesting character, Lady Bertram.

Mrs. Bennet receives my highest award as the Worst Mother in Jane Austen. Try as I will, I cannot discover in her a single redeeming feature. She dotes on her youngest daughter, that young ruffian Lydia; she is proud of Jane's beauty in the same way that a *procureuse* may reckon up the material gains which beauty may bring to her house; she is indifferent to Mary and Kitty (so are we, but still!); and I should not be surprised to hear in confidence that she positively disliked her enchanting daughter Elizabeth—until of course, the advent of tall rich Mr. Darcy as Elizabeth's accepted suitor. Then indeed, running on in a style that proved she had not even the intelligence to hide her gross sense of values, Mrs. Bennet reveals herself once and for all.

> "O my sweetest Lizzy, how rich and how great you will be! What pin-money, what jewels, what carriages you will have! . . . O my dear Lizzy! pray apologize for my having disliked him so much before. I hope he will overlook it. Dear, dear Lizzy. A house in town! Everything that is charming! Three daughters married! Ten thousand a year! O Lord! what will become of me? I shall go distracted."
>
> . . . Elizabeth, rejoicing that such an effusion was heard only by herself, soon went away. But before she had been three minutes in her own room, her mother followed her.
>
> "My dearest child," she cried, "I can think of nothing else. Ten thousand a year, and very likely more! 'Tis as good as a lord! And a special licence—you must and shall be married by a special licence. But, my dearest love, tell me what dish Mr. Darcy is particularly fond of, that I may have it tomorrow."
>
> This was a sad omen of what her mother's behaviour to the gentleman himself might be.

How deeply we sympathise with Elizabeth's premonition. Bad enough to have a thoroughly stupid mother, but stupidity can sometimes be concealed; bad enough to have to flinch from the innate vulgarity of every thought and wish that sprang from Mrs. Bennet's soul and found utterance in her speech; yet hardest of all to endure a mother who will constantly put her daughters to open shame in front of those before whom they would desire their parents should make the fairest impression. I imagine Jane Bennet was not as keenly perceptive as Elizabeth, or lacking her sense of humour, was perhaps also spared that agonising knowledge which Elizabeth had to endure so often, of their mother's making herself supremely ridiculous.

Especially when Mr. Darcy visited Longbourn in Bingley's company; and Mrs. Bennet cold-shouldered him, unaware that he had been the means of rescuing Lydia from her situation as Wickham's mistress, but ostentatiously displayed the utmost graciousness to Mr. Bingley (who might still marry Jane). She declared to Mr. Bennet that she hated the very sight of Darcy (probably because he made her feel small): " 'Thank heaven,' " (talking of Wickham) " 'he has *some* friends, though perhaps not so many as he deserves.' "

> Elizabeth, who knew this to be levelled at Mr. Darcy, was in such misery of shame that she could hardly keep her seat. . . . At that instant she felt that years of happiness could not make Jane or herself amends for moments of such painful confusion.

I made a statement just now without substantiating it; that Jane, despite her sweetness of disposition, was less perceptive than her sister Elizabeth; but I base it on a remark directly after her happy betrothal to Bingley: "I must go instantly to my mother," she cried. "I would not on any account trifle with her affectionate solicitude. . . ." How even the most loving daughter in the world could have spontaneously alluded to her mother's barefaced and embarrassing pursuit of Bingley as her "affectionate solicitude," only a slight degree of stupidity can explain. Jane was indeed a darling, but she had not inherited her father's brains.

Mrs. Bennet's total failure as a mother must be held largely accountable for Mr. Bennet's partial failure as a father. She set up an irritable reaction against fatherhood which he would not or could not strive to overcome. Whatever her inner feelings, Elizabeth remained a respectful daughter, remembering always what was due to her mother. If ever pertness were justified (and Elizabeth *was* a trifle pert), it might have been justified had she used it on Mrs. Bennet; especially as her father offered a bad example by continually making game of his wife in front of his daughters. Four of them did not know what he was at; the fifth, his favourite, Lizzy, knew all too well; it stands to her credit that she never took advantage of it.

Jane and Elizabeth were as one in regretting their mother's lavish indulgence of Lydia, and its probable consequences. They did their best to rouse Mr. Bennet to a sense of responsibility in the matter, but all he remarked was that Lydia would never be easy till she had exposed herself in some public place or other: " '. . . and we can never expect her to do it with so little expense or inconvenience to her family as under the present circumstances.' " Presently, however, seeing that Elizabeth was deeply in earnest over the danger to Lydia's wild volubility, her unchecked flamboyant character, he did take the trouble to reply more seriously. Elizabeth could not be wholly reassured by her father's argument that at Brighton Lydia would find her own level as a common flirt of no importance and hardly any fortune; she had not the pettiness of nature to be gratified when Lydia's father, later on, was forced to acknowledge how right they had been, and what evil consequences had sprung from his own perpetual attitude of amused detachment:

> . . . on her briefly expressing her sorrow for what he must have endured, he replied, "Say nothing of that. Who should suffer but myself? It has been my own doing, and I ought to feel it."
>
> "You must not be too severe upon yourself," replied Elizabeth.
>
> "You may well warn me against such an evil. Human nature is so prone to fall into it! No, Lizzy; let me once in my life feel how much I have been to blame. I am not afraid of being overpowered by the impression. It will pass away soon enough."

At least Mr. Bennet never hoodwinked himself into delusions concerning his offspring:

"They have none of them much to recommend them," replied he—"they are all silly and ignorant like other girls; but Lizzy has something more of quickness than her sisters."

"Mr. Bennet, how can you abuse your own children in such a way?" . . .

"From all that I can collect by your manner of talking, you must be two of the silliest girls in the country. I have suspected it some time, but I am now convinced."

His dry attempts to debunk Mrs. Bennet's ebullient aspirations may only have reached that stage from exhaustion during the earlier years when their five daughters were still young enough for the guidance they were never to receive; his wit may have been the outcome of despair. Yet it is a bad father who before his children are born, can expose them to the misery of such a mother.

Pride and Prejudice is undoubtedly a love story; veined with love, brilliant with love, tender with love's misunderstandings and reconciliations. Nevertheless, we have just as much reason to call it a family story, and to add an aunt and uncle to the group: Mr. and Mrs. Gardiner. They take an active share in whatever happens to the Bennets, but in contrast to the Prices' Aunt Norris, prove such a delightful couple, so sensible, so ready to give pleasure to their nieces and assist them in any trouble, that we marvel how Mrs. Bennet could possibly have achieved a brother like Mr. Gardiner; it would seem biologically impossible; they spring from quite a different social strata. Elizabeth, who is not free from a little natural snobbery, exults in exhibiting these most desirable relations to Mr. Darcy when he encounters them walking through the grounds of Pemberley:

It was consoling that he should know she had some relations for whom there was no need to blush. She listened most attentively to all that passed between them, and gloried

> in every expression, every sentence of her uncle, which marked his intelligence, his taste, or his good manners.

With her Aunt Gardiner, Elizabeth is on terms of liveliest intimacy and confidence; they write each other charming letters, more like sisters than aunt and niece. Although they have children of their own, the Gardiners seem imbued with a strong sense of responsibility towards the Bennet daughters, a sense lacking in both Mr. and Mrs. Bennet. Any uncle and aunt might have been happy to invite an Elizabeth to accompany them on their tour of Derbyshire, but not every uncle or aunt would have seen it as their duty to have had a bouncing unrepentant Lydia to stay with them at their house in Cheapside during the ungrateful period between her elopement and marriage. Nobody could link Sir Thomas Bertram and Mr. Bennet as prototypes in their outlook on the responsibilities of parenthood, but at this one moment they express exactly the same views: Sir Thomas will not receive Maria back at Mansfield Park after that lovely woman has stooped to folly; and in a rare moment of firmness, Mr. Bennet informs his wife that:

> "Into *one* house in this neighbourhood they shall never have admittance. I will not encourage the imprudence of either by receiving them at Longbourn."

Nor, by the way, would he advance so much as a guinea to buy a trousseau for his daughter: Mrs. Bennet simply could not believe it; to her, marriage scarcely seemed valid without new clothes.

The Bennet girls had another uncle and aunt who lived in the military town of Meryton, close by; a proximity wildly exciting to Lydia and Kitty, though not to their elder sisters. Aunt Philips was Mrs. Bennet's sister; we may readily believe it; a vulgar good-humoured woman, married to "broad-faced, stuffy Uncle Philips, breathing port wine." " 'My aunt Philips,' declared Lydia to Jane and Elizabeth, 'wants you so to get husbands you can't think.' "

Darcy also has an aunt, well mixed up with the plot of *Pride and Prejudice*. She is better known as Lady Catherine de Bourgh. An intolerable woman, overbearing and interfering, who exploits her aunthood even to the extent of visiting Elizabeth Bennet, and in a scene where she becomes abusive as any fishwife, informing her that a match with her nephew—

> "to which you have the presumption to aspire, can never take place—no, never. Mr. Darcy is engaged to *my daughter*. Now, what have you to say?"
>
> "Only this—that if he is so, you can have no reason to suppose he will make an offer to me."

Not unnaturally, Lady Catherine was stumped. I will do her the justice of supposing, however, that her interest in her nephew does not spring entirely from motives of snobbery; she seemed genuinely quite fond of him. And in the last chapter after a long interval:

> . . . her resentment gave way, either to her affection for him or her curiosity to see how his wife conducted herself, and she condescended to wait on them at Pemberley, in spite of that pollution which its woods had received, not merely from the presence of such a mistress, but the visits of her uncle and aunt from the city.

How surprising that the formidable Lady Catherine de Bourgh can be slipped into our Dotage Collection; but most of these dragon ladies have their weak spot tucked away under the scales, and Lady Catherine ceases to be a dragon when she refers to her daughter, her only child, Anne de Bourgh. Anne is a pale thin little thing without character or individuality; in fact, naughty Elizabeth chooses to approve of her appearance on the grounds that she would do very well for Mr. Darcy because "she looks sickly and cross." So it is rather touching when Miss de Bourgh's doting mother, unable to find anything outstanding to praise in her daughter's actual merits or performances, remarks of Elizabeth's musical talent:

"Miss Bennet would not play at all amiss if she practised more, and could have the advantage of a London master. She has a very good notion of fingering, though her taste is not equal to Anne's. Anne would have been a delightful performer, had her health allowed her to learn."

I am puzzled how to reconcile my preference for Mrs. Dashwood—nay, my selection of her as the Best Mother, with the fact that she may qualify for that position and yet cannot be passed out of quarantine free from a suspicion of Dotage. She dotes on her second daughter, Marianne; nothing less could have so blinded her to Marianne's shocking bad manners and heedless pursuit of her own way without any regard even for her nearest and dearest. Marianne is never reprimanded or controlled except tentatively by her elder sister Elinor; and the good sense and prudence of an elder sister is rather unfairly apt to sound priggish when she has to usurp the duties of a mother towards a spoilt child:

"Oh my dear mother, you must be wrong in permitting an engagement between a daughter so young, a man so little known, to be carried on in so doubtful, so mysterious a manner! *I* long to inquire; but how will *my* interference be borne!"

Having duly blamed Mrs. Dashwood for her all too loving indulgence of Marianne, I can now give substance to my bold assertion that in less obvious respects she deserves high praise. In a sense, her own happy temperament is her best ally; she never oppresses her daughters by complaints of the present or apprehension for the future, genuinely seeing no reason for either; though her husband, the girls' father, died on the second page of *Sense and Sensibility,* and they had to leave their home, their large property and estates, to manage on a very reduced income, living quietly in a cottage lent them by a relation. Plain misfortune can always better be endured than misfortune heightened by injustice and disappointment, but

Mrs. Dashwood had to put up with both. The reasons for which her husband, through no fault of his own, had been unable to provide adequately for his family after his death, are somewhat complicated; he had recommended them to the care of a son by a former marriage, who by an arbitrary arrangement of wills and deaths had succeeded to everything; he talked himself out of the necessity to help his father's second wife and his three half-sisters, in one of the best comedy scenes of rationalisation and self-delusion ever invented (Why, by the way, does Jane Austen refer to his stepmother as his mother-in-law?).

But Mrs. Dashwood's sanguine spirits, her gaiety and natural facility to look on the bright side of things, are more valuable than a hundred estates of the size of Norland:

> . . . no temper could be more cheerful than hers, or possess, in a greater degree, that sanguine expectation of happiness which is happiness itself.

Yet, when the author goes on to remark:

> But in sorrow she must be equally carried away by her fancy, and as far beyond consolation as in pleasure she was beyond alloy—

I simply do not believe it; Mrs. Dashwood recovers her spirits just when it is natural and not merely heartless that they should revive; and from then onwards her adaptability, no less than her desire that her daughters should not be made melancholy, recommend her as the most excellent of mothers, whose buoyancy Elinor has certainly to restrain a little when it leads to joyful planning for immense architectural improvements in their new home; but who inspires an atmosphere at Barton Cottage so free from strain and quarrelling, so affectionate and busy, that I am convinced the affection of her daughters and of the faithful servants who have accompanied them, are a direct result of contact with an unselfish mother and mistress, even at such close quarters as is suddenly forced upon them all by their change of fortune. As for her impulsive optimism, that in itself is lovable; we may gauge it by comparison with Marianne, equally impulsive and not in the very least lovable: she has inherited the optimism without the unselfishness. You will have perceived by now that Mrs. Dashwood is one of my favourite heroines in Jane Austen, and that I am yielding to a sad lack of self-control in quoting at length without any proper excuse or justification, my favourite of her speeches:

> "Perhaps in the spring if I have plenty of money, as I dare say I shall, we may think about building. These parlours are both too small for such parties of our friends as I hope to see often collected here; and I have some thoughts of throwing the passage into one of them, with perhaps a part of the other, and so leave the remainder of that other for an entrance; this, with a new drawing-room, which may be easily added, and a bedchamber and garret above, will make it a very snug little cottage. I could wish the stairs were handsome. But one must not expect everything; though I suppose it would be no difficult matter to widen them. I shall see how much I am beforehand with the world in the spring, and we will plan our improvements accordingly."

You must agree with me that these are not only the words, but the thoughts of an enchanting woman: "I shall see how much I am beforehand with the world in the spring" . . . Mrs. Dashwood will always be beforehand with the world in the spring.

When Elinor and Marianne receive Mrs. Jennings' invitation to stay with her in London, do we hear their widowed mother complain drearily that but for Margaret she will be left nearly alone in the cottage and how dull and desolate that will be, but she does not wish to stand in the way of their pleasure, so (with a heavy sigh) they had better go and enjoy themselves? Not a word in that vein; only too anxious that their pleasure may be unshadowed by any fears for her, she is at some pains to invent a number of plausible reasons why their absence at this period was the very thing she most desired.

Adaptability, gaiety, unselfishness and a warm affectionate disposition—I need add no more to my estimate of Mrs. Dashwood except a footnote to the effect that I discern a second cause for disagreement between Jane Austen and myself: not only does she love Fanny Price, whom I do not love at all, but she does not love Mrs. Dashwood as I do, and is forever jibing at her for her tendency to exaggerate the moment's emotional opportunities. If ever we meet, I must have it out with her on both these counts.

When Elinor and Marianne accept Mrs. Jennings' invitation to quit the West Country and come up to stay with her in Berkeley Square, we are told that Elinor wondered at her own situation:

> . . . so short had their acquaintance with that lady been, so wholly unsuited were they in age and disposition, and so many had been her objections against such a measure only a few days before! But these objections had all, with that happy ardour of youth which Marianne and her mother equally shared, been overcome or overlooked . . .

Yet Mrs. Jennings improves so much on closer acquaintance, that possibly Miss Austen was not aware herself in the early chapters of the book how much sturdy kindness and loyalty (and sense of decency, too, in all that really mattered) were concealed by a superficial lack of manner, of delicacy and tact. Apart from all that, Mrs. Jennings emerges as a good mother to her two extremely tiresome daughters, one of them insipid and one giggling. A touch of Dotage is shown towards Charlotte, the giggling one: over the mantelpiece of the spare room was hung a landscape in coloured silks, worked by Charlotte while still at school. Mrs. Jennings was the sort of mother and grandmother who came to the rescue in moments of emergency, never sparing herself; and her warm active solicitude when Marianne was struck down with a serious illness in the Palmers' house, had that rounded maternal quality to confirm our good opinion of the lady, and amply atones for any lack of refinement when we first meet her.

Of the behaviour of another mother in *Sense and Sensibility,* Mrs. Ferrars, a woman mean and rotten in heart, Mrs. Jennings remarks: " 'Well! that is *her* revenge. Everybody has a way of their own. But I don't think mine would be to make one son independent because another had plagued me.' " In spite of her importance to the plot and dénouement, we cannot, however, take Mrs. Ferrars seriously as a mother; unfair to Edward, doting on Robert, snobbery her motivating power, she really does not exist at all. Mrs. Allen in *Northanger Abbey* remarks several times: " 'Really I have not patience with the General,' " until she gets tired of saying it. So might I repeat: "Really I have not patience with Mrs. Ferrars," without being at all convinced that she is worth my indignation. Whereas I *can* be indignant with Elinor (though in the main I am exceedingly fond of her) when in favour of declining Mrs. Jennings' invitation, she can say to her mother: "she is not a woman whose society can afford us pleasure, or whose protection will give us consequence."

Had Mrs. Ferrars ever come alive, she would be runner-up to Mrs. Bennet in my choice of the Worst Mother, and that in spite of Mr. John Dashwood's encomiums of her as the best: " 'A most excellent mother . . . Mrs. Ferrars has a noble spirit' "—for which he adds reasons to stagger us, though to him they serve as the purest evidence.

A few of Jane Austen's less successful characters, such as Mrs. Ferrars, have been fashioned merely for their plot value. She whittles them out of wood, bids them live, but I imagine does not worry overmuch if they refuse to obey her bidding. Mrs. Churchill is another of these useful puppets. Both exist for the same purpose: the cruel parents who will not allow their son to marry the girl of his choice. Edward Ferrars is destined by his mother's ambitions to be the husband of Miss Morton, Lord Morton's daughter, with a fortune of thirty-thousand pounds; which is another reason for Mr. John Dashwood to assert her claims as a peerless mother; though to Mrs. Jennings she appeared "nothing more than a little proud-looking woman of uncordial address," a summing-up which for a moment does certainly give her a momentary flicker of life.

The great Mrs. Churchill, had she ever come to hear of it, must have been equally positive in forbidding any attachment between the nephew who was also her adopted son, and a dowerless girl destined to earn her own living as a governess; a mere granddaughter of poor Mrs. Bates. Frank Churchill was so certain that no representations could be of the slightest avail in making Jane Fairfax, his sweet Jane, acceptable at Enscombe as his bride, that he never even gives his aunt a chance of violent refusal, but instead takes the less honourable course of persuading Jane Fairfax to a secret engagement. In the letter where at length he explains himself, excuses himself, accuses himself to Mrs. Weston, he writes:

> "But you will be ready to say, What was your hope in doing this? What did you look forward to? To anything, everything—to time, chance, circumstance, slow effects, sudden bursts, perseverance and weariness, health and sickness,"

and goes on to plead that

> "I have the honour, my dear madam, of being your husband's son, and the advantage of inheriting a disposition to hope for good which no inheritance of houses or lands can ever equal the value of."

Yet, as Mr. Knightley points out to Emma while reading the letter, though Frank Churchill inherits his father's sanguine temper, Mr. Weston's upright and honourable exertions have been omitted in the son. Frank Churchill's "exertions" were all bent towards self-indulgence and on saving his bacon. They are alike and unlike, and the young man was far luckier than he deserved in the death of his aunt and the subsequent kindness of his uncle.

Mrs. and Miss Bates, dearest of people in their capacities of aunt and grandmother, cannot elude the Dotage collection. Both dote on Jane Fairfax, not altogether without reason; in birth, intelligence and fineness of perception she does seem their superior; though oddly enough, drawn as a heroine she emerges as a bore; whereas Miss Bates, drawn as a bore, represents in our eyes—not exactly a heroine, but a character whose garter Jane Fairfax is not fit to wear. I mention garters deliberately; for, exasperated by this all too visible dotage, Emma does flippantly remark to Harriet that Miss Fairfax cannot as much as knit her aunt a pair of garters nor send her grandmother a pattern for a stomacher but one hears of nothing else for a month. Harriet agrees, of course, but I suspect she was slightly shocked; she may have wistfully reflected that it would be nice to have relations, an aunt or a grandmother, best of all a mother, who might have been equally infatuated with her smallest, homeliest achievement.

Harriet Smith was of doubtful birth—

> . . . the natural daughter of somebody. Somebody had placed her, several years back, at Mrs. Goddard's school, and somebody had lately raised her from the condition of scholar to that of parlour boarder. This was all that was generally known of her history.

Emma's romantic impulsive point of view therefore immediately touched up the situation and coloured it according to her own fancy and desire, arguing with Mr. Knightley that the unknown father must certainly be a gentleman and a gentleman of fortune; she influences the girl accordingly to reject Mr. Martin and the Abbey Mill Farm, and to look higher and higher in the social scale, moving up from Mr. Elton to Frank Churchill . . . until Harriet's imagination takes too great a leap and fixes on Mr. Knightley himself.

> Harriet's parentage became known. She proved to be the daughter of a tradesman, rich enough to afford her the comfortable maintenance which had ever been hers, and decent enough to have always wished for concealment. Such was the blood of gentility which Emma had formerly been so ready to vouch for! It was likely to be as untainted, perhaps, as the blood of many a gentleman; but what a connection had she been preparing for Mr. Knightley, or for the Churchills, or even for Mr. Elton! The stain of illegitimacy, unbleached by nobility or wealth, would have been a stain indeed.
>
> No objection was raised on the father's side; the young man was treated liberally; it was all as it should be.

A comfortable state of affairs, which is right and proper in the last few pages of a Jane Austen novel; but what a curious point of view is revealed in the line "decent enough to have always wished for concealment." A point of view obviously so acceptable to the century, that it did not occur even to a satirical mind to question or to ridicule it. Considering, therefore, that from all "decent" points of view Harriet is an orphan, she acquires the best possible parent when she marries Mr. Martin, that honest yeoman; for without being told very much about Mrs. Martin, an impression is somehow conveyed of a sturdily independent woman, knowing how to command her children's respect, not seeking to scramble into the class above her own; nor, by making an undue fuss over a matter of illegitimacy, taking steps to kill the happiness of her only son. Harriet was made most kindly welcome at the farm while still a homeless parlour-boarder at Mrs. Goddard's school; and when she took a fancy to their very pretty little welch cow, Mrs. Martin, not devoid of imagination, said that as she was so fond of it, it should be called *her* cow; a perfect way to give happiness to a simple warm-hearted child without any live possessions of her own. Exalted by the patronage of Miss Woodhouse, she later pays a formal call on the Martins, strictly limited to a quarter of an hour; and we are again given an impression that no reproaches are spoken, no resentment shown, only a touch of natural dignity appears in her hostess at this ill-judged *visite de convenance*; and even so, stiffness is momentarily dispelled by—

> Mrs. Martin's saying, all of a sudden, that she thought Miss Smith was grown, had brought on a more interesting subject and a warmer manner. In that very room she had been measured last September with her two friends. There were the pencilled marks and memorandums on the wainscot by the window.

We have seen Mrs. Morland and Mrs. Martin can be given full marks not only as mothers, but in the more difficult rôle of mothers-in-law; Mrs. Dashwood to complete the trio in that capacity. With a certain trepidation we must contemplate dear Mr. Woodhouse as father-in-law to Mr. Knightley, after his marriage with Emma. In another chapter I have already gone into the matter, so it had better not be attempted here, where anyhow it is as a father that we are to view him. I will try and remain unprejudiced by my personal infatuation for Mr. Woodhouse, for he was *not* a good father to Emma and Isabella, if "good" in this context is to mean sensible, protective, self-sacrificing, a rock in times of need, a reasonable intellect to guide Emma's education and general outlook.

He had truly the kindest heart in the world; was ever a loyal generous neighbour and friend to those of Highbury less fortunate than himself, an old gentleman of breeding, a nature utterly foreign to sentiments malicious, cruel or vindictive; with a childlike dependence in those whom he trusted, combined with an unworldliness that in some of its manifestations of surprise and alarm brought him very near to being a borderline case. None of these otherwise endearing qualities make for good fatherhood; Emma deserved a halo and the Royal Humane Society's medal for never retorting while he fidgeted nervously over the hundred potential dangers that (he was convinced) beset her every hour. His uncritical admiration of his strong firm cheerful young daughter established him as leader and head of the Dotage class. Had she lived, Mrs. Woodhouse must have been both mother and father to Emma, as we surmise she was both husband and wife to Mr. Woodhouse; an image of her which is not merely guesswork; for discussing the problem with Mrs. Weston, Mr. Knightley says: "'In her mother she lost the only person able to cope with her. She inherits her mother's talents, and must have been under subjection to her.'"

Jane Austen is not interested in very young children. Mr. Woodhouse, Sir Walter Elliot, Sir Thomas and Lady Bertram, all the procession of parents, good, bad and indifferent who have passed through this chapter in review, are middle-aged or elderly fathers and mothers to the grown-up heroes and heroines of her stories; somehow it is not possible for her to concentrate with much interest on parents whose offspring are still in the nursery, and according to her notions should be kept there until claimed by the schoolroom, and kept in the schoolroom with their governess until the formal decree of society that they are of an age to come out. So children whenever they appear are sketched in with a slightly disapproving air. Mary Musgrove (for instance) is depicted as a young mother too easily exasperated, too selfishly hysterical to have any success in coping with her tiresome little Charles and Walter; their father could manage them better, but only when his wife was not present to interfere. Lady Middleton spoilt her children, giving in immediately to all the whims and screams of her sweet little Anna Marie, petting and apricot marmalade freely applied; yet we would just rather see Lady Middleton human and partial than in her usual listlessly polite state of half-alive. The children of Mr. and Mrs. John Knightley, Henry and John, Bella and little Emma, are better behaved, on the rare occasions when we meet them in their grandfather's house; it cannot be that Isabella does not coddle and indulge them; Mr. John Knightley as good as says so; but his more robust methods would provide a counter-irritant, and I dare say they will grow up very well. The Price children, Sam and Charles and Tom and horrid little Betsey, noisy and disobedient, pay no heed to their father's bellowing or to their mother's whimpering complaints; but then what chance have they had in that household? I expect we should have liked the Morland tribe of juveniles had we seen more of them, but Mr. and Mrs. Morland have already received their mead of praise as parents. In Miss Austen's novels, children are more or less synonymous with savages, and she hustles them out of sight as soon as possible, coolly taking for granted that her views on the subject are incontestable. The sight of a rational person ever sitting down to read for their own enjoyment a book about children—*Alice*, or *The Wind in the Willows* or an E. Nesbit story—would have filled her with incredulity, then with amazement, then with an emotion which I am so unwilling to awake even for a moment in my beloved Miss Austen that perhaps it is well she and I have been divided by nearly a hundred years from meeting in the flesh.

CHAPTER VI

"Four and Twenty Families"

SHEILA KAYE-SMITH

JANE AUSTEN is primarily a family novelist. She writes of family life. Her characters function as members of families. Her heroes and heroines are not solitary figures of mysterious origin, as in so many of the lesser novels of her day—when foundlings were apt to appear on any doorstep, and vast residences housed one single unknown. They have background if they have nothing else, and their stories introduce us into a complete society: It is a society of families. "I know," says Mrs. Bennet, anxious to impress Darcy with the largeness of her circle— "I know that we dine with four and twenty families."

Here and there some man—Mr. Elton, Mr. Knightley, Colonel Brandon—may live alone, but he is only awaiting matrimony and his absorption into family life of some sort. And these are the exceptions. Mostly the heroes as well as the heroines belong to good-sized families.

For the families are generally large, though Jane Austen, who does not judge these things by the timid standards of our day, acknowledges only two of them as such. Catherine Morland, we are told, was one of ten children, and "a family of ten children will always be called a fine family, where there are heads and arms and legs enough for the number." The Prices in *Mansfield Park* were also a large family, though only once are they called a fine one. That was on the Sunday when Henry Crawford walked with them all to the Garrison Church. "The family were now seen to advantage. Nature had given them no inconsiderable share of beauty, and every

Sunday dressed them in their cleanest skins and best attire. . . . Sunday made her a very creditable and tolerably cheerful-looking Mrs. Price, coming abroad with a fine family of children." Earlier we know she had written to her sister Bertram a letter "which spoke of such a superfluity of children, and such a want of almost everything else," that it was decided at Mansfield Park to relieve her at least of one of them.

Another family which must have been nearly as large, though its numbers are never specified, is the Musgrove family in *Persuasion.* Here we have Charles, the eldest son, who has married Mary Elliot, and the two sisters next him in age —Louisa and Henrietta. We hear also of "poor Richard" who died at sea, and get a glimpse of several smaller boys and girls home for the Christmas holidays. "On one side was a table, occupied by some chattering girls, cutting up silk and gold paper; and on the other were tressels and trays, bending under the weight of brawn and cold pies, where riotous boys were holding high revel; the whole completed by a roaring Christmas fire, which seemed determined to be heard, in spite of all the noise of the others." It is true that all the children did not belong to Mr. and Mrs. Musgrove—there were the little Harvilles and the two children from the cottage. Nevertheless "it was a fine family piece," in spite of Lady Russell's comment as she departed— "I hope I shall remember in future not to call at Uppercross in the Christmas holidays."

In such big families there is nearly always a pairing off among the children of brothers and sisters nearest in age or most alike in temperament. Such a pairing was natural between William and Fanny Price. Their love and happiness in each other's society is a golden thread running through *Mansfield Park,* from that first letter which Edmund helped Fanny to write to the journey to Portsmouth when "everything supplied amusement to the high glee of William's mind, and he was full of frolic and joke in the intervals of their high-toned subjects, all of which ended if they did not begin, in praise of the Thrush . . . or speculations upon prize-money, which was to be distributed at home, with only the reservation of enough to make the little cottage comfortable, in which he and Fanny were to pass their middle and latter life together."

Actually, in spite of their devotion, there could not be more dissimilarity between their characters. Fanny is timid and serious, William is merry and bold. But it is often contrasts that agree, and in spite of their very different reactions—for instance—to riding on horseback, it is possible to believe in "their eager affection in meeting, their exquisite delight in being together, their hours of happy mirth and moments of serious conference."

Crawford was right in seeking his way to Fanny's heart through William. Anything done for William was more than done for Fanny, and as gratitude was one of her strongest emotions he felt sure of making at least some progress when he offered to mount her brother on one of his own hunters. But "she feared for William, by no means convinced by all that he could relate of his own horsemanship . . . that he was at all equal to the management of a high-fed hunter in an English fox-chase; nor till he returned safe and well, without accident or discredit, could she be reconciled to the risk, or feel any of that obligation to Mr. Crawford for lending the horse which he had fully intended it should produce."

He was more successful when through Admiral Crawford he worked the difficult job of "making" William as a lieutenant. " 'Has this been all *your* doing, then?' cried Fanny. 'Good heavens! how very, very kind! Have you really—was it by *your* desire?— I beg your pardon, but I am bewildered. . . . How kind! how very kind! Oh, Mr. Crawford, we are infinitely obliged to you.' "

It was his goodness to William that embarrassed her refusal of his hand and gave him hopes which even he might have been unable to cherish had she been free to speak her mind.

William, for his part, naturally "lamented that his sister's feelings should be so cold towards a man whom he must consider as the first of human characters, but he was of an age to be all for love, and therefore unable to blame; and knowing her wish on the subject, he would not distress her by the slightest allusion."

It is interesting to compare with William and Fanny Price that other brother and sister pair in the same story. In many ways Henry and Mary Crawford seem equally devoted, but Henry's selfishness has already shown itself in a refusal to give Mary a settled home, as he easily could have done at Everingham. "To anything like a permanence of abode, or limitation of society, Henry Crawford had, unluckily, a great dislike: he could not accommodate his sister in an article of such importance; but he escorted her, with the utmost kindness into Northamptonshire, and as readily engaged to fetch her away again, at half an hour's notice, whenever she were weary of the place."

This is typical of his attitude towards her and Mary does not seem to resent it, which is unusual, for the selfish do not generally understand the selfish. She talks of "Henry who is in every other respect"—that of writing letters—"exactly what a brother should be, who loves me, consults me, confides in me, and will talk to me by the hour together. . . ." No wonder Edmund says, "She speaks of her brother with a very pleasing affection." But there is truth in Fanny's reply, "I cannot rate so very highly the love or good nature of a brother who will not give himself the trouble of writing anything worth reading to his sisters, when they are separated. I am sure William would never have used *me* so."

She is right. Henry will do anything for Mary as long as it does not put him to any serious inconvenience. He will ride with her and talk with her, he will fetch her harp from Northampton in his own barouche, and "he is always giving me something or other. I have such innumerable presents from him that it is quite impossible for me to value, or for him to remember, half." But he will not write her a letter worth reading or give her a settled home, because the first would be too much of an effort and the second would interfere with his personal liberty.

Her affection for him is more disinterested. He always comes first—if not before herself, then before anyone else. "She loves no one but her brother," says Fanny in a moment of bitterness, speaking more truth than she knew, for Mary, after a mere gesture of disapproval, had left him to his own devices with her heart. " 'Well, you will have opportunities enough of endeavouring to recommend yourself, for we are a great deal together.' And without attempting any further remonstrance, she left Fanny to her fate."

She will not interfere with his pleasures, even when they are likely to hurt "as good a little creature as ever lived." But on a later occasion her compliance is of a different order. She is genuinely delighted when his pursuit of Fanny becomes serious. It is true that she "was in a state of mind to rejoice in a connection with the Bertram family, and not to be displeased with her brother's marrying a little beneath him." But she is also delighted for his sake. "You will have a sweet little wife; all gratitude and devotion. Exactly what you deserve."

Loyally she does all she can to further his suit. Yet there is a perversity in her even here, for she is anxious to bring about and witness his meeting with Maria Rushworth. "Henry," she writes to Fanny, "has some idea of going into Norfolk again upon some business that *you* approve, but this cannot possibly be permitted before the middle of next week, that is, he cannot anyhow be spared till after the 14th, for *we* have a party that evening. The value of a man like Henry on such an occasion is what you can have no conception of . . . He will see the Rushworths, which I own I am not sorry for—having a little curiosity—and so I think has he, though he will not acknowledge it."

So, thanks to her, Henry meets Maria Rushworth again

and the old trouble is restarted, with disastrous consequences. We are not told if Mary and Henry saw much of each other after the elopement. We read that she found a home with Mrs. Grant, for "Mary had had enough of her own friends, enough of vanity, ambition, love and disappointment, in the course of the last half-year, to be in need of the true kindness of her sister's heart, and the rational tranquility of her ways." But except for the fact that she "was long in finding anyone who could satisfy the better taste she had acquired at Mansfield, or put Edmund Bertram out of her head," we hear no more, and in this connection there is no mention of Crawford. Did he disappear out of her life? I doubt it. But we are not told.

Mansfield Park gives us, perhaps, the fullest and most richly contrasted exposition of the brother-and-sister relation, but brothers and sisters play their parts also in *Northanger Abbey*. Here again Jane Austen delights in contrast. On one side we have the warmly devoted James and Catherine Morland, on the other the unspeakable Thorpe and his sisters— "I did not come to Bath to drive my sisters about." James and Catherine are not unlike William and Fanny. She is artlessly delighted with his sudden appearance in Bath, imagining that it is expressly on her account. "How good of you to have come so far on purpose to see *me*." "Indeed, Catherine, I love you dearly," says James, with perfect sincerity, but knowing that he has come for a very different reason. Later on, when he has been jilted by Isabella Thorpe, the depths of Catherine's grief, the warmth of her attachment, make a new inroad on Henry Tilney's heart. "To have so kind-hearted, so affectionate a sister, must be a comfort to him under any distress."

Henry himself is a devoted brother, the friend and supporter of a sister who without him would have been friendless and lonely. A most unsatisfactory father has brought them to depend on each other for family graces that should have come from him. There is of course the elder brother in the 12th light dragoons ("the hopes of the nation"), but he is never really in the picture, though Eleanor would appear to be very fond of him too, if there was any truth in Henry's teasing during that marvellous walk round Beechen Cliff. Frederick exists only for the very proper purpose of paying Isabella Thorpe in her own coin.

As for Isabella, she is, like Mary Crawford, "complaisant as a sister," but her complaisance is much less disinterested. To help her brother John in his courtship of Catherine is also to help her own courtship by Catherine's brother James. A slightly similar situation exists in Mansfield Park, but it is rooted in a very different soil. Isabella imagines Catherine to be an heiress, whose money will be useful to the Thorpes in a double flow from her and from James. When she realises that the financial tide is not a particularly strong one she becomes as perfunctory about Catherine's lover as she does about her own. "I confess as soon as I read his letter, I thought it a very foolish, imprudent business, and not likely to produce the good of either."

John, for his part, had no very high notions of brotherly behaviour. When they met in Bath "he slightly and carelessly touched the hand of Isabella" and his attitude to her throughout is casual and contemptuous, as indeed it is to his other sisters. Not only did he proclaim that he had not come to Bath to drive his sisters about "and look like a fool," but when he was obliged to drive one of them he proclaimed that his reason for choosing Maria instead of Anne was because Anne had such thick ankles. "I dare say she will not be in good-humour again this month," gloats Maria.

The Thorpes are not an amiable family—selfish, envious, quarrelsome, teasing without affection. It is not often that Jane Austen deals with such. Her families are usually united, and even though, like the Bennets, they may contain deleterious members, there seems to be no real conflict among them. Besides the Thorpes I can think only of the Elliots and here the disunion is of a different nature. Elizabeth, coldly selfish, pairs with her father, whose vanity and snobbery are akin to hers. Anne, sweetly unselfish, is to a certain extent exploited by Mary, but also warmly valued. I am inclined to wonder a little if Elizabeth's and Sir Walter's contemptuous indifference to Anne is really true to life. I feel that she would be too useful to them to be neglected. But then they both required flattery, and she was no flatterer, which explains both their indifference to her and their predilection for Mrs. Clay, whose "low" origins and undistinguished appearance would otherwise have affronted their illusions of grandeur.

Elizabeth and Anne are the only pair of sisters not on really good terms with each other. The relationship of sisters in the other novels never sinks lower than friendship and often touches heights of true devotion. It is a relationship of which Jane Austen is specially qualified to write, for she was herself a devoted sister to Cassandra. Their affection was lifelong—only death divided them. She valued her brothers too, and owed much to Edward's help and interest in her literary career. But Cassandra was her special friend chosen out of that large family to be nearest and dearest to her. So it is not surprising—apart from her preference for writing of women rather than of men—that in her novels the relationship of sisters is more common than that of brothers and sisters, and certainly than that of brothers—which, except for a very slight approach in John and George Knightley, she mostly ignores.

2

The novels abound in pairs of sisters. The most celebrated, of course, are Jane and Elizabeth Bennet. Here we have two girls who cannot have been unlike Jane and Cassandra Austen. Elizabeth has many qualities that we know were Jane's—her ready wit, her sharpness of eye and occasionally of tongue, her salty taste for human folly, coupled with her enjoyment of a good flirtation. Cassandra on the other hand had much of Jane's "candour," an unwearying sweetness which I must confess—when it becomes, as it often does, irrational—can irritate me. I am always grateful to Elizabeth for her comeback at Jane after the latter has been excusing both Darcy and Wickham on the grounds that "interested people have perhaps misrepresented each to the other." "Very true, indeed," says Elizabeth: "and now, my dear Jane, what have you to say on behalf of the interested people who have probably been concerned in the business? Do clear *them,* too, or we shall be obliged to think ill of somebody."

By the way, both my collaborator and I have marvelled at the reckless manner in which Jane Austen has bestowed her own name on the characters of her imagination. Jane Fairfax and Jane Bennet, both important figures . . . it must have been difficult for Jane to write so much about Jane; and it has certainly added some confusion to the preceding paragraph.

The attachment between the Bennet girls is the attachment of opposites, which can be so very much stronger than the attachment of like to like, since it is based on no surface attraction but on the deep, strong needs of a character incomplete without its complement. The same attachment exists between the Dashwoods in *Sense and Sensibility,* but here the contrast is a different one. There is less "candour" and sweetness in Elinor than wisdom and tolerance, combined with extremely good manners, and as for Marianne, the measure of her forbearance is even less than that of her common sense and her manners make one wonder how they could have survived so long in such a well-bred family.

The contrast in fact is as in the title, between Sense and Sensibility, and it is a tribute to Jane Austen that we, her readers, soon become equally attached to both. At a first reading, I confess that I thought Elinor a prig, but as one becomes familiar with the formality and sententiousness of some of her expressions, one realises that these belong less to her than to her author's inexperience. I imagine that fragments of Elinor and Marianne still survive in the dialogue, which is —at least at the beginning of the book—more stiff and less alive than in the other novels. I think, too, that the idea of priggishness is suggested by Elinor's being so exceedingly old for her age. She is only nineteen, yet she is temperamentally the oldest of the Dashwood family, and is treated as such by Mrs. Jennings, who, when she chooses to make what she considers an improper remark, delivers it in an aside to Elinor, "for fear of shocking the young ladies." No doubt the charming irresponsibility of her mother had forced her into an early sedateness. Certainly she behaves with a prudence and self-control quite extraordinary in one of her years.

Marianne, on the other hand, considers prudence and self-control as vices and deliberately cultivates their opposites. Yet we love her too. We forgive her intolerance, her rashness, her bad manners, for the sake of her charm. Here is indeed a triumph for the author, for no quality is more difficult to convey than charm. In nine cases out of ten—indeed in ninety-nine out of a hundred—we have to take the author's word for it that the heroine is charming. There is nothing in the text to convince us.

I think one reason for our assenting to Marianne's charm is the same as that for which we assent to her sister's restraint —it is never suggested to us as an external quality of fascination, but as the true, natural expression of a deeply loving nature. For Marianne loves deeply and passionately, not only her lover, but her mother and her sisters. Elinor can always sway her by appealing to her affections. Once she is able to prove that Willoughby's offer of a horse would be an embarrassment to her mother, then Marianne is willing to renounce the darling gift, though dear to her both for its own sake, and the sake of the giver. Also, on that other occasion, when she realises that the solitary horseman she had run to meet was not, as she had so fondly thought, the returning Willoughby, her disappointment is at once wiped out by the discovery that he is her sister's lover, Edward Ferrars. "He was the only person in the world who could at that moment be forgiven for not being Willoughby; the only one who could have gained a smile from her; but she dispersed her tears to smile on *him,* and in her sister's happiness forgot for a time her own disappointment."

Elinor's devotion to her, though calmer, is equally great. In all the six novels I know of no more moving scene than that in which Elinor attempts to comfort her on the receipt of Willoughby's letter. "She saw Marianne stretched on the bed, almost choked by grief, one letter in her hand, and two or three others lying by her. Elinor drew near, but without saying a word; and seating herself on the bed, took her hand, kissed her affectionately several times, and then gave way to a burst of tears, which at first was scarcely less violent than Marianne's. The latter, though unable to speak, seemed to feel all the tenderness of this behaviour, and after some time thus spent in joint affliction, she put all the letters into Elinor's hands; and then covering her face with her handkerchief, almost screamed with agony. Elinor, who knew that such grief, shocking as it was to witness it, must have its course, watched by her till this excess of suffering had somewhat spent itself."

Her devotion also takes the unobtrusive, self-denying turn of covering up with her own attentions and civilities Marianne's frequent rudenesses and neglects. On the journey up to London with Mrs. Jennings, during which Marianne "sat in silence almost all the way, wrapped in her own meditations . . . Elinor took immediate possession of the post of civility which she had assigned to herself, behaved with the greatest attention to Mrs. Jennings, talked with her, laughed with her, and listened to her whenever she could." Truly Elinor was a wonderful sister.

There is another pair of sisters in the book, and here—as in *Mansfield Park*—we are given a contrasting type of the same relationship. Not that Anne and Lucy Steele are on bad terms with each other—as I have said, Jane Austen seldom shows us a family at war within itself—but their attachment is of an inferior quality to that of Elinor and Marianne. Lucy can speak sharply to Anne, and Anne can play eavesdropper on Lucy—a return match, one gathers from her remarks to Elinor. Moreover, Lucy can borrow her sister's money and run off to marry Robert Ferrars, leaving her to find her own way home as best she can. Yet Lucy apparently readily forgave her the *gaffe* which resulted in their being both turned out of the John Dashwoods' house. "I never saw Lucy in such a rage in my life. She vowed she would never trim me up a new bonnet, nor do anything else for me again, so long as she lived; but now she is quite come to, and we are as good friends as ever. Look, she made me this bow to my hat, and put in the feather last night."

A similar sort of relationship, though more decorous and well bred as befits a more exalted situation, is to be found in *Mansfield Park*. Here Maria and Julia remain throughout on what might be called cold good terms with each other, except for a brief interlude of rivalry over Henry Crawford. When that is over, they recover "much of their former good understanding," and Maria is glad to have Julia as a third on her honeymoon, both at Sotherton and at Brighton. They "were at least sufficiently friends to make each of them exceedingly glad to be with the other at such a time."

Another pair of sisters engaged in rivalry are Louisa and Henrietta Musgrove in *Persuasion*. But here the situation is altogether different. They are both apparently in love with Captain Wentworth, but it is all so light-hearted that their interests never really clash, so that here there is no real test of their mutual affection. The emotion they so lavishly displayed is not love, but a sort of admiration—something akin to the excitement a film or radio star can arouse today in the hearts of worshippers who are united rather than disunited by their common devotion.

Henrietta's behaviour when Louisa has her accident on the Cobb is certainly that of a loving sister, for "sinking under the conviction" that Louisa was dead, she "lost her senses too." I originally thought of using this episode in an earlier chapter, as one of the few in the six novels in which our sense of modernity gets a jar, for the behaviour of all concerned is by present-day standards a little hysterical. In an accident there will always be some who lose their heads, and certainly Mary's collapse is no surprise, but that Henrietta, such a bright, merry, healthy outdoor girl, should fail in this manner belongs to an older pattern of female behaviour. Even when she recovers consciousness, she is utterly useless, for she was unable "to remain in Louisa's room, or to look at her, without sufferings which made her worse than helpless." Still, without question she is a devoted sister.

None of these family relationships is at all complicated. There is no probing of hidden motives or buried strifes. Jane Austen reproduces rather than analyses the life she saw all round her, in her own family and in the families of her friends. In a smaller, more restricted society than we have today, family unity was stronger, but also more inclusive, for "in-laws" were then definitely within the family circle instead of on the fringes of it as they so often are now. The words Father, Mother, Sister, Brother could imply a relationship by marriage as well as by blood. "My brother Hayter," says Mrs. Musgrove, speaking of her sister's husband, and when Isabella Thorpe becomes engaged to James Morland the "first effusion" of her and Catherine is "the happiness of having such a sister." "You will be infinitely dearer to me, my Catherine," says Isabella, "than either Anne or Maria," and though "this was a pitch of friendship beyond Catherine," she takes and seeks to give comfort later, when she has to declare the impossibility of her ever marrying John Thorpe, in the thought that "we shall still be sisters." "Yes, yes," blushes the disingenuous Isabella, as she thinks of Frederick Tilney, "there are more ways than one of our being sisters."

Another disingenuous lady writes to Jane Bennet: "I really do not think Georgiana Darcy has her equal for beauty, elegance and accomplishments; and the affection she inspires in Louisa and myself is heightened into something still more interesting from the hope we dare to entertain of her being hereafter our sister. . . ." "Shall you like to have such a brother?" asks Elizabeth of Jane when she has announced her engagement to Darcy. No "in-law," you see, and though later on in *Northanger Abbey*, Henry Tilney uses the term, it was more commonly applied to what we should now call a step-relationship. Mrs. Dashwood is John Dashwood's mother-in-law, and Frank Churchill is the son-in-law of Mrs. Weston. Thus the wicked stepmother of the fairy tales and the vexatious mother-in-law of the comedians share a confused origin.

But if in-laws are brought more closely into the family circle, cousins are regarded as further outside it than they would be today. It is remarkable how many cousins in the novels marry or think of marriage. Nowadays such marriages are regarded as bad for the race and seldom contracted without comment or criticism. But no one criticises or even comments on the eugenics of the marriage of Fanny and Edmund, though they were first cousins. Henrietta Musgrove marries her first cousin, Charles Hayter, and Anne Elliot's reasons for not marrying Mr. Elliot have nothing to do with their first cousinship. Here again we have the difference between a large, more or less homogeneous society which can offer plenty of marriage choices to its members, and a small community made smaller still by drastic class distinctions.

3

The tightness and closeness and warmth of family life that Jane Austen depicts would lead me to expect few instances of external friendship. Friendships between men and women would then be unknown and unthinkable apart from courtship, and friendships between men, Jane Austen, on her system of never describing anything of which she has no personal knowledge, leaves strictly alone. But, except *Sense and Sensibility,* each of the novels supplies at least one instance of close friendship between women.

In *Northanger Abbey* the main instance is, of course, a parody. The friendship between Catherine Morland and Isabella Thorpe mocks at the intense female associations of the Gothic novels rather than at women's friendships in general. It is a case of the heroine and her confidante. But it is also the case of the more intense, silly, unbalanced type of friendship, which has no real basis in sense or character. Good-hearted, sweet-minded little Catherine has nothing in common with the cold-hearted, false, mercenary Isabella. With the latter the whole thing is dictated by self-interest, with the former it is part of the enthusiasm and innocence of her nature. But the two different springs blend in the same fountain.

> The progress of the friendship between Catherine and Isabella was quick as its beginning had been warm; and they passed so rapidly through every gradation of increasing tenderness, that there was shortly no fresh proof of it to be given to their friends or themselves. They called each other by their Christian name, were always arm in arm when they walked, pinned up each other's train for the dance, and were not to be divided in the set; and, if a rainy morning deprived them of other enjoyments, they were resolute in meeting, in defiance of wet and dirt, and shut themselves up to read novels together.

The friendship, largely owing to the sweetness and impercipience of Catherine's nature combined with the fact that she is associated with both the young men Isabella considers marrying, keeps intact longer than might be expected. But when at last it dissolves on Isabella's jilting of James Morland, his sister has surprisingly few regrets.

> "I suppose," says Henry Tilney mischievously, "that in losing Isabella you lose half yourself: you feel a void in your heart that nothing else can occupy. Society is becoming irksome . . . you feel that you have no longer any friend to whom you can speak with unreserve; on whose regard you

can place dependence; or whose counsel, in any difficulty, you could rely on. You feel all this?"

"No," said Catherine, after a few moments' reflection. "I do not—ought I?"

Not only has her disillusion in Isabella been growing subconsciously through the weeks, so that its final appearance in consciousness is not unprepared for, but she has by this time a friend whose true worth has never shown more clearly than now. Eleanor Tilney's attraction doubtless began because she was "near the rose," but Catherine has long learned to love her for her own sake. Their friendship, true and doubtless lifelong, though entirely lacking the demonstrations of the earlier one with Isabella, stands as a model of what "a true friendship" should be. My collaborator blames Eleanor for her behaviour over Catherine's expulsion from Northanger Abbey, but it is very difficult to see what else she could have done. If the carriage had been a car and Woodston could have been reached by a telephone call, she might well have done something more effective for her friend's preservation, but cut off from Henry by twenty miles and no intermediaries save servants who would doubtless have been afraid to disobey the General, I do not see how she could have attempted a stronger defiance. Anyway, it is profitless to discuss what it would have been possible to do in an impossible situation, and Eleanor's friendship has been proved on steady lines from her first appearance. We may indeed rejoice that it was she and Catherine and not Catherine and Isabella who finish the book as sisters.

Northanger Abbey has perhaps the closest study of friendship in any of the novels. But only one, I think, is without some instance of it. There are no women friends in *Sense and Sensibility*. Elinor and Marianne stand alone and are apparently all-sufficient to each other. Lucy Steele's professions of friendship of course are worthless; her proclaimed regard for

Elinor does not exist even in her own imagination. Jane Bennet's imagination, however, is the setting of her friendship with Caroline Bingley in *Pride and Prejudice*. For a time it flourishes there, and Jane persuades herself that it has nothing to do with Caroline's brother. It is Caroline herself who disillusions her and provokes what Elizabeth approves as "the most unforgiving speech that I ever heard you utter." Later on, however, when Jane is engaged to Bingley and receives her future sister-in-law's congratulations, which "were all that was affectionate and insincere," "she was affected . . . and could not help writing her a much kinder answer than she knew was deserved."

A very different kind of friendship is Elizabeth's for Charlotte Lucas. This is a sober, sensible affair, which survives a blow at the heart. Elizabeth frankly acknowledges to herself that Charlotte can never be the same to her after her venal, cynical acceptance of Mr. Collins. Nevertheless she behaves like a true friend in giving her all the support, both verbal and practical, in her power, and making what must have been a sacrifice of time and inclination in going to stay with her for six weeks after she was married. The most ardent affection could hardly have done more.

We hear, however, nothing about Charlotte at the end of the book. Her name is not among those to whom Elizabeth gave hospitality at Pemberley, and indeed we can hardly believe that Darcy would have tolerated Mr. Collins as a visitor. Nor would Elizabeth certainly have required her, as she herself had been required, to interrupt an uncongenial *tête-a-tête*. So we can imagine that after her marriage they drifted apart—Charlotte doubtless learning to find her compensations in the "olive branch," or more probably, olive branches.

In *Emma* we are given one instance of true friendship, and two of another sort. I have already—in an earlier book—cited the friendship between Emma and Mrs. Weston as an ideal friendship between two women.

> There was not a creature in the world to whom she spoke with such unreserve as to [Mrs. Weston]—not anyone to whom she related with such conviction of being listened to and understood, and being always interesting and always intelligible, the little affairs, arrangements, perplexities and pleasures of her father and herself . . . half an hour's uninterrupted communication of all those little matters on which the daily happiness of private life depends was one of the first gratifications of each . . . the very sight of Mrs. Weston, her smile, her touch, her voice, was grateful to Emma.

This quotation brought me a letter from a correspondent who pointed out that, such perfect confidence existing, it is odd that Emma should have concealed from her friend her hopes for Harriet Smith and Mr. Elton. He also mentions their common but uncommunicated hopes for Emma and Frank Churchill, but this I do not think was a matter they would have discussed. There were many reasons why neither of them should mention it.

But I am not so sure about the other. Now I reflect upon it I think it really is strange that Emma discussed Harriet with no one but Harriet. She would not have found her friend unsympathetic, and obviously the situation was one in which advice would have been helpful, to say nothing of a little more contrivance than Emma was able to produce single-handed. Nor do I believe that Harriet would have objected. I can only think that Emma in this showed a little of her vanity, and wanted to act alone, to be the sole matchmaker and source of happiness. Or some subconscious doubt of the reasonableness and eligibility of it all may have silenced her. But I still find it a problem—a problem which did not occur to me till it was introduced from outside. So it is just possible that it did not occur to the author.

Emma's friendship with Harriet is the reverse of that for Mrs. Weston. In the latter she looks up, in the former she looks down. Harriet's inferiority, combined with her docility, is a satisfying meal for Emma's self-esteem. Mr. Knightley was right when he said: "I do not know what your opinion may be, Mrs. Weston, of this great intimacy between Emma and Harriet Smith, but I think it a bad thing." It was bad because it ministered to the weaknesses of each, and gave both of them some exceedingly wretched moments, which did not spoil their lives only because Emma was sufficiently wise at heart and Harriet sufficiently foolish to escape their logical effects. Emma's blindness is only temporary, and as for Harriet—"there was no preventing a laugh . . . Emma must laugh at such a close—such an end of the doleful disappointment of five weeks back—such a heart—such a Harriet!"

The friendship between Emma and Jane Fairfax—so much more suitable, apparently, than that between her and Harriet Smith, or even between her and Mrs. Weston—does not really exist, though it is frequently talked of, especially by Mr. Knightley. He admires and pities Jane, and sees her as just the right companion for Emma, of the same age and the same tastes. But Emma will have none of it. "I must be more in want of a friend, or an agreeable companion, than I have yet been, to take the trouble of conquering anybody's reserve to procure one. Intimacy between Miss Fairfax and me is quite out of the question." She also privately acknowledges another reason—that Jane Fairfax is really the gifted accomplished young woman she would like to be thought herself.

No doubt her vanity reinforced a personal antipathy, but—leaving out this consideration, which Emma herself was aware of—I am on her side. There was between the two girls a general lack of sympathy and personal accord which would have made true friendship impossible. Jane's reserve—though there is at the moment a special need for it—is evidently not an entirely new characteristic. She is by temperament cold and repressed. I cannot bring myself to like her, and I do not see why Emma should be expected to do so, just because they happen to be of the same age and live (in Jane's case, only occasionally) in the same village. Yet when her engagement to Frank Churchill was made known, Emma—

> bitterly regretted not having sought a closer acquaintance with her, and blushed for the envious feelings that had certainly been, in some measure, the cause. Had she followed Mr. Knightley's known wishes, in paying that attention to Miss Fairfax which was in every way her due; had she tried to know her better; had she done her part towards intimacy; had she endeavoured to find a friend there instead of in Harriet Smith; she must, in all probability, have been spared from every pain which pressed on her now . . . supposing even that they had never become intimate friends; that she had never been admitted to Miss Fairfax's confidence on this important matter—which was most probable—still, in knowing her as she ought, and as she might, she must have been preserved from the abominable suspicions of an improper attachment to Mr. Dixon, which she had not only so foolishly fashioned and harboured herself, but had so unpardonably imparted.

This is right and this is handsome. All the same, I do not see that Emma need reproach herself for being unable to *like* Jane Fairfax.

In *Persuasion* there is a friendship not unlike that between Emma and Mrs. Weston. Lady Russell was probably more her mother's friend than she was Anne Elliot's. Nevertheless, there is a close friendship between them and the older woman has the deepest possible influence on the younger's life. This friendship suffers as recorded, by the fact that Lady Russell never really comes alive. She is one of the novel's least satisfactory delineations, which is a pity, as she is also one of the most important, and the work suffers through our difficulty in understanding Anne's deference to her, Anne's affection for her, Anne's anxiety as to her final acceptance of Captain Wentworth.

But the friendship is strong enough to show up the true

colours of that between Elizabeth Elliot and Mrs. Clay. Here again we have a friendship based on the need for flattery, but —as was not the case with Harriet Smith—there is on the other side a foundation of self-interest. Mrs. Clay in fact is much smarter than the woman who condescends to her, and Elizabeth—unlike Emma—is likely to suffer all her life for having stooped to such an inferior connection.

> It cannot be doubted that Sir Walter and Elizabeth were shocked and mortified by the loss of their companion; and the discovery of their deception in her. They had their great cousins, to be sure, to resort to for comfort; but they must long feel that to flatter and follow others, without being flattered and followed in return, is but a state of half-enjoyment.

Or, as Mrs. Bennet more tersely puts it, "I hate such false friends."

CHAPTER VII

Seven Years Later

G. B. STERN

LOOKING back on any seven years of our own life, they afford plenty of evidence that no state of happy-ever-after can remain fixed and static, like a *tableau vivant* just as the curtain falls.

Jane Austen's gift of creating characters that, once we know them, are forever quick and not dead, has as an inevitable consequence bequeathed us these characters in a Last Will and Testament of which oddly enough she was unconscious, though she signed it herself. For our fancy, restless and insatiable, will not allow them to stay in peace at the point where the author leaves them. She has less right than we have to speculate on their future state, for it is she, that teasing creature, who is responsible for planting an appetite that cannot be fully enough satisfied; cannot allow us to say "Let us think no more of Catherine and Henry" etc., and so be done with them. Even could we grant her that time will not alter her heroes and heroines in constancy, once she has seen them as far as the threshold of blissful wedlock, yet what of their relations and friends, guarded by no such golden laws as heroes and heroines? What, for instance, of the Minor Characters, always apt to wander beyond the author's control, and how much more when bidden stand out of the way for the grand finale, where all misunderstandings are made right, all lovers united with as little delay as possible?

Except perhaps in the case of Henry Tilney and Catherine Morland. There indeed, a whole twelve months was to separate them from the perfect felicity of an immediate marriage. And having settled Catherine and Henry, after such a truly terrible test of their endurance, we begin to speculate under what conditions the General will allow them to remain settled in their happiness. Jane Austen herself was, I suspect, not entirely free from anxious preoccupation with General Tilney; the final pages of *Northanger Abbey* are cloudy with apprehension as to his conduct and permissions; you cannot create a roaring tyrant and then put him to sleep till kissed awake in a hundred years or so; the General had no spinning-wheel. Nor can you kill off all fathers, just to make sure nothing may interfere with the permanent prettiness of our *tableau vivant* at fall of the curtain. You will note my temerity in interfering with Miss Austen's own far too easy, far too optimistic solution (flung out in a personal letter) of the Hartfield situation in *Emma*. Useless to believe that fortune is so obliging as to slay such an amiable valitudinarian as Mr. Woodhouse, whose expectation of life, besides being proverbial in terms of a creaking door, is usually also of the longest duration, as any insurance company will testify. Of *course* he does not die in two years simply because no Mr. Knightley in the world, however devoted, could have survived residence with such a father-in-law for even two years and a week. Someone, certainly, had to die in the nick of time to solve the problem; someone—but not Mr. Woodhouse.

And furthermore, though Jane Austen has the undoubted right to dispose of Dr. Grant by three great institutional dinners, entirely for the purpose of bringing Edmund to the living at Mansfield, she cannot possibly have imagined that some sort of trouble and upset will not in time develop from the future she throws out for Mrs. Norris and Maria: Mrs. Norris is not likely to acquiesce for ever in the establishment Sir Thomas has formed at a safe distance from Mansfield; she is not sufficiently tame to acquiesce in anything; and besides, we are specifically told that her temper gets worse every day.

"My dear Lady Bertram" cried Mrs. Norris, "it is not my habit, you know, ever to consider my own wishes, otherwise

I should not have put myself to the prodigious expense and discomfort of coming all this way into Northamptonshire by coach (and the state of the roads you would hardly believe), so that I might discuss with you and Sir Thomas what he had best do about our poor dear Maria. For I assure you that the state of her temper from the moment it was settled I should devote my life to her, and so far from Mansfield and my own home—but I am not one to cry over spilt milk or make reproaches, I hope, to overindulgent parents. For you know, sister, Maria was spoilt, excessively spoilt, when she was still at home, and *I* never thought she could compare with dear Julia, who, you will remember, was always my favourite. But it was to oblige you and Sir Thomas that I went to shut myself up in utter seclusion and endeavoured to make the best of it with Maria. I have everybody's good at heart, but my health and spirits have suffered too much and I can do no more."

Lady Bertram, sitting on the sofa and indolently caressing Pug, did not allow herself to be too perturbed, though she could have desired that Baddeley might somehow have better contrived to have given her warning of this unexpected and unwelcome arrival. "I trust, sister," she put in, hardly raising her voice, "that things are not so very bad with you neither, considering. Sir Thomas, I know, did all in his power for you to be comfortable when he formed this establishment."

"Lady Bertram, I make no complaints. There were many suggestions I might have made at the time, but I was too upset at leaving Mansfield at all, and my dear little home at the White House just across the Park. I am not used to living so remote and private and with so little society, though naturally Maria's unfortunate *situation* made anything else impossible. But I say nothing of it. Had she not been placed in my charge I make no doubt I should have had callers enough, but Sir Thomas was only too ready that she should quit Mansfield for a neighbourhood where the disgrace she had brought upon her family need not affect them in any way.

Had her parents received her at home and countenanced her—but no, Fanny was the one to be considered, Fanny must not be exposed, Fanny must be sheltered and protected with every scruple, and I hope he was pleased when his own son could find no greater match than his own cousin, a little nobody from Portsmouth."

"Indeed, sister, Sir Thomas was very pleased and so was I. I am excessively fond of Fanny, you know, though Susan has grown up a fine girl, and in some ways even more useful to me. She has happier nerves than Fanny."

But it was not to discuss the indigent Prices that their Aunt Norris had travelled such a long way, so she contented herself with "Fanny was always sly and a creep-mouse," and then, abandoning that, returned to her main project, which was no more and no less than to persuade Sir Thomas and Lady Bertram to install her back where she had every right to be, at her own home which she had sacrificed two years ago to do them such a great service as to live with Mrs. Rushworth after she had been divorced. Once more Mrs. Norris aspired to be the guiding spirit of all concerns at Mansfield Park; consulted in every crisis, Sir Thomas' right hand, and Lady Bertram's most energetic counsellor. Above all did she look forward to keeping a sharp eye on Fanny and Edmund, lately installed at the Parsonage, and by frequent reminder of how things had been in her own day while her husband was yet alive, with hints of all the economies that had been practised there and so sadly allowed to lapse, contrive to make Fanny feel herself a failure as a wife and mistress of a home, as she had been (according to her Aunt Norris) in everything else.

Lady Bertram listened to the project unfolded, but said nothing of the White House having a tenant of some duration who certainly would not suffer himself nor his family to be evicted to make room for her sister Norris. A curious emotion was kindling in her breast, usually so unused to all emotion. Were it not completely alien to what we have always heard of Lady Bertram, we might venture a guess that it was the maternal instinct, the same solicitude as had been awakened at the sight of her elder son's sufferings during Tom's illness of over seven years ago. All she said, however, was: "Is Maria well? I asked in my letters, but you only told me of yourself in your replies."

"Sister, I trust that I am the last to be unsympathetic, and had Maria been really ill and not merely the victim of her own temper which as you know produces in appearance very much the same effect, I should not have spared myself, I should have nursed her day and night. That she should have grown a great deal thinner is only natural considering the mortification with which she heard of Mr. Rushworth's second marriage."

"Is she thinner? That is bad. I do not like to hear it."

Mrs. Norris was beginning to lose her own temper under the provocation of Lady Bertram's refusal to become interested in her own return to Mansfield. "I have kept a good table," she began, "that is, with the slender means at my disposal."

"Not so slender, I think, sister, from what Sir Thomas told me of the allowance he made."

Mrs. Norris would dearly have loved to reply that she had not touched Sir Thomas' generous allowance, but had supported Maria and the full establishment of servants on her own pitiful little income, eked out by excellent management; but she was afraid lest this might be repeated presently to Sir Thomas on his return home, and that he might then, not unnaturally, prove the contrary. So she changed the subject as rapidly as she could by glancing aside at her patience with Maria's tears and tantrums and generally ungrateful behaviour, for who was she now to give herself airs?

"Tears," asked Lady Bertram. "Does she cry?"

"Lord yes, and you may imagine that is no very great entertainment for me. But then who considers me, and whether I am fagged or out of spirits?"

"I do not above half like her crying so much."

Mrs. Norris ignored this. "I collect Sir Thomas will be home this evening?" she enquired impatiently.

"You will have retired to bed, sister; you must be tired from your journey."

"Then I must see him tomorrow as early as may be. For the sooner I am back in Somerset to pack up my things, the sooner I can be settled again at the White House. You will not be sorry, I dare say, to have your embroidery set to rights for you again?"

"Susan does that very well. What were you going to suggest for Maria, if you do not wish to stay with her any more?"

Mrs. Norris was not very wise at detecting fine shades of manner, but even *she* thought it would not come amiss if instead of disparaging her niece, she were to speak a few words to show a kinder feeling. "Why to be sure, I had not forgotten Maria; that was part of my wish to speak with Sir Thomas, that I might advise him. She should have someone to control her who can be firmer than I and will not suffer her to have her own way in everything. I have been too soft-hearted to remind her of all she has thrown away by her wicked folly—Sotherton and the London house and the regard and esteem of all our friends; but give her a companion who would not hesitate to draw her attention to this, and maybe we still need not despair of some amendment. I have done my duty and I am worn out. You will not have me long at the White House, and when I am dead—"

Suddenly Pug, the third of her line, came to the rescue. It was hardly to be supposed she could be barking in such ecstasy at the notion of Mrs. Norris dead, though she was a sensible little creature and less somnolent than her mistress. She was fond of cake, fond of Baddeley, fond of Susan; and the entrance of the tea equipage, with Susan to preside, was what had brought her from the sofa with a bound. Susan Price concealed whatever was disagreeable at the sight of her Aunt Norris, and attended to the wants of both ladies, while discoursing pleasantly with her dear Aunt Bertram on her six little nieces and nephews at the Parsonage, who were also, of course, Lady Bertram's grandchildren. The two eldest, Edmund and William, were twins; Fanny, next to arrive, was a puny child, as Aunt Norris was delighted to hear; Thomas and Sophie, who had followed Fanny, caused some anxiety as well, from a tendency to putrid throats directly the open weather gave place to sharper winds. But at last in little Mary the youngest (born a year ago) they seemed to have produced a fine healthy little romp.

Mrs. Norris, pouncing into the conversation, enquired whether little Mary had been named for Miss Crawford? "Not but that I always thought, to be sure, that Edmund would have done much better there, and that with a little contriving it would not have looked so shocking. You had but to take my advice and not send for Fanny back from Portsmouth in such a hurry, and this unfortunate match need never have happened. You could not have expected that dear sweet-tempered boy not to take pity on her when she was forever thrusting herself under his notice. I said at the time, you will remember, Fanny is safe in her father's house and she had better remain there. But I do wonder that she permitted Edmund to *name* a child Mary."

"There is no great harm in the name," said Lady Bertram, paying no attention.

But not in the least afraid of her Aunt Norris, Susan spoke out in a fearless tone: "Fanny chose the name herself, Aunt Norris. She dearly loved our little sister Mary who died; and as for Miss Crawford, I do not suppose either Fanny or Edmund gave her a thought. Why should they?"

Aunt Norris reddened. She had forgotten her sister Price had had an extra daughter, who if she had grown up would undoubtedly have been but a charge and an expense to Sir Thomas and probably to herself as well but she would have contributed her widow's mite towards bringing her up and putting her out in the world. And now here was her niece Susan speaking so disrespectfully, with an alarming independence that boded ill for the poor young man whom she was shortly to marry; a lieutenant in the navy, a friend of her brother William's. What a family!

Having made an excellent tea, Mrs. Norris announced her intention of going to lie down. "And though it is not at all warm for the time of the year, I do beg, sister, that you will not put yourself to the trouble of ordering a fire to be lit in the big spare room on my account. I dare say I shall do very well, and compared with the discomfort and cold I have had to endure in that great gaunt house where I have been kept prisoner by my own good heart for the past seven years—"

"Sir Thomas!"

His wife's indolent voice, so rarely lifted, always commanded his courteous attention. He had already been holding forth for some half hour on the impossibility of allowing his sister-in-law to return to Mansfield, admitting that his opinion of her had sunk ever since the day of his return from Antigua; he confessed that previous to his journey, he had considerably overrated her sense and most wonderfully borne with her manners, but afterwards she had regularly lost ground in his esteem. And he reminded his wife, though softening his phrases as far as he could to spare her feelings, that to be relieved from her perpetual company was too great a felicity to be hastily forfeited. It would not be possible even had they wished it, Sir Thomas rolled on, to ask their excellent tenants at the White House to quit for a mere whim; and if not at the White House, where else could Mrs. Norris stay? She had too independent a disposition, added Sir Thomas quickly, to wish to make her home in the same house with themselves; and besides, did not her Ladyship think that they might not see their dear son Edmund and their dear daughter Fanny as often at the Park, nor continue their relationship with the Parsonage with such peace and felicity, were the new arrangement to be made? As for all their happiness in their grandchildren, in dear little Edmund and William and Fanny, and Thomas and Sophie and Mary, it was not to be supposed that Mrs. Norris would learn to control her dislike and irritation at seeing them overrunning the very rooms and garden and shrubbery where she herself, prior to the death of her husband and the arrival of the Grants, had reigned supreme. "That we must provide Maria with another, a kinder and more patient companion cannot be denied, and I will make it my business to make enquiries immediately. Whatever has happened, I cannot forget that she is my daughter, and as such, however distant her home must always be from ours, she cannot be allowed to remain unprotected. As for your sister Norris, another establishment must be formed for her." Sir Thomas, though mightily improved and mellowed by misfortune in the past and happiness in the present, was yet a little disposed to believe that all problems could be solved by the simple expedient of forming establishments. Another establishment should certainly be formed for Mrs. Norris at some distance from Maria and from Mansfield Park. He meditated for a moment: "I have heard of Yorkshire as a salubrious climate, unless of course she would prefer my assistance to try further afield. Her great energies must not be wasted." He reflected again. The thought of his sister-in-law removed from him by a long sea-journey became too attractive to be resisted. Antigua . . . he had interests in Antigua. Had not Mrs. Norris at one moment spoken of herself as a great traveller, and expressed a desire to see the world? As for Maria, he remembered hearing of a Mrs. Annesley, a well-bred, agreeable-looking woman with the highest recommendations from Mr. Darcy of Pemberley, whose sister Georgiana had been her especial charge. Might not Mrs. Annesley be persuaded to take Mrs. Norris' place? A handsome salary would be offered her; he, Sir Thomas, would interview her himself, for it was essential she should be acquainted with the delicate situation in which Mrs. Rushworth had contrived to place herself by her ill-judged elopement with Mr. Crawford seven years ago. She would then, he said, be better able to make allowances for the lack of society, the isolation, the coldness of the neighbouring families, their reluctance to permit their own young people to approach one on whom the cold shadow of disgrace must ever lie—

It was at this point that Lady Bertram interrupted him. "Sir Thomas!"

"Yes, my dear?"

"I have quite settled in my mind what we are to do. And I tell you what, Maria shall come back and live with us at home. Do you not think that would be the best plan?"

"Only to think," began Catherine, "that this is the very room—"

She stopped. Her husband glanced at her with twinkling eyes, for indeed this was the very room from which Catherine had emerged, at the sound of footsteps, during her first disastrous stay at the Abbey, blushing and embarrassed at her notion that here she might have found proof that General Tilney had been guilty of murdering Mrs. Tilney.

Now here they were sitting in great comfort before the bath-stove, the western sun of a fine December afternoon pouring through the two sash windows; and Henry kindly conniving at his Catherine's hasty change of subject, they discussed the arrangements for the Christmas house-party at Northanger Abbey. For the General, a doating grandfather, had insisted on having all four children around him, three belonging to Catherine and Henry, and one, a fine boy, the future little Viscount, Eleanor's only offspring. "And tomorrow the viscount arrives and my dearest James—oh, and your brother too—"

"*Your* dearest Frederick," put in Henry, gravely teasing her, for he knew how little a favourite Frederick was with his young sister-in-law.

Catherine was silent.

"And by the next day, which is Christmas Day, our children and Eleanor's too, I make no doubt, will all be in bed from the over-stuffing of sugar-plums and rich cake, to say nothing of brawn and cold pies which my father appears to think is the truest way of showing his affection and partiality, together with staying up an hour or even two hours later than we have ever permitted them in their own homes; getting into every sort of mischief and holding high revel, and altogether so noisy and wild from overindulgence that I should continually be punishing them, only that my father will not hear of punishment. In his eyes they are all perfect."

"Yes, indeed, *how* he has changed. He has a whole roomful of playthings for them, and told me he could hardly bear not to present them until Christmas. He is so generous now, so good and sweet and kind, I could not have believed it; I cannot now imagine him performing any gross or discourteous action." She was thinking of that terrible evening when the General had come home unexpectedly from London to give orders that Catherine was to be turned out of the house without explanation, without escort or protection, by 7 A.M. the very next morning.

"I could wish," Henry remarked, "that he were also a little more judicious in his treatment of the children. My mother would never suffer us to be so spoilt, and see how we have benefited; you could not find two people in the whole of the county so gifted nor so sensible nor with such elegant manners as Henry and Eleanor Tilney."

Catherine most earnestly agreed, and Henry burst out laughing. Nevertheless, an incurable romantic, she chose to maintain her delusion that because General Tilney, once the ogre of her wildest fancies, now devoted most of his life to undoing any good with his grandchildren that might have been achieved during his absence by their parents, tutors and governesses, his whole character must therefore have been changed to benevolence; though she could not but be glad that he showed himself even more often in the ancestral home of his daughter Eleanor, than in theirs, to interfere with the education of the future Viscount, his especial pride, surpassing by several degrees of snobbery the pride he had in the Woodston children, born in a mere country parsonage.

"Hark! Is that a carriage? Can it be that the Viscount was able to leave London earlier than he expected?"

"I dare say, if it is to get away from business and be with his wife." Henry was excessively fond of his cheerful young brother-in-law whose pleasing address, happy readiness of conversation, and easy spirits were in such contrast to the manners and disposition of his quiet sister Eleanor, that were he not assured that beneath this gay exterior lay a constant heart and an exemplary devotion to his wife and son, he might have been disposed to like him a great deal less.

The bustle of arrival and the general sound of commotion seemed to indicate, however, that the arrival was for them and not for Eleanor, even before the butler threw open the door and announced: "Miss Isabella Thorpe."

Here was a matter for surprise indeed, and a surprise that was far from pleasant to either; for Henry from the first had not attached any importance to Miss Thorpe's honesty nor her heart, and had been at some pains to disengage his Catherine from ingenuous admiration of the worldly minded young woman with whom she had struck up such a friendship after their first encounter at Bath. Though he had had but little success until Isabella herself had been obliging enough to aid him by jilting Catherine's brother James, for whom she had professed such disinterested affection, in favour of no other than Henry's elder brother Captain Tilney, undeniably a better match in fashion and fortune than poor young James Morland. Had anything been needed to complete Catherine's sad disillusion, it was when Isabella herself, treated with scant fidelity by Captain Tilney, had sought in vain to reinstate herself with her dearest James by protestations of affection for the latter, and abhorrence of the former. At that time it was to be supposed that Catherine would not again let herself be imposed upon by falsehood and shallow artifice.

But it is ever the weakness of honesty that it cannot believe in the absence in others of those principles which to them are as natural as life itself. And as Isabella advanced to throw herself in Catherine's arms, pouring forth a flood of pleasure in their reunion, Henry saw with apprehension that for all her six years as a wife and a mother and mistress of his establishment, Catherine was still disposed to let herself be influenced by a tale of distress.

"Oh my dearest creature, my sweetest Catherine, so I look upon you again. You are dearer to me than anybody can conceive and I am only amazed that I could have lived so long away from you. Of your generous heart I need not ask whether I am welcome. Were I not so agitated—but no matter. Were our situations reversed, were I the mistress of a grand establishment such as yours, it would be exactly the same, my first care would be that you should be made happy. Nay, I am the wretchedest creature alive—" Here Miss Thorpe shed a few tears, and was assisted by Catherine to an easy chair by the fire, her cloak loosened, her bonnet undone, her wrists gently chafed with lavender water, and orders given that refreshment should be brought. Henry, however, taking little notice of her pleading look, merely rang for a servant to take these, and continued watchful, unwilling to leave the two alone until he was satisfied not only as to the brief duration of Isabella's stay, but also as to her motives and their effect upon his wife. Soon it became clear that Isabella had no intention of leaving in the immediate future. She had cast herself upon their hospitality, having first visited Woodston, where she had been informed that Mr. and Mrs. Henry Tilney were spending Christmas at Northanger Abbey; and the object of her visit, concealed in a profusion of compliments and inconsistencies, was to enlist her friend's good offices with the General on behalf of the young man to whom she was betrothed, a junior lieutenant in the -shires, recently stationed not many miles away in the little garrison town of M——.

"My sweet Catherine knows that of all things riches are the most abhorrent to me—my wishes are so moderate that the smallest income would be enough; grandeur I detest, and a lack of constancy is my aversion. I beg you will not believe that I would be less faithful to my Edgar if we had to wait ten long endless years before we could afford to marry. It is for his sake that I desire a speedier promotion than any young man can obtain without influence. With the recommendation of General Tilney, the thing is done, he is made. I would not for all the world—"

She was interrupted by the entrance of the General himself, in his benevolent character as grandfather, uproariously attended by four children between the ages of two and six, one on his back throttling him, the others clinging to his arms and urging him to send away the two harassed nursemaids in the background, whose suggestions of bedtime long past were as little minded by the General as by his troupe of rebels. Eliza even dared go so far as trying to remove from little Catherine's hand a large sweetmeat; but screaming that Grandpa had given it to her, the little girl crammed most of it for greater safety into her mouth, and glared defiance at poor Eliza.

Isabella Thorpe at once burst into exclamations of admiration for the children, without even waiting for an introduction to General Tilney. She could not control her transports over the little angels, declaring that in beauty and intelligence they far surpassed any children she had ever known. The General beamed upon her, and desired Catherine to make him acquainted with her fair friend; while Henry came to the aid of the two agitated nursemaids, and with a father's authority, profiting by the General's interest temporarily removed elsewhere, succeeded without too much ado in packing them all off to bed.

"Unfortunately," remarked Henry later that evening, in conference with his sister over the disastrous intrusion which promised to mar their Christmas peace, "unfortunately she is more beautiful than ever. Already she has won our father's admiration, and recommended herself both by flattery and by insinuations that she was alone and penniless and but for her beloved Catherine friendless as well."

Nevertheless, his sister shrank from adopting the bold means by which Henry had proposed ridding themselves of such an incubus. "Could Catherine do nothing?" she hazarded. "Surely if she were to go to the General and tell him of Miss Thorpe's past behaviour, not only with her own brother but with ours, how all her protestations were hollow, her promises empty, her disposition fickle and avaricious, and her mind set on the vulgar project of winning a husband at all costs who would keep her in luxury and that no consideration for truth, no delicacy would turn her from her purpose, surely then—?"

"Do you seriously imagine," interrupted Henry somewhat ruefully, "that my darling wife with her simple honest nature would really go to the General with such a tale? No, already her warm heart has forgiven her friend; already she is wondering if we have not been too harsh these many years, and what can she do to make poor Isabella feel that at Northanger Abbey she is at home, at any rate till Christmas be over? The General gave the invitation, and Catherine warmly seconded it."

"I thought," remarked Eleanor, troubled, "that once her eyes had been opened, her native good sense—"

"There is something in the air of an Abbey that is always disposed to work against my Catherine's good sense. The influence is too romantic; presently we shall have her hunting anew for Laurentina's skeleton. No, Eleanor, we shall get no help from Catherine. You will have to consent to my plan, you will have to go to our father and do as I suggest. You are his darling; he will listen to you."

"Only since I am married," replied Eleanor, with a shrewd stab at her father's weakness for titles.

His son shrugged his shoulders. "True: her ladyship, my daughter the Viscountess. As for little Charles, he will be ruined if your Christmas stay were to last longer than a se'nnight. When does your ladyship expect my brother-in-law, the Viscount?" mimicking the General.

Eleanor smiled and replied: "Tomorrow, when your other brother-in-law is also due to arrive, and our own brother Frederick."

"Miss Thorpe will have a fine dashing choice of admirers, past, present and future."

"I have no fears for my husband," said Eleanor with a happy smile.

"Nor I. Besides, she cannot marry him, and it is an establishment she is after. As mistress of Northanger Abbey, she would have wealth and consequence more than she ever dreamt of. Frederick has already jilted her; he does not jilt twice in the same place, it does not amuse him. Nor will she give him the opportunity; she is clever enough for that. As for poor James, he is a Morland with Catherine's own trusting innocent heart, always ready to be imposed on and to suffer afresh. But she will profit by his admiration."

"Men are such foolish creatures."

"Aye, fools and rogues every one of us—always excepting, dear Eleanor, your husband. Amazing that thus far no adventuress has captured our father. I do not think that even your easy-going Charles would relish such a near connection with Miss Thorpe. Eleanor, I tell you the danger is urgent. If you will not take an active share in what I have suggested, at least allow me to represent you to my father as too distraught; at least let me pretend to be your ambassador."

And to this at last his sister gave her reluctant consent. She let herself be swayed by Henry only when her judgment informed her that his was rational and his apprehensions well founded. He was so far from being defunct in understanding that she could trust his present alarm, especially as her own strong desire was to see the fair Isabella safely away from the Abbey before their Christmas house-party should be complete.

His plan was simply as follows. He would go to the General and inform him that to allow the beautiful adventuress and his titled son-in-law to meet under the same roof might easily prove fatal to Eleanor's happiness. That Miss Thorpe had had no other idea of forcing herself into the Abbey and employing Catherine as her tool. That Eleanor was at that very moment of hearing the news pacing the room weeping and distraught, but relying on her father's sense of protection to rid her of this peril to her honour and the fortunes of her noble son. Remembering his father's surprising credulity seven years ago when he had returned home post-haste after hearing in London some incredible tale against Catherine Morland—yes, from John Thorpe, brother of this very Isabella, Henry did not scruple to hint at rumours of some secret attachment which had existed between Isabella Thorpe and the Viscount, long before the latter's unexpected accession to the title. The General's love of a lord was his paramount weakness, and you had only to play upon that.

It is to be feared that Henry Tilney loved a tale for its own sake, as well as for the benefits it might effect. Had he not teased Catherine, long ago, with his story of the Abbey haunted by the ghost of the wretched Matilda, vilely murdered in its haunts, her woeful memoirs might have been recognised sooner by Catherine as no more than a washing-list left behind by the valet of Eleanor's future husband. What Henry had to do now was a trifle more difficult, but he did not despair of success.

Pale and trembling, Catherine came to the door of Isabella's room. She could hardly speak connected words to tell of her dreadful errand. Explanation and apology were impossible; for the General's commands had been too loud, too peremptory to allow of any pleading. It was the tyrant back again, the tyrant of Northanger Abbey whom she had believed gone forever. He would brook not the slightest mitigation of his orders; hospitality was nothing to him. Miss Thorpe was to be turned from his doors. The hour was fixed for early the next morning, the carriage ordered to be there at seven o'clock, without any considerations even of decent civility. Catherine had asked in a faltering voice how Isabella had offended him? The volume of sound by which the General replied would have shaken the stoutest walls, but it lacked coherence.

It was not to be supposed that Isabella would help her dearest Catherine to overcome her distress; on the contrary, she added to it by every means in her power. When at last she was made to understand what had occurred was past mending, her swelling indignation was at first inclined to name Catherine herself as the author of all her ills; at the very least, Catherine had revealed herself a weak timid creature and a disloyal friend; however, all was not lost yet; if Catherine were at least half as sorry as she declared herself to be, could she not leave the Abbey and accompany her wretched friend to her own home at Woodston, vowing that she preferred not to stay herself where her friends were so harshly treated? "Then be sure your husband will follow you to make every apology in his power, and we can all be as miserable as may be together; we need not depend on the General; his intolerable lack of civility must be its own punishment. I never thought him handsome, nor his cockscomb of a son. Your dear brother is worth a thousand of such. Can we not send him word that he is to come direct to Woodston instead of to the Abbey?"

In a low voice Catherine murmured something about her children being an objection. She could hardly suppose that Henry would delight in a Christmas spent under his father's displeasure, away from his family, with the company only of Miss Thorpe to console him, but this she hardly dared to offer to Isabella's complacence. Fully half an hour had to be spent in convincing her that neither at Northanger nor at Woodston could she remain an uninvited guest. And then what reproaches were hurled at poor Catherine! What devices to wound her. To be sent forth thus, to travel alone and unattended, exposed to every insult, to travel by post, penniless—

Here at least her friend could assist. Henry was a generous husband, and Catherine promised to accommodate Isabella with all she could spare.

Upon this they parted, with so much coldness on the one side that it was all poor Catherine could do to bring herself shortly after six the next morning to appear at Isabella's door and offer assistance in packing her trunk; for on retiring to her room the evening before, and finding a maid to wait upon her, Isabella had imperiously ordered her to unpack and hang her clothes in the dressing-closets so conveniently adjoining. She was barely ready when a servant announced that the carriage was there. Walking down the corridor like a queen going to her execution, she flung at Catherine this final philippic: "I could not have cared more for you had you been my sister, and it is as a sister that I hope you will never be happy while you remember the pain you have given to your unhappy Isabella who forgives you with all her heart. Adieu."

The wheels of the carriage rolled away. Catherine stood on the steps of the Abbey gazing after it, bewildered, sore, guilty, penniless, exhausted, and yet could it be, quite amazingly relieved?

"Neither my caro sposo nor me would endure it for a single moment," declared Mrs. Elton.

She was discussing the rumours which had been flying round Highbury for some time, that all was not well between Mr. and Mrs. Knightley of Donwell Abbey, and that the cause of trouble, at least from Mr. Knightley's point of view, was precisely that they were *not* at Donwell Abbey, but for the past seven years residents at Hartfield, Mrs. Knightley's previous home; for she positively refused to break her promise to her father that her marriage would deprive him of nothing but rather give him a cheerful addition to her company in the person of a friend whose strength, resolution and presence of mind must be commendable to him when his spirits were low.

"No, not for a single moment."

And Miss Bates, drinking tea at the Vicarage, for once found nothing to reply; her usual volubility could find little pleasure in the troubles of her friends, and such close friends as Mr. Woodhouse and his daughter and Mr. Knightley. She tried indeed to divert Mrs. Elton's gleeful hopes of complete ruin to the happiness of Emma Knightley (whom she disliked with all the force that envy acting on a small nature could summon up), by an attempt to give news of her niece Jane from whom she had recently had a letter. "—Wait, I will read it to you. I think I have it by me."

But Mrs. Elton would have none of sweet Jane Fairfax since her marriage to Frank Churchill removed her from the neighbourhood. Jane as a dependent needing Mrs. Elton's recommendations for the post of governess to anyone of her circle who would allow wax candles in the schoolroom was all very well, especially as her patronage served to mark her contempt for Emma Woodhouse's own protégée of seven years ago, Harriet Smith, now Mrs. Martin of the Abbey Farm. She had only invited poor Miss Bates, living alone in Highbury since her mother's peaceful death, in order to hear more of any bad news that might be in circulation from Hartfield. So Miss Bates might return her niece's letter to her reticule, for it could not command a hearer.

"Rather him than me, I said to Mr. Elton—a'nt I daring? —at the time when the marriage was first spoken of. Not but that I have a great liking for that dear old Mr. Woodhouse, quite a beau of mine. But poor Mr. K., his infatuation must sink, indeed from all accounts it has sunk already this long time. Not living in his own home, nor master of his own family—Aye, 'twas a sad business from the start."

Her vulgar complacency would have been odious to any but Miss Bates, the kindest creature in the world, and always too ready to believe the best of everyone, even Mrs. Elton.

"Mark my words, I said to Selina when I was visiting at Maple Grove a se'nnight ago; I remember we were in Mr. Suckling's barouche-landau at the time paying a call on Mrs.

Bragge— Mark my words, I said," and Mrs. Elton nodded significantly. "—And as for all this talk of his having but now gone to London to see his brother Mr. John Knightley who is indisposed, I do not believe a word of it. I have the greatest horror of gossip, as you know, nobody could be more at pains than me to disbelieve half I hear, but when Mrs. Hodges has positively told Mrs. Stokes of the Crown who passed it on to our Wright who thought it no less than her duty to come to me about it— There was quite a set-to between Mr. and Mrs. Knightley at Donwell only last Thursday when she went to visit the children, and afterwards when she returned to Hartfield and he remained behind, Mrs. Hodges could hear him tramping up and down, up and down in the library, and none of the children durst go near him, he had such a brow on him when at last he came out; poor little mites." Mrs. Elton paused with a fit of coughing, so that Miss Bates was able at last to put in eagerly:

"Oh, but indeed—No more, I thank you, such a noble tea — Indeed I cannot think that our good Mrs. Stokes or perhaps Mrs. Hodges heard aright. Our dear Mr. Knightley— such an excellent father—to be sure his patience can have been a little tried now and then, his manner a little quick; but he has too much respect for his father-in-law, even though at times it may be a little difficult—our kind Mr. Woodhouse's fears for his digestion, gruel served every evening, the eggs a minute and a half too lightly boiled for her husband's taste, Mrs. Knightley told me. We cannot all fancy the same cooking, and I remember my dearest mother once having a sad disappointment over a fricassee that Mr. Woodhouse had had sent away for fear it might not agree with her—but I'm thankful to say her digestion was always of the strongest or she could not have lived so long. We have so excellent a neighbour in Mr. Woodhouse, my mother always said; all our family are remarkably fortunate; look at Jane— she and Mr. Frank Churchill, that child of good fortune, Miss Woodhouse calls him— I mean Mrs. Knightley, my poor memory!— Where was I? Oh yes, Jane, she has the best of homes with his uncle, and though it is true that I did not think her looking well last time I was at Enscombe, they invite me so often and always such attention paid me I declare I am sometimes quite ashamed—a little pale and silent, and I am not sure that a married woman should be so taken up with her music, but Mr. Churchill cannot be held responsible for that—he would not discourage Jane from playing, not by any means—her own instrument, the finest that can be procured—but I forget, you already know it: it used to stand in our sitting-room. Was it not you who said that a married woman however accomplished if she does not neglect her pianoforte must neglect her husband?"

Miss Bates had talked herself to a standstill on the various topics flowing like tributaries into the main stream; but she could hardly have hit on one more unfortunate to the Knightleys than a married woman's neglect of her husband. Determined not to let Mrs. Elton or anyone else know that she was secretly a little alarmed at finding Mrs. Frank Churchill so very pensive, especially when her husband was by, and taking so little pleasure in his flow of spirits and rattle of conversation that had previously delighted her, Miss Bates was now to face what was only a degree less distressing—the possibility of a disastrous finish to the wedded happiness of dear, wilful, high-spirited Emma Woodhouse. Really, none of the young couples who had entered the conjugal state with such felicity seven years ago were in a state to be viewed with complete satisfaction by their friends and well-wishers—unless it might be Mr. and Mrs. Robert Martin.

Nobody with any perception, however, could have named Mrs. Elton as a well-wisher of poor little Harriet Smith; and she was not to be drawn now, even to Miss Bates' comment on her increasing plumpness since presenting Mr. Martin with his sixth child. Mrs. Elton preferred to keep her eyes fixed on the pitiful situation of Mr. and Mrs. Knightley: "I hold the arrangement very cheap, very cheap indeed; and only your precious Miss Woodhouse would have thought of it to spare herself trouble, that her children should live in one place and she and her husband in another. To be sure she calls it sparing her dear father the discomfort, but if she is so full of consideration, need she have run after poor K. seven years ago? She had always meant to catch him if she could, and I was extremely concerned for him then and did not hesitate to say so. A shocking plan for him to live together with his wife in a house belonging to her, or as near as makes no difference. It could not fail to spell ruin to any marriage, and with her temper—well, and now at last we see the end of it—they are obliged to separate. I collect he is to stay at Donwell and she at Hartfield, and when she comes over to see the children he has obliged her to promise she will send him word beforehand, that he may be out. A very awkward business. For one cannot wish for Mr. Woodhouse to die, as no doubt *she* does every day of her life."

But in her lack of delicacy Mrs. Elton had gone too far, and Miss Bates would by no means suffer such an allusion; the death of an old friend of so many years, or his daughter's desire for it, were equally to be repudiated with all the energy at her command. And shortly afterwards she took polite leave of Mrs. Elton.

Disappointed to find her friend Mrs. Knightley gone to Donwell, Harriet remained talking awhile by the fire with Mr. Woodhouse. Her gentle voice and pretty manners never came amiss with him, and when she enquired for Mrs. John Knightley's fine family of five, their grandfather always had much to tell of their health and of the sad mistakes of their apothecary, Mr. Wingfield: Ah, if they would only call in Perry, especially as in his opinion little Bella's throat had never quite recovered from its weakness of seven years ago, a weakness which he persistently ascribed to the unhealthy effect of sea air.

Harriet agreed. She would not know how to do otherwise. It was almost a matter of regret to Mr. Woodhouse that her children, with a sensible father and grandmother to combat any nervous fears for their health, and Abbey Mill Farm for their playground, so rarely gave any cause to summon Mr. Perry. She was able to report, however, that Mr. Martin's mother had been suffering from a touch of gout, for which Mr. Perry had recommended Constantia wine. Naturally Mr. Woodhouse was warmly gratified, and with all this, forgot to wonder why Emma had not yet returned from her daily visit to her children at Donwell. "I do not often go myself. The drive is a little fatiguing and I do not above half like to take the carriage out in this dismal weather, except indeed to Randalls. Our old James does not mind taking the horses to Randalls; his daughter is housemaid there, Hannah, a civil pretty-spoken girl. Our poor Miss Taylor—that's Mrs. Weston, my dear, but she will always be Miss Taylor to me—was happy to have Hannah about her when she went from Hartfield. Ah, that was a sad business. Emma will not have it so, but I shall always say that Mr. Weston is too rough with their little Anna. He forgets that she is not a boy; an excellent father, our Mr. Weston, but little girls should not be treated like little boys." He sighed, and moved his chair two inches further back from the fire. "Are you sure you do not feel a draught, my dear?"

"No indeed, Mr. Woodhouse, there is never any draught at Hartfield. I always say it is the most comfortable house to visit." Yet secretly, even Harriet wondered that with so much to say of his grandchildren in Brunswick Square, and even of Mrs. Weston's only daughter Anna, and with such kind interest in the Martin family, he should have so little to relate of his other grandchildren, Emma's little boy and girl. He saw them but rarely, and then their natural high spirits produced a fatigue that his nerves could ill endure, though he had never complained of the noise and romping of Isabella's two schoolboys, Henry and John, when they had been brought to stay with him at Hartfield. Odd indeed, meditated Harriet as she made her adieus, for she could not wait longer to see Mrs. Knightley (she had promised Mrs. Weston to call)—odd indeed that he seemed quite resigned to Cassy and George living at Donwell in charge of their nurses and governesses and housekeeper, visited every day by their parents; rarely enquired for them, and received with tolerable calmness any news of misadventure or childish ailments without even recommending Mr. Perry forty times an hour. What could he have against them? Finding no answer in her own mind, Harriet asked this of Mrs. Weston presently when they were comfortably seated together at Randalls, and after she had conscientiously delivered all Mr. Woodhouse's affectionate messages.

Mrs. Weston believed she knew the answer to Harriet's speculations, but thought it more prudent not to say that Mr. Woodhouse had never been fully reconciled to Emma's marrying, even though it had not taken her away from him; a fear might persist that one day the claims of husband and children would supercede his own. She was wise enough to perceive that what looked like indifference, in reality could be ascribed to jealousy, or if his gentle disposition were not capable of so strong a passion, at least to a hope that by not often seeing Cassy and little George, he might pretend to himself that they were not in existence. When Isabella married Mr. John Knightley, Mr. Woodhouse still had his Emma to be mistress of Hartfield; he was first with Emma, his peace was secured, nothing could ever separate them; therefore Mr. John Knightley could be allowed a wife, children and a home in London. He was not the rival his brother had become. Something of this, but not much, Mrs. Weston explained to Harriet.

"That is very bad," Harriet agreed solemnly; and then her thoughts taking a new direction— "I am very fond of Mrs. Martin; *she* lives in *our* house, but I do not think me and Mr. Martin could bear it were it otherwise. I do not see how Mr. Knightley bears it to live always at Hartfield. Would it not be better if Mr. Woodhouse removed to Donwell?"

Mrs. Weston was silent for a moment. The weight on her mind had been growing for some time past, that all was far from well with her dearest Emma. It would be a relief to share her apprehensions with Harriet, who was far more sensible from seven years of Mr. Martin's constant companionship than she had been as a young girl. "It would kill him to be moved. I do not know what is to come of it all."

"Nor I indeed. Dear Mrs. Weston, do you think Mr. Knightley is to blame for consenting, when they married, that while her father was alive they should always live at Hartfield?"

"No-one is to blame. Mr. Woodhouse could not be left alone without a daughter, and yet to postpone the wedding until— It was not to be thought of."

"Does it not strike you," Harriet offered her opinion timidly, "that Mr. Woodhouse, though of course he has to be very very careful, is now in better health than he has been these many years?"

It *had* struck Mrs. Weston. It had struck a great many other people in the neighbourhood, fearful that Mr. Knightley's endurance could not forever endure the strain. Not so easy to see, but clearly visible to Mrs. Weston, as ever Emma's dearest friend and confidant, was the fact that Emma herself in a different way was suffering from the arrangement, and in her mind accused Mr. Knightley of being unreasonable. Not that he ever failed in respect to his father-in-law, but there was a settled melancholy in his manner now, so that the burden of keeping Mr. Woodhouse cheerful and entertained fell mainly on Emma herself; how therefore could she devote her whole energy and attention to her other home and her children at Donwell? Emma showed the strain increasingly, not by impatience with her father, but in a more dangerous direction, with the husband whom she loved so dearly.

"What is to happen?" asked Harriet naively; adding— "I

mean if nothing happens soon? It is unthinkable, is it not, that Mr. Knightley should go away?"

"Go away? Harriet, what are you thinking of? Mr. Knightley go away? He who could hardly ever bear to leave Donwell for more than a night when business took him to London? You've been hearing gossip."

"Aye, if it were that, I should not take much account of it all; they are forever gossiping at Highbury. Mr. Martin will not allow me to go where I am likely to meet Mrs. Elton, and I am not sorry; she has been no friend to me." Harriet spoke with a little air of dignity that did not become her ill.

"Then why do you think Mr. Knightley may be going away? Is it from something he has let fall to your husband? Do not be afraid, Harriet, you may trust me; we are too fond of our friends, I hope, at Donwell and at Hartfield; we would not harm them for the world."

Harriet was reassured that no blame would attach to her for repeating what had recently caused her such alarm, that Mr. Knightley had given her husband certain directions for the farming of his land around and about Donwell Abbey in the near future, in case, he had said, something occurred to take him out of England.

The sudden entrance of Mr. Weston broke into their conversation. He was not in his usual sanguine spirits, nor as glad to find company to be entertained; it was plain he had but just heard some bad news. His greeting to Harriet was grave and preoccupied, and so unlike his natural manner that without further ado his wife besought him not to keep them any longer in suspense.

"Presently, my love," he replied. "All in good time. Bad news will always keep, you know." And then in an undertone clearly audible: "Presently, when we are alone."

"Good heavens," cried Harriet, breaking in, "My husband! Mr. Martin! Something dreadful must have happened. I beseech you, Mr. Weston, do not wait. I charge you, tell me instantly."

"No, indeed, upon my honour, you are mistaken. It is not in the smallest degree connected with Mr. Martin. For all I know, he does very well indeed."

Harriet's knees gave way. She sat down again and had to be relieved with hartshorn before she was able to pay attention to Mr. Weston's grave news.

It was soon told however. Mr. John Knightley was dead.

He had for some time been far from well, and Mr. Wingfield had ordered him to rest, but paying no heed and with a very important case on his hands, he went into court, made an eloquent speech and collapsed from heart-failure. It was over almost at once.

Through all the first agitation which must be felt on behalf of any such close friends of the two families, the shock, the enquiries as to poor Mrs. John Knightley and who was with her and how she did, and did his brother know and had Emma departed at once to support her sister or had she first felt it her duty to break the news to her father at Hartfield? —through all this, it could not be denied that a thought had come into the minds of both Mrs. Weston and Harriet Martin; which however indecorous to the sadness of the occasion, could not be wholly suppressed.

"How very very fortunate for poor Mrs. John Knightley," said Harriet earnestly, some half hour later, "that at least she and her children will not be left wanting a home; that there will be such a warm welcome waiting for them with her father at Hartfield."

Mrs. Weston dared not reply, so ashamed was she of the unreasoning joy that for a moment had swelled her heart at the thought that here was the only solution of the problem they had been discussing, the only possible manner of perfectly contenting Mr. Woodhouse and thus saving the happiness of Mr. and Mrs. Knightley. Her beloved Emma, with her duty done and with no regrets, would shortly be free to devote herself to her own family in her own home at Donwell.

Nothing of course, of these far too early speculations could be spoken of without impropriety. It did not even need any self-command on Mrs. Weston's part after this one irrepressible sigh of relief, to devote all her present thoughts to Isabella; much as she may have endured in recent years from the temper of a husband whose naturally irritable disposition had deteriorated in illness for which he had no patience, it was yet not to be supposed but that she must sincerely mourn him.

Mr. Weston, however, who until Harriet spoke had not realised what favourable changes might be brought about in their neighbourhood, now leapt upon this aspect of the news she had so innocently revealed. He spoke almost gaily: "True, too true. She will be coming home to Hartfield. Aye. I had not thought of that." And among the many causes of satisfaction, he was just about to enumerate the confidence Mrs. John Knightley had in Mr. Perry, who, her husband's prejudice removed, could now be called in for herself and her family whenever she saw fit, when he was recalled by his wife's gentle murmur of reproof.

"Very well, my love. Very right. Nothing can as yet be settled and certainly nothing must be said outside our little circle. You can set your mind at rest on that. I wonder if Miss Bates is at home if I were to call round?"

Though Jane Austen had chosen to conclude these three of her books, *Mansfield Park, Northanger Abbey* and *Emma,* in a panorama of peace, weddings and happiness, the wicked characters confounded and the hero and heroine freed from all misunderstandings, nevertheless as far as I was concerned I was left unsatisfied, oddly sure that we had not really heard the last of it. Why, Jane Austen had not even told us where and how she had placed Isabella Thorpe at the end of *Northanger Abbey;* and that young woman was one of nature's catfish; presently she would start threshing round, troubling the peaceful water and the inhabitants of the ocean bed. . . . And if Isabella's creator had been somewhat remiss in finally disposing of her at any rate without a hint towards a rich marriage, a husband who would keep her in order and stand no nonsense, then it was up to me instead to make sure for my own peace of mind that wherever she might choose to intrude her opulent egoism, Isabella had made it impossible for herself to stage a dramatic reappearance with a hard-luck story, either at Northanger Abbey itself or at the Parsonage.

Nor could the establishment have remained static which Sir Thomas had formed for his daughter Maria far enough from Mansfield Park for Aunt Norris and her pretty ways to have grown dim in retrospect. Like Isabella Thorpe, Aunt Norris was not that sort of a woman; once at least she would have tried to burst apart the serene state of affairs at Mansfield Park; great Birnam Wood would eventually come to Dunsinane. Seven years was a long time for such a pair; they would have been at the extreme end of their tether, the rope stretched taut. So here again I had this compulsion to attend to the matter myself, to play Providence and slip the idea into Sir Thomas' head that Antigua might be a convenient place of exile for an unwanted sister-in-law; and to prompt Lady Bertram's drowsing maternal instinct into sudden aloe blossoming. Naturally I had not the audacity in these two books to invent wholly on my own initiative; I took hints from Jane Austen and used them, that is all; gratefully and with sincere humility following up her delineation of character. But I do not believe that the amazing vitality with which her power had endowed them, could die and cease to function merely at the arbitrary announcement: The End.

Most of all, Emma demanded some solution denied her by Jane Austen, that would carry with it as far as human prescience may stretch, a grant of permanent happiness. Emma's rapture was on the shortest lease; only now, after I have despatched Mr. John Knightley to a painless death and so given Mr. Woodhouse his elder instead of his younger daughter to live with him at Hartfield, only now can I begin to accept for the latter a fair chance of living happy-ever-after.

But in the other three books, *Pride and Prejudice, Sense and Sensibility* and *Persuasion,* we can surrender to the paradisal promises of the last chapter, without a compulsion to raise questions: "Yes, but wouldn't Mrs. Norris—?" "Yes, but after all, Isabella—"; "Yes, but Mr. Knightley—?" In these other three, if I pick out here and there at random something which might have happened at the end of seven years to one or other of the characters, it is not because it was almost bound to happen, but for little better reason than to divert myself. In fact there is no real need for me to butt in at all; and if you care to join me in the idle pastime, let it be with an apology to Jane Austen; an appeal that she may be tolerant (for instance) over fancy playing round an idea that Mrs. Bennet had died about four years after successfully marrying off her two elder daughters to rich and indulgent husbands. I like to speculate on Longbourn and Meryton and Pemberley with Mrs. Bennet dead and buried, although no provision is made in *Pride and Prejudice* that she should thus have succumbed in the flower of her middle age; we are not told she was delicate (except, of course, several times by herself); she overate, of course, but not to that extent. And even if Mrs. Bennet had not died, Darcy and Elizabeth, Bingley and Jane could still have been happy, as her two sons-in-law had prudently seen fit to remove their wives as far as possible from their old home to estates in Derbyshire; where, we are told, Mr. Bennet used to delight in arriving often and unexpectedly; and where Lydia and Wickham would certainly have been a perpetual nuisance, but that Darcy could be trusted to deal unsentimentally with spongers and parasites. Thus most of the loose ends are tied up in the last pages of *Pride and Prejudice*. Georgiana, Wickham and Lydia, Kitty, the Gardiners, even Mary Bennet: "she was necessarily drawn from the pursuit of accomplishments by Mrs. Bennet's being quite unable to sit alone. Mary was obliged to mix more with the world, but she could still moralize over every morning visit."

Nicely to mix my metaphors, the curtain falls on a landscape where there are no catfish; and if, bound by my own formula, I have limited myself to raising it again only seven years later and not a day before, I must loosen control of decorum—though only for a few moments—to record an earlier scene of really indecent rejoicing, handshakes of mutual congratulation and juvenile back-slapping between Darcy and Bingley, on first receiving the news that their buxom mother-in-law had painlessly passed away: "Oh *boy!!*" repeated over and over again. . . . And then, composing their faces, proceeding gravely together to support Elizabeth and Jane in their bereavement.

And Mr. Bennet? What would be his reactions? We have already seen many times that they were never quite what we expected; and without being too arbitrary, I believe we can draw a conclusion that as a man he was susceptible to female charms (in the plural, not the singular) or he could never have married Mrs. Bennet; it could hardly have been her intellect or her good breeding that attracted him. Such men as Mr. Bennet obstinately follow type; and his type, as we have seen, lay in the direction of a pretty fool, unreasonable, vain, capricious, good-humoured enough if not thwarted; the very type, in fact, to bring out all his latent sarcasm once he had committed the initial idiocy of sealing her as his blushing bride.

Therefore, seven years after the last chapter of *Pride and Prejudice,* and three after Mrs. Bennet's demise, Darcy and Bingley are again bidden startle their wives with a piece of news from Longbourn. This time it arrives via Mrs. Gardiner. And their stunned amazement may be imagined on hearing that Mr. Bennet was for the second time about to enter into matrimony . . . with Mrs. Forster, widow of Colonel Forster; a bouncing young woman addicted to frivolous parties, extravagant shopping and practical jokes, who at one time had been an intimate friend of his daughter Lydia.

The same wayward desire which had led me to plan an untimely death for Mrs. Bennet merely because I had always wished to see her dead every time (in the course of *Pride and Prejudice*), she had opened her mouth, now leads me, via a similar orgy of self-indulgence, to announce that seven years after the end of *Sense and Sensibility*, Mrs. Dashwood, dear, gay, enchanting, unselfish Mrs. Dashwood is also marrying again; as good a match as you would wish to see, and from the point of view of material consideration, a very much handsomer, richer and nobler husband than had fallen to either of her daughters Elinor and Marianne; more intelligent, too, with a sense of humour lacking in both Edward Ferrars and Colonel Brandon. Mrs. Dashwood has ever been such a favourite of mine, and I was so surprised that Jane Austen (and everyone in the book) had taken it for granted that all her chances were over after the death of Mr. Dashwood, that I simply cannot check my longing to reward her with such a husband . . . and particularly to rouse the astonishment of her daughter Marianne. There, in fact, I believe we may seek what film producers call the motivation in my case. I was angry, not amused, that Marianne, silly, ignorant little chit, convinced she knew everything and knowing literally less than nothing, should in one of the early chapters of *Sense and Sensibility* have unhesitatingly relegated her white-haired tottering parent (at the age of forty-one) to the back seat, to the topmost shelf. I was surprised, too, that by never as much as mentioning an admirer for Mrs. Dashwood, from the first chapter to the last, Jane Austen should carelessly have seemed to endorse Marianne's verdict. "This'll be a shock to the young woman," I said to myself grimly, yet with irrepressible relish visualising the scene of Marianne's being told the news—(I think solemnly by Colonel Brandon).

However, we should probably have received more support from Jane Austen had it been not customary at that period for ladies to have their hands sought in marriage during their forties; unless by fortune-hunters in need of a wealthy wife.

We have Jane Austen's word for it that Marianne and Colonel Brandon were to live happy ever after—

> Colonel Brandon was now as happy as all those who best loved him believed he deserved to be;—in Marianne he was consoled for every past affliction;—her regard and her society restored his mind to animation, and his spirits to cheerfulness: and that Marianne found her own happiness in forming his, was equally the persuasion and delight of each observing friend. Marianne could never love by halves; and her whole heart became, in time, as much devoted to her husband, as it had once been to Willoughby.

I am not disposed to tamper with the pronouncement; it will satisfy me enough to know that Mrs. Dashwood has come into her own though she could not have had any notion of how I chafed at the subsidiary rôle assigned to her, for she was ever the least conceited of women, with a gift for self-sacrifice so cheerfully fulfilled that it never created uneasiness in those about her. The only other disturbance that I can see foreshadowed on those revealing last pages, lay in the statement that Willoughby made Marianne his secret standard of perfection in woman; and many a rising beauty would be slighted by him in after days as bearing no comparison with Mrs. Brandon. This practice surely would be bound to cause talk? More than talk; hot scandal. Willoughby has an ever jealous wife to fan the flame, and the beautiful Mrs. Brandon herself is "thrown away"—(thus the town would figure it out)—on a husband so many years older than herself, so formal, so heavy, who, when the open weather broke, always took the precaution of wearing a flannel waistcoat against his twinges of rheumatism. Rumour would always be heightened by Marianne's scornful refusal to behave discreetly and with due regard for the world's opinion. Belonging to the school that believes there is nothing so dead as a dead love, I am convinced that having once been disillusioned, Marianne would never again find Willoughby dangerous; her loyal mother and her sister Elinor would rally to her aid; Colonel Brandon would gloomily challenge the most offending backbiter to a duel, and the whole thing would die down.

Of all the happy endings in Jane Austen's stories, none is so unassailable as *Persuasion.*

Yet, though the author has not left the future of Anne and Wentworth exposed to the slightest apprehension, we may perhaps discover, again merely for amusement's sake, one or two odd bits of conjecturing to be done round the outer rim. Seven years must have decided once and for all whether Mrs. Clay, that clever Penelope with her web, has indeed succeeded in netting for herself the name of Lady Elliot. We are given a strong hint, in the last chapter, that though the future Sir William had prevented her from being the second wife of the present Sir Walter, he might after all be wheedled and caressed into marrying her himself. . . . However, as I estimate Mr. Elliot's intelligence and his sense of self-preservation very high indeed, I do not think this in the least likely to occur; you cannot easily hope to make a dupe of a man who is watching you narrowly all the time to know whether you are about that very thing. Sir Walter could be tricked by flattery, because his vanity put him into the pachydermatous species. My guess is that Mrs. Clay will get over her unprofitable infatuation for Mr. Elliot, return to Sir Walter, and this time pull it off. It could very well happen six years after the end of *Persuasion*, so that seven years after, we may greet a little heir to Kellynch, proudly inscribed in Sir Walter's copy of the Baronetage, whilst in the distance we listen to the pleasant sound of Mr. Elliot gnashing his teeth. . . .

Fairly improbable, too, that Louisa Musgrove and Captain Benwick should continue blissfully mated, once she has fully recovered from her fall off the Cobb at Lyme. As Jane Austen says, it was originally propinquity that drew them together; otherwise they were wholly incompatible. We need not let them part with any violence, at the end of seven years; the Musgrove as a large united family are too good-humoured, too noisy and insensitive even to notice if one among them is gradually absorbed into their midst, and swallowed. Is Captain Benwick a type of worm that turns? No, I think not. He will go to sea; he will come home again; he will find women to listen while he reads poetry aloud. . . . he will begin to write poetry himself. A slim volume will be published—and not read by any save his brother-in-law, Charles Musgrove, who might try out of sheer kindness; but he would be sadly put to it to discover what it all meant. . . . And presently he would toss it aside, and ask Captain Benwick if he would care for a ratting expedition?

The true end of *Persuasion* blends all the shining quality of a fairy tale with such sturdy reality in the weave, that we are glad to recognise how difficult it would be for us to tease out any of the threads to make a loose end. When Anne and Frederick are reunited at last, and go wandering up the streets of Bath, higher and higher, oblivious of passers-by, it is as though they were held inside music, safe in the curve of a pearl. No harm can pierce through. Nor would it be anything but morbid for us to imagine either prematurely taken from the other by death. They will live till they are very old. They will be perfectly happy always. Perhaps they will die in the same hour.

CHAPTER VIII

"A Complete Party of Pleasure"

SHEILA KAYE-SMITH

THE SOCIAL life of small villages is often very much more intense than that of large cities. The absence of other, commercial sources of entertainment compels the inhabitants to seek relaxation in their own homes and the homes of their neighbours. So, as all the chief characters in Jane Austen's novels live in what we should now call small villages, it is not surprising to find them involved in all sorts of social occasions.

I confess that this social life is for me one of the great attractions of the novels. It is the complement and extension of the family life, and gives me an exhilarating sense of participation. I love to go with the heroines to their balls and parties, to accompany them on their dinner visits and even their morning visits, though these are often mere visits of duty and ceremony. I am not socially minded, and perhaps the real attraction of these engagements lies in the fact that I can watch without actually taking part. Probably in actual presence I should not enjoy myself at all. The conversation is never brilliant, the playing and singing would probably seem amateurish in comparison with the radio, and the only other diversion, unless it were dancing, would be cards—all this rather dimly by candlelight, in rooms warm only within a few feet of the fire.

But out of it the author has made a powerful magic, and whether we go to a ball at Netherfield or at the Crown Inn, to dinner at Randalls or at Mansfield Rectory, to an evening party in Bath, a strawberry picnic at Donwell Abbey, or only pay a call on Miss Bates, it is all delightful.

Emma is the novel most fruitful in this sort of entertainment; which is perhaps surprising, for Mr. Woodhouse is very much a recluse— "I am not fond of dinner-visiting. I never was"—and according to Mrs. Elton the standards of the village were not high. "She was a little shocked at the want of two drawing-rooms, at the poor attempt at rout-cakes, and there being no ice in the Highbury card-parties." But I never close the book without feeling that I have been in a sort of social whirl—from that first Christmas Eve dinner, when it snowed and Mr. Elton behaved so strangely and deplorably, to that last picnic on Box Hill, when the sun shone and the strange deplorable behaviour was Emma's own.

For between these events there is the dinner at the Coles', the dinner given at Hartfield for Mrs. Elton, the ball at the Crown, the rather strange little tea-and-games party at Hartfield, when "disingenuousness and double dealing" seemed to meet Mr. Knightley at every turn, and then the strawberry picnic at Donwell, to which "under a bright mid-day sun, at almost Midsummer, Mr. Woodhouse was safely conveyed in his carriage, with one window down."

These festivities do not sound wildly exciting. They make, perhaps, a decidedly middle-aged appeal, and any modern young person reading the book might feel sorry for Emma of whose winter and summer engagements they formed the sum. But Emma is a character so vital, so alive, that she seems to carry with her everywhere her own entertainment. Certainly, by all standards, her life was monotonous, dull and sometimes even lonely. But we never find her depressed —except when outside events, such as Mr. Elton's behaviour in regard to Harriet, or her fears and regrets for Harriet and Mr. Knightley, combine to depress her. It is this vitality which makes her society so enjoyable, and as we always go into company with her, no matter who else may be present or absent, we are interested in what interests her and enjoy what she enjoys. Which is everything except the picnic on

Box Hill, from that indeed I come away with feelings nearly as dejected as her own.

Emma is the only novel which features picnics, though one is planned in *Sense and Sensibility*—"a party was formed for going on the following day to see a very fine place twelve miles from Barton . . . cold provisions were to be taken, open carriages only to be employed, and everything conducted in the usual style of a complete party of pleasure." That party did not take place, owing to Colonel Brandon's unaccountable summons to London; which may have been just as well, for the month was October, rather late for picnics, and "it had rained very hard for the last fortnight." Elinor we know "was prepared to be fatigued, wet through, and frightened." Only Sir John Middleton could have made such a plan. Perhaps it is the winter setting of most of the novels which accounts for the scarcity of picnics as a whole.

The most general form of entertainment was a dinner party, and let this not be confounded with the brief encounters that dinner parties are now. A properly conducted dinner party swallowed up almost half the day. "Here are we," grumbled John Knightley to Emma, "setting forward to spend five dull hours in another man's house." No doubt they would arrive at Randalls soon after four o'clock, for we know that Mr. Woodhouse liked his dinner early, and though on this occasion the snow sent them home before the usual time, a normal dinner-party would not end before nine or ten. We hear that the dinner at the Coles' finished with an impromptu dance—following on a musical entertainment provided by Emma and Jane Fairfax. The dinner itself probably lasted about as long as an Edwardian dinner of several courses. For though the courses were only nominally two, each "course" contained so many separate dishes that they must have taken some time to eat. I do not suppose that the dinner at Randalls approached in quantity those gargantuan feasts we read of in *Tom Jones* and Parson Woodford's *Diaries*. But I have no doubt that besides the saddle-of-mutton that

Mr. Weston carved there would be a couple of birds, and some well-filled "corner dishes." At the Coles', who did not have to consider the effect of the sight of so much unwholesome food on Mr. Woodhouse, there would probably be more; though not so much, perhaps, as on Dr. Grant's table at Mansfield Parsonage, where Mrs. Norris was convinced "of its being impossible among so many dishes but that some must be cold."

In Jane Austen's circle there would not be that long session of the men after dinner, that in a more hard-drinking society often made it impossible for them to join the ladies. We read that at Randalls Mr. Woodhouse "very soon followed them into the drawing-room. Neither wine nor conversation was anything to him; and gladly did he move to those with whom he was always comfortable." The other three sat on a little longer over "Mr. Weston's good wine," to the subsequent undoing of Mr. Elton. In those days the men did not leave the dining-room in a body. Later on we hear at the Coles of Frank Churchill's coming out "the very first of the early."

At the Coles a sort of inferior party assembles after dinner for tea, very much as in later times inferior guests used to be asked in to coffee. Sometimes the interval between tea and dinner would be a long one—Emma had been for an after-dinner walk with Harriet and Mr. Knightley when she met Miss Bates with Jane Fairfax and Frank Churchill, and knowing that "it was exactly the sort of visiting that would be welcome to her father, pressed them all to go home and drink tea with him." But in *Pride and Prejudice* we find Elizabeth Bennet making tea directly after dinner. Mr. Woodhouse's hours, of course, were unfashionably early, and as the dinner-hour grew later and later—once in the novels it touches six o'clock—the interval between dinner and tea necessarily grew less.

There are a number of dinner parties in *Pride and Prejudice*. Mrs. Bennet we know was hospitably inclined; even her own brother and sister when they stayed with her "did not once sit down to a family dinner," and the embarrassment of Lydia's return with Wickham was softened by "having very frequent parties at home. These parties were acceptable to all; to avoid a family circle was even more desirable to such as did think than such as did not." But I do not find the dinner parties in *Pride and Prejudice* as stimulating as those in *Emma.* The company is not as good, and the occasion is more perfunctorily and vaguely dealt with, so that we have not that sense of participation which I find so fascinating.

I have that sense very much indeed in *Mansfield Park,* especially at the dinner party at Mansfield Parsonage to which Fanny is invited to accompany Edmund, greatly to the surprise of both her aunts and the indignation of one of them. It is a most significant occasion, for Fanny has never been asked out to dinner before. "Being the *first* invitation, it should be accepted," says Edmund. "So strange!" says his mother, "for Mrs. Grant never used to ask her." Is it they or their creator who forgets that Fanny has dined at the Parsonage once before. "Pray is she out, or is she not?" asks Mary Crawford earlier in the book. "She dined at the Parsonage with the rest of you, which seemed like being out; and yet she says so little that I can hardly suppose she *is.*" I wonder if this is to be ranked with the apple blossom in strawberry time which is Jane Austen's only certain slip in a matter of fact.

In spite of knowing that she was "sure of seeing or hearing something there to pain" her, Fanny eagerly looked forward to the engagement, "though going only half a mile and only to three people, still it was dining out, and all the little interests of preparation were enjoyments in themselves." Of course Aunt Norris did her best to spoil it all for her: "I hope you are aware that there is no real occasion for your going into company in this sort of way, or ever dining out at all; and it is what you must not depend upon ever being repeated. . . . And I must observe that five is the awkwardest of all possible numbers to be sitting down to table . . . and though Miss Crawford is in a manner at home at the Parsonage, you are not to be taking place of her . . . and if it should rain—which I think exceedingly likely, you must manage as well as you can, and not be expecting the carriage to be sent for you . . ." and so on and so on.

It is a great relief when Aunt Norris is proved wrong about the carriage and a number of other things as well. Fanny "must submit, as her own propriety of mind directed, to being the principal lady in the company, and to all the little distinctions consequent thereon." Moreover, Edmund admired her dress— "I like those glossy spots"—and there was so much conversation at table in which she was not required to take a part, "there was so much to be said between the brother and sister about Bath, so much between the two young men about hunting, so much of politics between Mr. Crawford and Dr. Grant, and of everything and all together between Mr. Crawford and Mrs. Grant, as to leave her the fairest prospect of having only to listen in quiet, and of passing a very agreeable day."

In *Northanger Abbey* there are no dinner parties. The heroine finds her entertainment at the Bath Assemblies, the Rooms and the Theatre. We gather that evening parties rather than dinner parties were fashionable in Bath, for in the stiffer circles of *Persuasion* the Elliots "gave no dinners as a rule." Their time was spent in "the elegant insipidity of evening parties," and when Mary and Charles Musgrove came to Bath with his parents, Elizabeth had a struggle "between propriety and vanity." She knew she ought to ask them all to dinner, but "she could not bear to have the difference in style, the reduction of servants, which a dinner must betray, witnessed by those who had always been so inferior to the Elliots of Kellynch. . . . Old-fashioned notions—country hospitality—we do not profess to give dinners—few people in Bath do—Lady Alicia never does; did not even ask her own sister's family, though they were here a month. . . . I will ask them all for an evening; that will be better; that will be a novelty and a treat. They have not seen two such drawing-rooms before."

As it happens, she was right, at least as far as her own sister was concerned. "Mary was completely satisfied. She was particularly asked to meet Mr. Elliot, and be introduced to Lady Dalrymple and Miss Carteret; and she could not have received a more gratifying attention."

Anne we know enjoyed the party too. But her reasons were not Mary's—or Elizabeth's.

> Glowing and lovely in sensibility and happiness and more generally admired than she thought about or cared for, she had cheerful or forbearing feelings for every creature round her. Mr. Elliot was there; she avoided him, but she could pity him. The Wallises; she had amusement in understanding them. Lady Dalrymple and Miss Carteret; they would soon be innoxious cousins to her. She cared not for Mrs. Clay, and had nothing to blush for in the public manners of her father and sister. With the Musgroves, there was the happy chat of perfect ease; with Captain Harville the kind-hearted intercourse of brother and sister; with Lady Russell, attempts at conversation, which a delicious consciousness cut short; with Admiral and Mrs. Croft, everything of peculiar cordiality and fervent interest, which the same consciousness sought to conceal;— and with Captain Wentworth some moments of communication continually occurring, and always the hope of more, and always the knowledge of his being there.

Which all goes to show how independent a party can be of the actual givers of it.

There are evening parties too in *Sense and Sensibility*, once the story has shifted from the orbit of "country hospitality." In London Elinor and Marianne go into public with Lady Middleton, and it is at an evening party chaperoned by her that Marianne has her disastrous encounter with Willoughby. "They arrived in due time at the place of destination, and as soon as the string of carriages before them would allow, alighted, ascended the stairs, heard their names announced from one landing-place to another in an audible voice, and entered a room splendidly lit up, quite full of company and insufferably hot." Except for the fact that "Lady Middleton sat down to Casino," it was not unlike a Victorian or Edwardian "crush." Later on, when the dreadful scene was over, and Marianne "continued incessantly to give way in a low voice to the misery of her feelings," Lady Middleton—in whom good breeding often took the place of good feeling—"though in the middle of a rubber, on being informed that Marianne was unwell, was too polite to object for a moment to her wish of going away, and making over her cards to a friend, they departed as soon as the carriage could be found."

There is another evening party later on in the book, to which Elinor and Marianne were unwillingly taken by Mrs. John Dashwood, owing to the donor having "allowed her fancy so far to outrun truth and probability, that on merely hearing the name of the Miss Dashwoods, and understanding them to be Mrs. Dashwood's sisters, she immediately concluded them to be staying in Harley Street." So she sent them "cards of invitation, as well as for their brother and sister, to a small musical party at her house."

This party was not entertained, as such parties were when I was young and probably would be now, by professional musicians, but by the performers who were "as usual, in their own estimation, and that of their friends, the first private performers in England." In those days professionalism of all kinds still had a taint.

Elinor was "neither musical nor affecting to be so," so she entertained herself—and us—with Robert Ferrars, whose conversation leads up to what is almost my favourite quotation in the six novels— "Elinor agreed to it all, for she did not think he deserved the compliment of rational opposition."

But evening parties were for Bath and London only, when

fashionable people had many engagements to fit in—had not the little company at Cleveland, as they talked of the friends left behind, "arranged Lady Middleton's engagements?" While Lady Russell had "fresh-arranged all her evening engagements" in order to meet Lady Dalrymple. For the longer evenings and larger hospitality of the country there were dinner-parties—and balls.

The novels abound in dances and balls of all kinds. There are the public balls that Catherine Morland attends at the Rooms in Bath, and the Assemblies frequented by the Bennets and their friends in Meryton. There are private balls given in private houses, and one private ball given in a public house. Then there are various little unpremeditated hops—a few couples dancing to the music of "violin players in the servants hall" or of a good-natured Anne Elliot or Mrs. Weston at the piano.

The one I enjoy most is the ball at Mansfield Park. This may seem a curious preference, for most people would not choose to go into company with Fanny Price. But the occasion has all the primal allurements of the Cinderella story. The fairy godfather waves his wand and the poor little drudge becomes the belle of the ball and the choice of Prince Charming. She wears her triumph so modestly, too: "she could hardly believe it. To be placed above so many elegant young women! The distinction was too great. It was treating her like her cousins! And her thoughts flew to those absent cousins with most unfeigned and truly tender regret that they were not at home to take their own place in the room and have their share of a pleasure which would have been so very delightful for them."

The Wicked Sisters, combined in the person of Aunt Norris, are defeated at the start, at the very inception of the ball. I sometimes call this the "Thank-your-uncle ball," because of Mrs. Norris' first reaction to its proposal. Sir Thomas' slow, measured speech to William had reached its climax: "A dance at home would be more eligible, and if—" when she breaks in: "Ah, my dear Sir Thomas, I knew what you were going to say. If dear Julia were at home, or dearest Mrs. Rushworth at Sotherton, to afford a reason, as occasion for such a thing, you would be tempted to give the young people a dance at Mansfield. I know you would. If *they* were at home to grace the ball, a ball you would have this very Christmas. Thank your uncle, William, thank your uncle."

But the slow, measured speech, like the tread of a policeman on his beat, marches on over her interruption. "My daughters have their pleasures at Brighton, and I hope are very happy; but the dance which I think of giving at Mansfield will be for their cousins." It is a comfort to know that Mrs. Norris' "surprise and vexation required some minutes' silence to be settled into composure."

Everything went right with that dance. Though her aunt's maid arrived too late to help her dress, "she did not dislike her own looks . . . and left her room at least comfortably satisfied with herself and all about her"—which was something that can seldom have happened to her before. One cause of satisfaction was that the necklace Mary Crawford had almost forced upon her, to wear with the amber cross brought by William from Sicily, would "by no means go through the ring of the cross." So she had hung it instead from Edmund's better loved gift of a plain gold chain—though in the generosity of relief she added the necklace as an extra adornment.

Then Edmund had cheered her with signs of being no longer quite so much "the dupe of Miss Crawford." He pours out his heart to Fanny. "She says it is to be the last time that she will ever dance with me. . . . She has never danced with a clergyman, she says, and she never *will*" and, when Fanny warns him: "Do not tell me anything now which hereafter you may be sorry for. The time may come—" he assures her "the time will never come. No such time as you allude to will ever come." No wonder that when the dance was due to begin "she had hardly ever been in a state so nearly approaching high spirits in her life. Her cousins' former gaiety on the day of a ball was no longer surprising to her; she felt it indeed to be very charming."

It is true that she was tired out before the end and Sir Thomas "gave his orders for her sitting down entirely." But when later on—again at Sir Thomas' command—she went upstairs to bed, and "creeping slowly up the principal staircase, pursued by the ceaseless country-dance, feverish with hopes and fears, soup and negus, sore-footed and fatigued, restless and agitated," she yet felt, "in spite of everything that a ball was indeed delightful."

Another ball, not quite so delightful for the heroine, is that given at Netherfield. If for Fanny's ball everything went right, for Elizabeth's everything went wrong. To begin with it rained determinedly for several days before, so that "the very shoe-roses were got by proxy." Then the ball itself was marred by the absence of the man she liked and the presence of the man she disliked. When Elizabeth found that Wickham was not there "every prospect of her own was destroyed for the evening." It was a grievous disappointment. Moreover, she was engaged to Mr. Collins for the first two dances —largely owing to a piece of ill-timed liveliness on her part —and "Mr. Collins, awkward and solemn, apologizing instead of attending, and often moving wrong without being aware of it, gave her all the shame and misery which a disagreeable partner can give."

She had others more congenial later, but in the end Mr. Collins was to rob her even of these, "For he continued most perseveringly by her side; and though he could not prevail with her to dance with him again, put it out of her power to dance with others." There were also unpleasantnesses of a different kind—Sir William Lucas' ill-judged remarks to Mr. Darcy about Bingley and Jane, Miss Bingley's rudeness on the subject of George Wickham, and finally the obsequious effrontery with which Mr. Collins insisted on introducing himself to Darcy when he heard he was a nephew of Lady Catherine de Bourgh. As for the supper interval, it appeared to Elizabeth "that had her family made an agreement to expose themselves as much as they could, it would have been impossible for them to play their parts with more spirit or finer success."

No, that is not the sort of dance one enjoys—or forgets, either.

Jane Austen herself, as we gather from the *Letters* as well as from the novels, enjoyed a good ball as much as anyone, and in *Mansfield Park* I think I catch an echo of her own life and custom in that meeting at Mansfield Parsonage which gave Fanny "an opportunity of talking over Thursday night with Mrs. Grant and Miss Crawford in a very handsome style, with all the heightenings of imagination and all the laughs of playfulness that are due to the shadow of a departed ball." She had been disappointed the day before when "she had talked to her aunt Bertram—she must talk to somebody of the ball; but her aunt had seen so little of what passed, and had so little curiosity that it was heavy work. . . . 'She could not recollect what it was she had heard about one of the Miss Maddoxes, or what Lady Prescott had noticed in Fanny; she was not sure whether Colonel Harrison had been talking of Mr. Crawford or of William when he said he was the finest young man in the room; somebody had whispered something to her—she had forgot to ask Sir Thomas what it could be.' "

But apart from discussing "departed balls," morning visits are not perhaps very entertaining. Emma did not particularly enjoy calling on Miss Bates, and "was considered by the very few who presumed ever to see imperfection in her, as rather negligent in that respect." Yet morning visits were not just the drab, perfunctory occasions they were afterwards to become as afternoon calls. Some were visits of ceremony and politeness, no doubt—such as those exchanged at Pemberley in *Pride and Prejudice*—but in many places they were the small change of social intercourse, the currency of those who could not afford more elaborate entertainment. That is why, no doubt, Miss

Bates had so many callers. The long interval between breakfast and dinner, which constituted the "morning," provided both leisure and appetite. Refreshments would always be offered—at Miss Bates's a baked apple or a slice of cake, at Miss Darcy's "cold meat, cake, and a variety of the finest fruits of the season," and there was no question of departure at the end of a quarter of an hour.

Men were nearly as assiduous callers as women. Indeed the social life of the period owed much of its intensity to the greater leisure and availableness of the men. They did not in those days leave the house at eight o'clock in the morning and return to it at six. Even those who "worked" as clergymen, lawyers or doctors, seem to have put in very few hours at their job. The most hard-working men I can find in the novels are John Knightley and Mr. Perry. They are the only two who ever seem to be "busy." The rest seem mostly to be leisured country gentlemen, whose main interest is sport and the administration of their estates. If they are not out with their guns or "showing zeal after poachers" as magistrates, there is nothing to prevent their accompanying the ladies on a morning visit, enjoying a dinner party from four o'clock onwards, exploring with Mrs. Elton to Box Hill, or dancing all night at Netherfield or Mansfield or the Crown at any time of the week.

This leisure and leisureliness are not ours. The pressure of life and work has squeezed our social intercourse into brief occasions. Our much wider circle of friends and acquaintances—for it is an irony of progress that we have so much more of the raw material of party-making both in things and people than our ancestors had—meets brokenly and briefly. So it is an escape not only from our work but from our own special sort of play when we go out to dinner with Emma, out dancing with Fanny or Elizabeth, to an evening party with Elinor and Marianne, or with Catherine "only go and call on Mrs. Allen"—finding amusement and stimulation even in what Henry Tilney rightly calls a "picture of intellectual poverty."

CHAPTER IX

"The Envelope Itself Was Likewise Full"

G. B. STERN

I IMAGINE that most authors will agree with me that there are two moods in which we reread our past works—if indeed, at intervals of years, we are driven for some obscure reason to reread them at all. Either we are plunged in despair at the brilliance of our achievement before schizophrenia and senile decay set in, and despair of such an effortless leap to peaks that now seem strangely unfamiliar as well as impossible; or the alternative mood, and I think a preferable one, is hot confusion and shame: how *could* I have written that? I must have been mad! . . . and hastily closing the volume, we comfort ourselves with the reflection that everyone who has read it has forgotten it, or at any rate, which is more important, forgotten the author.

But Jane Austen need never have suffered such reactions if she idly chanced to pick up any of her earlier works. I cannot remember that we are ever told in her letters that she did; she was never foolishly deprecating over her powers; even her famous remark about the "little bit of ivory two inches wide," was sensible and true. But she was too delighted with the stream of life as it swept past, to be heavily preoccupied with what had already been borne away several years before. When rarely she does take account of herself as a writer, in among the intimate personal chronicles of daily life, it is always her contemporary book that she mentions, never the day before yesterday's. How we could wish for a letter, say in 1802, which began: "Having nothing else beside me to read, my dearest Cassandra will be surprised to hear that

I actually spent half an hour over *Sense and Sensibility,* and was amazed at . . ." Amazed at what? That reflection, never written, must be left for ever unfinished; for here invention may not dare to tread.

Yesterday, then, I picked up *Speaking of Jane Austen,* and was somewhat amazed, not at my discovery mentioned there that many of the letters in her books could be modernized into conversations on the telephone; but that having said so, I should then have left it at that, and not expanded the idea more fully. By which I mean that it is odd I should not have allowed myself more fun with it.

We have only to think of the numerous letters her characters write, to realise how we of the twentieth century have taken to the telephone as ducks who take to water cease to be conscious from the first moment that they are swimming. Ringing-up finds an Austen equivalent in the constant little streams and runnels and freshets watering her pages, of compliments and congratulation, of sensational tidings good and bad, of announcements, condolences, acceptances, succulent gossip, apologies, insults, proposals, thanks, explanations, complaints, courtesies, introductions, repudiations, invitations, filial resignation, and so on for ever; nearly all, be sure, in fine pointed handwriting, often crossed and recrossed, and "The envelope contained a sheet of elegant, little, hot-pressed paper, well covered with a lady's fair, flowing hand."

Nevertheless, nobody can accuse Darcy's communications of having anticipated the telephone technique; he was incapable even of dashing off a spontaneous letter: "The effort which the formation and the perusal of this letter must occasion should have been spared, had not my character required it to be written and read." He then polysyllabically clears up the Wickham business in detail, which was certainly necessary and could hardly have been done without hurting himself almost as much as he hurt Elizabeth, for it involved the painful story of his little sister Georgiana's infatuation with the wicked young libertine. Could he have confined himself to that— But I have always felt, and still feel, that to write to a loyal, high-spirited girl on the inferiority of her family and their total want of propriety, was hardly a winning way of a man with a maid. Miraculously, Darcy survives, I shall always think in spite of and not because of his letter. Elizabeth read it swiftly once, in a state of extreme prejudice and agitation; then read it again, and "widely different was the effect of a second perusal." Darcy himself, on his second and successful proposal, though warmly ashamed of his first, apparently never had any doubts about the letter itself: " 'Did it,' " said he, " 'did it *soon* make you think better of me?' " the italics give his importunity a charmingly ingenuous air.

Frank Churchill, I am convinced, has the fluent temperament that not only would have made constant use of the telephone as a matter of course, but would have chafed more impatiently than any other selfish young man in Jane Austen if it were ever out of order, or if his autocratic aunt, Mrs. Churchill, forbade him to use it during certain hours of the night. Frank would have been perfectly capable of ringing up Mr. Woodhouse (from Richmond) at midnight, if the fancy took him, and gaily asking for Emma. He would only once have attempted it, however: Mr. Woodhouse must have trembled at the notion of ever using such a dangerous instrument himself, nor willingly have suffered any of his household to regard it as other than dynamite; but he always would have heard the bell, however far off, and however promptly it were answered. In that case, we might argue, would he ever have allowed it to be installed at Hartfield? Ah, but Emma could have persuaded him by adroit quotation from Mr. Perry, how necessary it was in case of any sudden illness, brought about, let us say, by eating a hard-boiled egg on Searle's evening out!

I never quite believed that Frank Churchill would have had the patience to write his overlong letter of explanation for all his past misconduct; apart from the fact that obviously it cannot hold for me, as for Emma, the irresistible charm of lines relating to myself, he must have known that he did not excel in any form of apology giving him so little chance to wheedle, to be persuasive, gallant, swift and eloquent in his own defence. For I am inclined to agree with Mr. Knightley's estimate of the young gentleman: Frank Churchill is too glib, too profuse in his self-condemnations. Mr. Knightley had remarked earlier in the book, "he can write a fine flourishing letter" on the occasion of his father's second marriage to Miss Taylor; but then, if ever, was a time when he should have come in person. Yet the letter seemed to satisfy the rest of their friends at Highbury, who were not so exacting.

> I suppose you have heard of the handsome letter Mr. Frank Churchill had written to Mrs. Weston? I understand it was a very handsome letter, indeed. . . . Mr. Woodhouse saw the letter, and he says he never saw such a handsome letter in his life. . . . He wrote a letter to poor Mrs. Weston, to congratulate her, and a very proper, handsome letter it was.

None of this cut any ice with Mr. Knightley, who although not aware of it himself, was already subconsciously disliking the very idea of Frank Churchill, and of his potential courtship of Emma Woodhouse, already in the air. So he condemned this fine, proper, pretty, handsome letter as brimming with falsehood: "his letters disgust me"; plain-speaking, indeed, with the not unnatural result of sending Emma to the opposite extreme of championing the absent Frank Churchill; in the argument which followed, near enough to a quarrel, Mr. Knightley made an excellent point: that any young man of delicacy should have recognised all the more the need to come in person, because the present Mrs. Weston had been a governess and not a lady of any consequence. "Your Frank Churchill is amiable only in the French, not the English sense." Swiftly Emma retorted: "You seem determined to think ill of him." "Me? Not at all," replied Mr. Knightley, displeased. The quarrel from first to last is beautifully handled for our diversion, and we are perhaps less disposed to quarrel with Mr. Frank Churchill for having originated it. "He is a person I never think of from one month's end to another," said Mr. Knightley.

Unfortunately for Mr. Knightley's temper, once a question of Frank Churchill and his letters got into the air, they were not allowed to be forgotten; his father, Mr. Weston, would by no means suffer it; he even turned up late at a party given by the Woodhouses in honour of the obnoxious Mrs. Elton ("A bride, you know, must appear like a bride") with a letter from Frank addressed to his wife: "he had met with it in his way, and had taken the liberty of opening it." Perforce the whole room had to know what was in that letter; Mr. Weston was not a man to believe in private communications; he cornered Mrs. Elton as being fresh blood; and she was well content to be cornered while she could keep his attention directed on herself and rally him archly as a sad fellow who opened letters directed to his wife. Thereupon followed one of Jane Austen's most delightful comedy scenes, with Mr. Weston determined to talk about Frank's letter and the major importance of Frank's impending arrival, and Mrs. Elton determined to talk about Mrs. Elton.

But we have not yet done with Frank Churchill and his letters. We are still at this party which Mr. Woodhouse and Emma gave in honour of Mr. and Mrs. Elton, but earlier, before Mr. Weston has arrived; in fact, we have not yet gone in to dinner. Mr. John Knightley, staying with his father-in-law, had met Jane Fairfax on her way to the post-office to fetch the letters. He reproves her, laughingly, for going out in the rain:

> "When you have lived to my age, you will begin to think letters are never worth going through the rain for." There was a little blush, and then this answer:— "I cannot expect that simply growing older should make me indifferent about letters." "Indifferent! Oh no; . . . . Letters are no

matter of indifference; they are generally a very positive curse."

"You are speaking of letters of business; mine are letters of friendship."

"I have often thought them the worse of the two," replied he coolly.

We know, of course (having read the book a mere once or twice) that she goes to the post-office to make sure that no one but herself should see her daily letter from Frank. Her blushes, her determined efforts to get away from the dangerous subject, speak of a guilty conscience. Jane Fairfax is not as good as he at leading a life of deception. Her expeditions to the post-office, to her dismay, become a main topic. Mr. Woodhouse had overheard enough to make him believe that she might have run the danger of wet stockings, so a great deal of kindly solicitude followed. Mrs. Elton was the next to join in; an officious woman: " 'The man who fetches our letters every morning (one of our men—I forget his name) shall inquire for yours too and bring them to you.' " The perfect Jane Austen touch: if we never heard any more of Mrs. Elton, we should know her now.

And we may indeed be thankful for the sake of the rest of Highbury, and especially Hartfield, that the telephone had not yet been invented, and that they were all spared hearing the ominous announcement: "Mrs. Elton is on the line and wishes to speak to you, ma'am; she says she will not keep you a moment." Only the Bateses would have been safe; they could not have afforded a telephone; again a merciful dispensation, for who would have had the heart to cut off Miss Bates before she had done? Yet who could have waited?

Jane Fairfax tried to escape from further questioning on her secret expeditions, by handing bouquets to the post-office as a "wonderful establishment": "So seldom that a letter, among the thousands that are constantly passing about the kingdom, is even carried wrong, and not one in a million, I suppose, actually lost." From there it is but a step to a discussion on handwriting in general and handwriting in particular; Mr. John Knightley has some interesting observations to make: "Boys have very little teaching after an early age, and scramble into any hand they can get." He says that his wife and Emma write so alike that he cannot tell them apart; to which his brother and Mr. Woodhouse each contribute a characteristic comment: "But Emma's hand is the strongest." "Isabella and Emma both write beautifully."

It is now Emma's turn. She begins a remark to the effect that Mr. Frank Churchill writes a beautiful hand— And stops, wondering whether she is equal to mentioning his name without confusion in that company? Then resolutely carries on, and finishes the sentence and the compliment.

" 'I do not admire it,' said Mr. Knightley. 'It is too small—wants strength. It is like a woman's writing.' " By now we are beginning to get quite a reasonable notion that Mr. Knightley is not passionately fond of Frank. But the whole room rises against him in protest. Emma wishes to produce a note of Frank's to prove her point. It is perhaps lucky for Mr. Knightley's trial of patience that dinner was just then announced, and the subject of letters which occupies most of this chapter and the next could be postponed.

When at last misunderstanding comes to an end, and Mr. Knightley (who will never be George to us any more than to Emma herself) announces his engagement to his younger brother, he receives only a somewhat cool letter of congratulation which has to be considerably softened in transit: "My Emma, he means no such thing. He only means . . ." etc. But Emma, a sensible young woman with a genuine sense of her unworthiness to wed this hero from Olympus, is not at all offended. I am always ready to be pleased with Emma, in spite of her many follies, for her reception of John Knightley's rather too blunt and disparaging remarks; it would have been so easy for her to bridle or shed a few tears or nourish a secret resentment, but she does no such thing, and when she says that she honours his sincerity in considering the good fortune of the engagement as being all on one side, she is entirely sincere. This is one of the few letters where we must guess at the actual text, from Mr. Knightley's confusion. It is a little odd that the author should slightly bore us (as well as Mr. Knightley) by writing out the full seven pages of Frank Churchill's letter to Mrs. Weston, when the substance necessary to the plot could have been given in half a page of narrative, and yet deny herself the treat of inventing Mr. John Knightley's much too blunt letter of so-called congratulation.

In Emma's unregenerate days, she used to calculate when it would be safe to visit the Bateses, midway between the arrival of letters from Jane Fairfax (Miss Bates' cultured, elegant and impeccable niece), so that she would not have to listen while the fond aunt read passages aloud: "One is sick of the very name of Jane Fairfax. Every letter from her is read forty times over." On one especial occasion, however, an unexpected letter had arrived out of turn that very morning, and Emma was caught, though she was polite enough to feign interest:

> "Have you heard from Miss Fairfax so lately? I am extremely happy. I hope she is well."
> "Thank you. You are so kind!" replied the happily deceived aunt, while eagerly hunting for the letter.

A discreet flicker of a look may well have passed from Emma to Harriet while Miss Bates went on to apologise for Jane's letter being so *short*: ". . . only two pages, you see, hardly two, and in general she fills the whole paper and crosses half." (I can remember letters arriving from abroad when I was a child, with a page of writing usually slanted across the original page in a very palimpsest, though the grown-up eye, trained by habit, seemed oddly to find no trouble in making it out.) Unconscious of what Emma was feeling, poor Miss Bates hurried on through a forest of irrelevance, to explain that in the normal course of things they would not have heard from Jane before next Tuesday or Wednesday. "Yes, so I imagined," said Emma . . . (and *we* can imagine a stifled giggle from Harriet at this point; Harriet, be sure, would have had little control over her giggles.) Miss Bates scampered on, telling them the whole contents of the letter, and finally proposed to read it aloud now that she had given them "a hint" of what it was about. But Emma, having had the substance, contrived to escape without any forfeit of manners; though poor Miss Bates was always a strain upon her patience or her sense of comedy, till in the famous picnic chapter, politeness snapped asunder and she laid herself open to Mr. Knightley's severest reproof.

Formal letters of that period had apparently to begin and not end with traditional protestations of this and that. When an answer had to be written declining Mrs. Coles's invitation to dinner, Mr. Woodhouse reminds his daughter to begin with his compliments, and "compliments" are in italics. Although he grieves at such an injudicious idea as this of his good neighbours— "I am not fond of dinner-visiting. I am sorry Mr. and Mrs. Cole should have done it," he has to admit that the invitation itself had been properly expressed. "They would have solicited the honour earlier, but had been waiting the arrival of a folding screen from London, which they hoped might keep Mr. Woodhouse from any draught of air." (Metaphorically, this whole book is to show how Mr. Woodhouse must be screened from any draught of air.) The good Coles were no sycophants, but they subscribed to the social order of things, and it was regarded as completely natural that Mr. Woodhouse's company at dinner should be almost too much of an honour; as natural as Mr. Weston's reminder that Emma's hurrying away would be more thought of than any other person's, and that it would wreck the party.

He (or she) writes "very properly" . . . the expression recurs through Jane Austen. During a discussion in *Sense and Sensibility* Elinor tries to urge Edward (for expedience' sake) to a letter of "proper submission" to his mother; though Edward argues stubbornly that considering all that has been done to him, he knows of no submission proper for him to make. Elinor, however, rationalises to such good purpose that though he still resists the idea of a letter, he was more willing to make "mean concessions by word of mouth." I must have read *Sense and Sensibility* fully thirty times, at a rough guess, before at the thirty-first I noticed the word "mean," and was surprised to find Edward so spirited and outspoken.

My favourite letters in *Sense and Sensibility* are written by Lucy Steele; though she can only amuse on paper, by the "twopenny post" (as Miss Austen is careful to inform us; might it have been recently installed, as the price of communications from one address in London to another?) Lucy begins her letters from Bartlett's Buildings in the third person, hoping "my dear Miss Dashwood will excuse the liberty I take of writing to her"; and swopping horses in mid-stream, "But I know your friendship for me will make you pleased to hear." Heavily stressing the great trials and persecutions that she and her dear Edward have suffered, the rest of the letter is chiefly employed to drag in constant references to "dear Mrs. Jennings" with whom the Miss Dashwoods were then staying in Berkeley Street. Mrs. Jennings herself saw nothing wrong with the letter when Elinor obligingly fell in with Lucy's obvious wish and gave it her to read:

> "Very well indeed, How prettily she writes . . . she calls me dear Mrs. Jennings, you see . . . that sentence is very prettily framed . . . it is as pretty a letter as ever I saw and does Lucy's head and heart great credit. . . ."

I would suggest that Mrs. Jennings might have been appropriately named Mrs. Gullible. Nevertheless she was not to remain forever a victim of guile; when Lucy jilts Edward, Mrs. Jennings writes to Elinor in a state of honest indignation, pitying poor Mr. Edward "who she was sure had quite doated upon the worthless hussy." The rest of the letter was unauthorised gossip in Mrs. Jennings' most intimate vein; the kind of letter, to be candid, that we still enjoy better than mere news. Mr. Dashwood's strains on the same topic were more solemn; Elinor's half-brother had few virtues to recommend him; he was pompous, stupid, mean, snobbish; yet he had the merit of believing in his wife and in his wife's mother; so when he writes that his poor Fanny was suffering "agonies of sensibility," Fanny Dashwood being considerably horrider than himself, we may marvel how she had gained such undiscriminating affection. His epistolary style reminds us pleasantly of Mr. Collins, that emperor of letter-writers.

But in *Sense and Sensibility*, the letters that matter most are those that sway the plot, and as usual Jane Austen makes considerable use of them. A letter is brought to Colonel Brandon at which he "changes colour," proving definitely—not before proof was needed—that he was a human being and not a dummy. Mrs. Jennings teases him to reveal what had so discomposed him, and Willoughby whispers to Marianne that he would "lay fifty guineas the letter was of his own writing." Over a hundred pages further on, we learn the ironic truth: the letter revealed that Colonel Brandon's ward had been seduced by Willoughby himself. Like many quiet men when really roused, Colonel Brandon rants like a barnstormer:

> Would he have been less gay or less happy in the smiles of your sister? No, he had already done that which no man who can *feel* for another would do. He had left the girl whose youth and innocence he had seduced, in a situation of the utmost distress, with no creditable home, no help, no friends, ignorant of his address! He had left her, promising to return; he neither returned, nor wrote, nor relieved her. . . . His character is now before you—expensive, dissipated, and worse than both.

The passion betrayed like wild music between her every written line to Willoughby would have been an unendurably painful confession of Marianne's love for him, were it expressed by any other medium than on the flat page; as well, therefore, that no telephone had as yet been invented, for Mrs. Jennings would certainly have had an extension in every room, and how could Marianne have controlled her raging impatience to hear Willoughby's voice, his very voice, speaking to her out of the unresponsive air? At first, as she confidently expected, in high delight at her presence in London; but then as her repeated calls would have failed to bring her this longed-for thrill—(assuming Willoughby had the luck not to answer the first call himself, and took mean precautions over all future calls)—ringing up more and more frantically and at ever briefer intervals: "But didn't you give him my message? You *can't* have. . . . Are you *sure* you got the name right?— I spelt it for you: D A S H W O O D, Miss Marianne Dashwood. . . . And my number? Please write it down *again*. And you *will* be sure to tell him as soon as he comes in, won't you? When did you say you expected him back?" . . .

If it had been painful for Elinor to watch her sister feverishly scribbling her heart out onto paper, how inexpressibly worse it would have been to have heard those young wretched tones appeal for one live word from him, only one, to break the increasing perplexity and suspense, the growing horror of doubt.

The rules of conduct that at the period held such sway over Elinor must make us smile a little, reflecting that not a little of her perturbation arose from Marianne's violations of propriety's code in writing to Willoughby at all and in such intimate terms, when they were not formally engaged. Her mother, Elinor thought, should have forbidden correspondence till she had fully enquired into the matter. Conventions apart, perhaps she was right; Marianne was so very young; as young as Catherine Morland, and not nearly as instinctively honest and dependable.

Mr. and Mrs. Morland were more justified when they indulgently permitted a clandestine correspondence between Catherine and Henry during the period that had to elapse, nearly a twelve-month, till General Tilney's consent could be won to the engagement. Probably they would have allowed an occasional trunk call; not too many. Trunk calls are, after all, a little more unsettling than letters.

Henry Tilney's letters to Catherine must have been great fun; we are sorry never to have been allowed a glimpse of even one of them. Instead, we would have been glad to forfeit another of these dull letters necessary to the plot, from Catherine's very dull brother James, telling her that all is at an end between himself and Miss Thorpe; she had jilted him, her head turned by the attentions of the dashing Captain Tilney, a much better match than a country clergyman's son still at Oxford. The interest of that letter was in the last line: "Dearest Catherine, beware how you give your heart." Catherine reads the sad news at breakfast at Northanger Abbey, the tears running down her cheeks; and presently, alone with Henry and Eleanor, is prompted by their solicitude to hand it over to them to read for themselves. . . . A moment of deep confusion and she tries to take it back "recollecting, with a blush, the last line." Catherine is so sweet.

As we have seen before, Jane Austen can rouse more excessive joy in her readers by these irrelevant letters, than by those explanatory, and (if she will again forgive me for the criticism) often rather colourless epistles by which she has chosen to solve her plots, rather than by dialogue: Edmund Bertram writing to his cousin Fanny a detailed account of his hopes and fears, his ups and downs, his perturbations and procrastinations on the question of making an honourable offer to Mary Crawford, forms a necessary part of the story's pattern. But how much rather would we hear of Lady Bertram, Sir Thomas and Mrs. Norris dealing with poor Mrs. Price, who had written them—

a letter which spoke so much contrition and despondence, such a superfluity of children, and such a want of almost everything else, as could not but dispose them all to a reconciliation. . . . The letter was not unproductive. It re-established peace and kindness. Sir Thomas sent friendly advice and professions, Lady Bertram dispatched money and baby-linen, *and Mrs. Norris wrote the letters.*

The italics are mine, and those are the letters that our aggravating author withholds from us. It is somewhat surprising that Lady Bertram did not write them, for in spite of her indolence, we know that she fancied herself in the epistolary art. There must have been hundreds of Lady Bertrams, nay, thousands of leisurely ladies at their escritoires all over nineteenth-century England, who were for ever "taking up their pens to communicate" and feeling it no hardship.

. . . "Sir Thomas, I have been thinking, and I tell you what: if we had a very much longer cord put on the telephone, I could speak on it very much more often, for then I would not have to move."

No, you will search in vain for this sentence in *Mansfield Park;* nor will you find Sir Thomas Bertram's courteous reply to her ladyship's lightest wish:

"Certainly, my dear, we will have the flex lengthened. But would you not find it too fatiguing?"

"Not the least little bit in the world; Fanny can put it all in order for me before I start to speak."

But Fanny would have proved of less use than a sick headache in dealing with the intricacies of the telephone exchange at Northampton, with TOL, TRU and TEL—or even the simplest local call; and with her Aunt Norris looking on. . . . And her Aunt Bertram would be gently insatiable; she would positively have enjoyed long, leisurely, languid conversations with all her acquaintance, on no urgent pretext, having no point at issue, but droning on and roundabout, sometimes even a little vague as to whether she were through to the right person. . . .

And I feel sure that Mary Crawford would have been one of those lively tongues also for ever on the telephone, for ever ringing up her friends, gaily babbling news and chatter: "My *dear*, what *do* you think . . ." and so forth. She writes several long gossiping letters to Fanny in Portsmouth, which are in essence clearly telephone calls; reporting parties, elopements, fragments of dialogue, her own opinions, her friend Lady Stornaway's opinions; warm-hearted spontaneous missives with that air of immediacy about them; if not dashed down at once, at that very moment, they would never have been written at all:

> "Fanny, Fanny, I see you smile and look cunning, but upon my honour I never bribed a physician in my life. Poor young man! If he is to die, there will be *two* poor young men less in the world."

As for this comment on the dangerous illness of Tom Bertram, the eldest son of the house, frankly and mischievously phrased, we are more shocked later on when Fanny betrays it to Edmund, than at Mary for writing it. Her knowledge of Fanny's character must have been faulty, or could she ever have written: "I see you smile and look cunning"? Propinquity forced those two girls towards a threadbare friendship which did in fact wear into holes at the very first strain put upon it; Fanny was disgusted at Mary's letters; and Mary never understood that she was something of a merry rake attempting to speak her own language to a prude.

Most of Fanny's stay at Portsmouth was spent in waiting for letters, dreading them, longing for them; one of them might bring her a recall to her beloved Mansfield, but another might give her news that Edmund had proposed to Mary and been accepted. Mostly they brought her what she did not want: Mary's news of her brother Henry's love for her. For indeed, Mary was tickled to death at Henry's courtship of Fanny Price; of her wonderful brother, so sophisticated, so sought after, yet infatuated as a schoolgirl might be with the Maths mistress, more than infatuated, besotted.

> . . . "Had you seen her this morning, Mary," he continued, "attending with such ineffable sweetness and patience to all the demands of her aunt's stupidity . . . her colour beautifully heightened as she leant over the work . . . her hair arranged as neatly as it always was, and one little curl falling forward as she wrote, which she now and then shook back."

. . . To do Mary justice, her rejoicing at Fanny's power over Henry's hitherto fickle heart is completely free from ambition or snobbery; nobody can say that little Fanny Price of Portsmouth could be a good match for a young man of fashion and fortune, and of such sparkling wit and address. She sent Fanny by Henry an affectionate note welcoming her into the family, and poor Fanny went through every agony in her attempt to answer the note suitably: ". . . your note, I know, means nothing; but I am so unequal to anything of the sort, that I hope you will excuse my begging you to take no further notice."

I like Fanny and Edmund best when she is ten years old, newly arrived at Mansfield Park, and he, in the eyes of his little cousin, a lordly young man of sixteen. It is really a very charming scene when he discovers her crying on the attic stairs, and taking great pains to discover the cause, comforts her by helping her to write to her favourite brother William; she had promised she would write first, but had not any paper and did not know how to set about the whole heavy business; a faltering we can understand in this great mansion which she was one day to love so well, but where she was now a waif and a stranger.

> . . . "I will furnish you with paper and every other material, and you may write your letter whenever you choose. . . ."
>
> "But, cousin, will it go to the post?"

"Yes, depend upon me, it shall: it shall go with the other letters; and, as your uncle will frank it, it will cost William nothing."

"My uncle!" repeated Fanny with a frightened look.

"Yes, when you have written the letter, I will take it to my father to frank."

Edmund prepared her paper, and ruled her lines with all the goodwill that her brother could himself have felt, and probably with somewhat more exactness. He continued with her the whole time of her writing, to assist her with his penknife or his orthography, as either were wanted. . . . He wrote with his own hand his love to his cousin William, and sent him half a guinea under the seal.

This particular passage was always a great puzzle to me when I read it as a child; for *Mansfield Park* was my first and only Jane Austen till I grew up. Ruling the lines, yes; my own lines had to be ruled; but how could he assist her with his penknife? And what was all this business of franking? Above all, was it safe to send half a guinea under the seal—although a lovely surprise for William? For quite a little time afterwards, I eyed all sealed letters with hopeful eyes, waiting for the gold half-guinea to emerge.

In two or three of her own letters, Jane Austen tells us rather more of *Mansfield Park* than of any of her other books. She writes of her brother Henry: "He admires H. Crawford; I mean properly, as a clever, pleasant man." And again in a letter three days later: "I believe *now* he has changed his mind as to foreseeing the end; he said yesterday, at least, that he defied anybody to say whether H.C. would be reformed or would forget Fanny in a fortnight." (Forget Fanny in a fortnight!)

In *Persuasion,* there are as far as I am concerned, but two memorable letters; and one of them only of consequence because it was never written: the unlucky omission of a letter of condolence from Sir Walter Elliot to his cousin Lady

Dalrymple in Ireland on the death of her husband, the Viscount. The agonies which arose from this apparent neglect of the proper ceremonials in a noble family may seem trivial to us, especially as it all happened long before the story opens, but once we are acquainted with Sir Walter it is not difficult to believe that the anxious business dogged his days and overshadowed his nights. We are told that it was not even his fault that the letter of condolence had never been sent; he was himself dangerously ill at the time. But the Dowager Viscountess Dalrymple had refused to hear any explanation of such ill-mannered neglect:

> . . . when poor Lady Elliot died herself, no letter of condolence was received at Kellynch, and, consequently, there was but too much reason to apprehend that the Dalrymples considered the relationship as closed.

However, we may all congratulate ourselves that the end of *Persuasion* does not leave us with this tragedy still not set to rights . . . to spoil all our happiness in Wentworth and Anne reunited. When Sir Walter and his eldest daughter Elizabeth let Kellynch and went to live in Bath, they saw in the paper one morning the announcement of the arrival of the Viscountess with her daughter, the Hon. Miss Carteret; and after giving themselves a fine headache apiece debating as to what should be done to be once more admitted as cousins, Sir Walter—

> at last wrote a very fine letter of ample explanation, regret, and entreaty, to his right honourable cousin. Neither Lady Russell nor Mr. Elliot could admire the letter; but it did all that was wanted, in bringing three lines of scrawl from the Dowager Viscountess. "She was very much honoured, and should be happy in their acquaintance." The toils of the business were over, the sweets began.

Mary Musgrove, who would have rung up continually from her deathbed, sends Anne in Bath a characteristic letter which was delivered personally, to Anne's great surprise, by Admiral and Mrs. Croft; the first part was all Mary's grievances, her querulous hints of favours that should be forthcoming, her little collection of slights (we can see Mary bridling in every sentence of the first half of the letter). The postscript contained a startling piece of news, which left Anne dizzy and incredulous; *Captain Benwick was to marry Louisa Musgrove.* Captain Benwick might marry whomever he pleased, for though he was supposed to have admired Anne, his attentions left her unmoved. But Louisa attached to Captain Benwick could only mean Louisa was not to marry Captain Wentworth. The news rolled away a nightmare, and Anne went about with a radiant tremor of hope in her heart: "She had some feelings which she was ashamed to investigate. They were too much like joy, senseless joy!"

Those who will have it that Jane Austen is no more than a frivolous drawing-room writer, with no power, no passion at her command, must surely admit the strong emotional content of these few moments in which Wentworth poured out his love in a letter, with Anne standing so near that he could have touched her, while she spoke of faithfulness with Captain Harville in a crowded sitting-room of the hotel at Bath: ". . . a slight noise called their attention to Captain Wentworth's hitherto perfectly quiet division of the room. It was nothing more than that his pen had fallen down." Her detractors should suspend their far too hasty judgment on her as a spinster lady with a talented pen to portray the visitings and gossipings of elegant ladies and gentlemen who live in the English countryside and appear so extraordinarily unaware that we were at war with Napoleon— (How often, I wonder, have I heard that particular proof of her emptiness of mind and soul trotted out and offered me with an air of extreme originality, as though the speaker had thought it out by himself and were the first to have noticed it. . . . And how odd, how very odd, how almost inconceivable that

Shakespeare wrote his lightest comedies of manners in such stirring times, and not even mentioned the Armada!)

Partial devotees exist who would give all the letters in all the novels of Jane Austen, for one little group which has lent its name to immortality. Will you leap to it, I wonder, or can I keep you guessing? What is it that we say when we have been staying with friends, perhaps for the first time, and there was no bedside lamp in our room, the mirror was hung so high on the wall that we could only see the top of our head in a bad light, we were woken at 7.30 A.M. by the children clamouring for attention, and brought early morning Indian tea when we drink China or none, the hot water is tepid and in meagre supply, the door rattles all night, and one's hot-water bottle was left cold and beseeching on our bed the evening before?— What do we say?— "Goodbye; thanks ever so much; I've adored it". . . And then (but not aloud) "Damn, *I shall have to write them a Collins.*"

So I had heard of Mr. Collins before I discovered the first Collins ever written: his own "Collins" to Mr. Bennet after receiving hospitality. At this point it occurred to me that such a famous letter deserved to be quoted, and I spent the next half-hour unprofitably hunting for it through the pages of *Pride and Prejudice.* On his verbal farewell after his second visit, when he had been accepted by Charlotte Lucas, he "wished his fair cousins health and happiness again, and promised their father another letter of thanks." "Another" betokened clearly enough that he had already written one letter of thanks following his first visit; and indeed, it seemed inconceivable that no actual "Collins" existed, after all I had heard and written and spoken on the matter. So I told myself that I must be under a spell of frustration, and the sooner I broke it, the sooner I could get on with this chapter. So again, summoning resolution and commonsense, I set to work industriously seeking the first Collins. My final report on the matter must still be that it has never existed . . . and for many years I must have been pursuing a delusion. The letter of thanks *is* mentioned. "The promised letter of thanks from Mr. Collins arrived on Tuesday, addressed to their father, and written with all the solemnity of gratitude which a twelvemonth's abode in the family might have prompted." . . . And I strove to recollect (in a worried way) how often I had recommended people who did not know Jane Austen's books as well as myself, to use it as a model of style and propriety for themselves when they sat down at their desks to fulfil a similar concession to usage and politeness.

Not that we are lacking in examples of Mr. William Collins' pre-eminence as a correspondent. It is plain from the one announcing his existence to Mr. Bennet and promising him the felicity of a personal visit, that he must reread them several times before he despatched them, his mind complacently stroking each polished phrase and meritorious sentiment.

> The disagreement subsisting between yourself and my late honoured father always gave me much uneasiness, and since I have had the misfortune to lose him, I have frequently wished to heal the breach; but for some time I was kept back by my own doubts, fearing lest it might seem disrespectful to his memory for me to be on good terms with any one with whom it had always pleased him to be at variance.— "There, Mrs. Bennet."

Mr. Bennet shares with us, and no doubt with Jane Austen, a never failing delight in the ridiculous aspect of human nature; and Mr. Collins appears to have provided sumptuously for his happiness. Elizabeth takes after her father in this; and until Mr. Collins upsets her by the persistence of his courtship, the two alone, out of all the Bennet family, are able to appreciate him from the right angle.

"Can he be a sensible man, sir?"

"No, my dear, I think not. I have great hopes of finding him quite the reverse. There is a mixture of servility and self-importance in his letter which promises well. I am impatient to see him."

"In point of composition," said Mary, "his letter does not seem defective."

The correspondence gets better and better as the book goes on. How it would have astonished Mr. Collins to be told that when he was not being fatuous and sycophantic, he was interfering and presumptuous. The very last letter that Mr. Bennet received from him was to warn him that his daughter Elizabeth has been receiving proposals of marriage from the nephew of Lady Catherine de Bourgh.

"After mentioning the likelihood of this marriage to her ladyship last night, she immediately, with her usual condescension, expressed what she felt on the occasion; when it became apparent that on the score of some family objections on the part of my cousin she would never give her consent to what she termed so disgraceful a match, I thought it my duty to give the speediest intelligence of this to my cousin, that she and her noble admirer may be aware of what they are about, and not run hastily into a marriage which has not been properly sanctioned."

Elizabeth might have said with Queen Victoria that she was not amused, though she had to force one reluctant smile, not to puzzle and disappoint her father by her lack of relish; he declared that much as he abominated writing, he would not give up Mr. Collins for any consideration; and fervently we agree with him. He was able to delay his reply till Darcy and Elizabeth were happily betrothed, and then had the satisfaction to send five lines which were as characteristically Mr. Bennet as the other had been Mr. Collins:

Dear Sir, I must trouble you once more for congratulations. Elizabeth will soon be the wife of Mr. Darcy. Console Lady Catherine as well as you can. But if I were you, I would stand by the nephew. He has more to give. Yours sincerely, etc.

Mr. Collins excels himself again in condoling with Mr. Bennet on Lydia's elopement. On mature reflection, I have decided to quote the whole of this letter in place of that one which apparently has never existed. It has been so carefully thought out, word by word, that it has convinced me beyond all argument that Mr. Collins himself, after pondering on what would be most consoling to a father's heart under those circumstances of extreme affliction, sat back at last, contented with what he had produced.

My dear Sir,— I feel myself called upon by our relationship, and my situation in life, to condole with you on the grievous affliction you are now suffering under, of which we were yesterday informed by a letter from Hertfordshire. Be assured, my dear sir, that Mrs. Collins and myself sincerely sympathize with you, and all your respectable family, in your present distress, which must be of the bitterest kind, because proceeding from a cause which no time can remove. No arguments shall be wanting on my part that can alleviate so severe a misfortune, or that may comfort you, under a circumstance that must be, of all others, most afflicting to a parent's mind. The death of your daughter would have been a blessing in comparison of this. And it is the more to be lamented, because there is reason to suppose, as my dear Charlotte informs me, that this licentiousness of behaviour in your daughter has proceeded from a faulty degree of indulgence; though, at the same time, for the consolation of yourself and Mrs. Bennet, I am inclined to think that her own disposition must be naturally bad, or she could not be guilty of such an enormity at so early an age. Howsoever that may be, you are grievously to be pitied, in which opinion I am not only joined by Mrs. Collins, but likewise by Lady Catherine and her daughter, to whom I have related the affair. They agree with me in apprehending that this false step in one daughter will be injurious to the fortunes of all the others; for who, as Lady Catherine herself condescendingly says, will connect themselves with such a family? And this consideration leads me, moreover, to reflect, with augmented satisfaction, on a certain event of last November; for had it been otherwise, I must have been involved in all your sorrow and disgrace. Let me advise you, then, my dear sir, to console yourself as much as possible, to throw off your unworthy child from your affection for ever, and leave her to reap the fruits of her own heinous offence.—I am, dear sir, etc.

This is not only a letter to make me believe in the flesh-and-blood existence of Mr. Collins, but as a natural corollary, to disbelieve in the very existence of an inventor of Mr. Collins. I can pay Jane Austen no greater compliment.

CHAPTER X

"The Labours of Her Inferiors"

SHEILA KAYE-SMITH

THE servants in Jane Austen's novels are in a very different situation from those in the books of the great eighteenth-century writers before her. What an important part servants play in *Tom Jones,* in *Humphrey Clinker,* in *Pamela* and *Joseph Andrews.* Indeed, in the last two they might be considered as the principal characters, with their masters and mistresses playing secondary parts. Whereas in the six Jane Austen novels servants have very little to do besides open doors, wait at table, curl hair, and such other things as are normally expected of them. Never at any time will there be the smallest chance of their marrying their masters or being pursued by their mistresses' dishonourable intentions. Both sides know their place and keep it.

Indeed, so shadowy are the servants' parts that at one time I doubted if I had enough material for a whole chapter. But I now see that there is a certain interest in the position they do not occupy as well as in the one they do. Their author's reticence illuminates her class and time. I will not call her snobbish, for that would be to take her out of her own period and put her into ours, where no doubt she—for her own part—would find what Emma deplored in Frank Churchill — "a confusion of rank bordering on inelegance of mind." But certainly times have changed, not only since her day, but between her day and that earlier one when Mrs. Honour shared the adventures of Sophia Western and Mr. B. wooed his mother's housemaid.

In the novels of Fielding, Smollett and Richardson the distinction is between High Life and Low Life, and it is a sharp distinction. No danger of any "confusion of rank" complicates the relations of Mr. B. and Pamela or of Lady Booby and Joseph Andrews. Indeed the whole interest of their respective stories lies in the fact that the characters are on different sides of a gulf. Is any bridge-building desirable? and if so, will it hold? Yes, says Richardson, No, says Fielding, and we have *Pamela* and *Joseph Andrews.*

With Jane Austen there was no question of gulfs but of grades. She was a member, and all the principal characters of her novels are members, of the newly emergent middle class—a class that fifty years earlier was almost unknown. In her time it had spread very widely over the eight million population of England, including at one end the baronetcy, with Sir Thomas Bertram and Sir Walter Elliot, at the other such vulgarians as Mrs. Elton, Mrs. Jennings and the Miss Steeles. Outside it are whole sections of the populace that she ignores completely.

She will not touch the aristocracy. In all the novels there are only two peers—Lord Ravenswood, who is little more than a shadow in *Mansfield Park,* and the Dowager Countess Dalrymple who has only a slightly more solid part in *Persuasion.* We find the same aloofness when we come to the masses. "The poor" exist mainly to be ministered to—to be sewn for by Fanny, visited by Emma, or "scolded into harmony and plenty" by Lady Catherine de Bourgh. None of them has even a one-line part—unless we include among them young Dick Jackson who comes "marauding about" Mansfield Park in hopes of a share of the servants' dinner and leads to Mrs. Norris' solitary impersonation act— "Mother had chanced to send him of a message to father and then father bid him bring up them two bits of board, for he could not nohow do without them."

But he does not speak with his own voice, nor—though the Jacksons were "very encroaching, I have always said so —just the sort of people to get all they can"—does he properly belong to that class provided for out of the Mansfield sewing basket. He was the son of the estate carpenter and would rank with the servants whose dinner he hoped to share.

Here is a class which is outside his author's province, but which she cannot ignore. She will, however, deal with it as little as possible, and achieves her end by taking it mostly for granted. This she is entitled to do by all the rules of her art. In the society she writes about there is no "servant problem." Men and maids abound—and to such an extent that their respective goodness and badness would cancel each other out. It is not until we get to the two-servant home of Mrs. Price that we have any discussion of the subject. Mrs. Price was so ill-served by Rebecca and her underling that her head was full of the badness of Portsmouth servants generally and she embarrassed her daughter with resentments and antagonisms unknown at Mansfield Park.

There no one troubled much about the servants except Mrs. Norris, who enjoyed interfering with them as much as she enjoyed interfering with everyone else. We even read of her "fresh arranging and injuring the noble fire the butler had prepared." And how she must have maddened the "good old coachman" when she burst into his room "just as he was putting on his wig," to give him unasked for and unneeded advice. She evidently belonged to that class which cannot let servants alone, for even at Sotherton she was "dancing about with the housekeeper," sponging gifts from her and delighting herself with the information that no wine was allowed at the "second table" and that two housemaids had been turned away for wearing white gowns.

Mrs. Norris had also, of course, servants of her own, though doubtless her establishment was a small one. There is more than one mention of Nanny, who was sent to fetch little Fanny Price to Mansfield from London. She is referred to as "my chief counsellor," so evidently she had some sort of a position with her exceedingly tiresome mistress. One would be interested to know what she thought of her, also the thoughts of the sick maid she went home to nurse, "with all the supernumerary jellies."

There are, as might be supposed, more servants at Mansfield Park than in the houses of the other heroines, but we know only one or two of them by name. There is Mrs. Chapman, Lady Bertram's "own maid," who was sent to help Fanny dress for the ball but arrived too late for more than civilities. "But Fanny felt her aunt's attention almost as much as Lady Bertram or Mrs. Chapman could do themselves." Then there is Baddeley the butler, of whom we get one human glimpse, when he appears to summon Fanny to Sir Thomas' room where Mr. Crawford is awaiting her.

> Instantly rising, she was preparing to obey, when Mrs. Norris called out "stay, stay, Fanny! What are you about? Where are you going? Don't be in such a hurry. Depend upon it, it is not you that are wanted; depend upon it, it is me. . . . It is me, Baddeley, that you mean; I am coming this moment. You mean me, Baddeley, I am sure; Sir Thomas wants me, not Miss Price." But Baddeley was stout. "No, Ma'am, it is for Miss Price. I am certain of its being Miss Price." And there was a half smile with the words which meant, "I do not think *you* would answer the purpose at all."

It is notable that such talk as there is about servants in the novels is mostly put into the mouths of the least admirable characters, as if Jane Austen anticipated the Victorian convention that "well-bred people do not discuss their servants." Besides Mrs. Norris and Mrs. Price, we have Lydia Bennet who went after dinner "to show her ring and boast of being married to Mrs. Hill and the two housemaids."

Mrs. Hill had attended Mrs. Bennet during the nervous spasms with which she marked her daughter's elopement with Wickham. Her family "left her to vent all her feelings on the housekeeper, who attended in the absence of her daughters," and though they

> were persuaded that there was no real occasion for such seclusion, they did not attempt to oppose it, for they knew that she had not prudence enough to hold her tongue before the servants, while they waited at table, and judged it better that *one* only of the household, and the one whom they could most trust, should comprehend all her fears and solicitude on the subject.

Mrs. Hill entered just in time to share her ultimate jubilations.

> " 'My dear Hill, have you heard the good news? Miss Lydia is going to be married; and you shall all have a bowl of punch to make merry at her wedding.' Mrs. Hill began instantly to express her joy. Elizabeth received her congratulations among the rest, and then, sick of this folly, took refuge in her own room."

Mrs. Elton is another character who shows no reluctance to talk about servants, and adds a special odious touch of her own in doing so. Jane Fairfax has got wet in going to the post to fetch her letters:

> "My dear Jane, what is this I hear?—going to the post-office in the rain!— This must not be, I assure you . . . there must be some arrangement made . . . the man who fetches our letters every morning (one of our men, I forget his name) shall inquire for yours too and bring them to you" . . . "Excuse me" said Jane earnestly, "I cannot by any means consent to such an arrangement, so needlessly troublesome to your servant. If the errand were not a pleasure to me, it could be done by my grandmamma's—"
> "Oh, my dear; but so much as Patty has to do!—and it is a kindness to employ our men."

No doubt in her more obscure Bristol days Miss Augusta Hawkins had not been used to servants, and even the comparatively modest establishment at Highbury Vicarage had gone to her head a little. Jane Fairfax provides another occasion for boasting—this time about her cook: "I should be extremely displeased if Wright were to send us up such a dinner as could make me regret having asked *more* than Jane Fairfax to partake of it." By the way, Wright's position in the Elton household is rather indeterminate, and I think that the confusion may be due not so much to her mistress as to her author. On this occasion she is obviously the cook, but at the ball at the "Crown," Mrs. Elton asks "how has Wright done my hair?" making her the lady's maid. It is not likely that the two offices should have been combined and I am wondering if here we have not another of those slips which rarely, very rarely, give other authors a feeling that in spite of all the rest they and Jane Austen are sisters under the skin.

Mrs. Elton reinforces her boasting of her own servants by sneering at those of other people. She observes that Mr. Knightley's servants are all "extremely awkward and remiss. I am sure I would not have such a creature as his Harry stand at our sideboard for any consideration. And as for Mrs. Hodges, Wright holds her very cheap indeed. She promised Wright a receipt and never sent it." Possibly Mrs. Elton still resented Mr. Knightley's very firm handling of her offer to organise his strawberry picnic. " 'Can I or my housekeeper be of any use to you with our opinion? Pray be sincere, Knightley. If you wish me to talk to Mrs. Hodges or to inspect anything'— 'I have not the least wish for it, I thank you.' 'Well —but if any difficulties should arise, my housekeeper is extremely clever.' 'I will answer for it that mine thinks herself full as clever, and would spurn anybody's assistance.' "

At Hartfield the servants are, needless to say, all the subjects of Mr. Woodhouse's affectionate solicitude. If James the coachman is to drive him half a mile to Randalls, compensation for his trouble must be found in the presence of his daughter as the Westons' housemaid. " 'You may be very sure,' says Emma, 'he will always like going to Randalls, because of his daughter being housemaid there. I only doubt whether he will ever take us anywhere else.' " Emma had perforce become an adept at such persuasions. Later on we hear her saying— " 'If [the ball] can be contrived to be at the Crown, papa, it will be very convenient for the horses. They will be so near their own stable.' 'So they will, my dear. That is a great thing. Not that James ever complains . . .' "

Mr. Woodhouse's fatherly care for James is equalled only by his filial trust in him. When he has been "talked into an aquiescence" of Emma's going to dinner at the Coles, he says, "We must let James know that the carriage will be wanted on Tuesday. I shall have no fears for you with him. We have never been there above once since the new approach was made; but still I have no doubt that James will take you there very safely."

Equally touching is his trust in his cook. A boiled egg may be safely offered to Mrs. Bates because "Serle understands boiling an egg better than anybody. I would not recommend an egg boiled by anybody else." Serle was to be trusted even with pork— "No stomach can stand roast pork . . . but very thoroughly boiled, just as Serle boils ours, and moderately partaken of, it is not unwholesome." Evidently Mr. Woodhouse believed in having his food well boiled, for Miss Bates tells the sad story of his sending away a "very delicate fricassee of sweetbread and asparagus, because it was not boiled enough." Even Serle, apparently, had nodded . . .

It is not to be expected that Jane Austen should give us any picture of those warm, friendly, interdependent relations between employers and their servants that other novelists have used to further both the plan and the human interest of their work. No Mrs. Honour shares the misfortunes of Catherine Morland, no Jeeves assists the wooing of Edmund Bertram with his great intellect. She would have said that the thoughts and speech of the "lower orders" were as far beyond her powers of reproduction as those of the house of Saxe Coburg and Gotha, which she had declined to touch even by royal command. But she was obviously aware that such cosy relationships existed, for, though never elaborated, they are suggested more than once.

There is clearly something of the sort between Mr. Knightley and William Larkins. We know that Mr. Knightley consulted William and deferred to his judgment, besides submitting to a sort of benevolent tyranny. When he promises Miss Bates another supply of apples, "for I have a great many more than I can ever use," he adds: "William Larkins let me keep a larger quantity than usual this year." Emma evidently realised the situation, for only a short time after Mr. Knightley had proposed, she cried: "Ah! there is one difficulty unprovided for. I am sure William Larkins will not like it. You must get his consent before you ask mine." William, on his side, delighted in his master's prosperity, even to the extent of being pleased to think that he had no apples left "to bake or boil . . . he was so pleased his master had sold so many; for William, you know"—it is Miss Bates speaking—"thinks more of his master's profit than anything."

We might have expected one or two of the numerous ladies' maids in the novels to be on similar terms with their mistresses. But we find only Mrs. Jennings taking "comfort in the gossip of her maid for the loss of her young companions," and on another occasion using her to satisfy her curiosity when Willoughby drives Marianne to Allenham. Apart from her we get none of those confidences which have so often made the lady's maid useful both in fiction and on the stage—only a hint of "flagrant indiscretion," when the elopement of Maria Rushworth and Henry Crawford is precipitated by circumstances that include "the maidservant of Mrs. Rushworth senior," who "threatened alarmingly."

To be without a personal maid was in those days and in those circles the exception. Even Jane and Elizabeth Bennet had some sort of a maid between them, for Mrs. Bennet, when she "ran into her daughters' room in her dressing-gown, with her hair half finished" to tell them Bingley had arrived, bids "Sarah come to Miss Bennet this moment and help her on with her gown. Never mind Miss Lizzy's hair." But though Darcy says "in a tone of gentleness and commiseration 'let me call your maid,'" when he finds Elizabeth shocked and shaken at the Lambton inn, I doubt if Sarah had accompanied her on that "tour of pleasure." She would have been wanted too much at Longbourn, to look after the other young ladies. It was, however, considered the proper thing that a lady's maid should travel with her mistress. Eleanor Tilney's maid occupied the middle seat of the chaise when the family moved from Bath, and we know that Dawson travelled with Lady Catherine de Bourgh, and did not "object to the barouche box."

Catherine Morland had no maid, or her journey home would not have been made at such a risk to safety and propriety. Nor did Marianne and Elinor Dashwood have anything in the nature of a personal attendant. Their modest household—four ladies living together on an income of five hundred a year—consisted of two maids and a man, which we hear is the same establishment as Jane Austen and her family maintained when they lived in Bath. That Mrs. Dashwood was the ideal mistress goes without saying, but is further attested by "the joy of the servants" when she and her family arrived at Barton, and by the easy chat with which Thomas makes known his experiences in Exeter.

Their manservant had been sent one morning to Exeter on business; and when, as he waited at table, he had satisfied the inquiries of his mistress as to the event of his errand, this was his voluntary communication: "'I suppose you know, ma'am, that Mr. Ferrars is married.'"

Nowhere else in the novels has a servant been allowed to state so much.

> Marianne . . . fell back in her chair in hysterics. Mrs. Dashwood . . . was shocked to perceive by Elinor's countenance how much she really suffered, and in a moment

> afterwards, alike distressed by Marianne's situation, knew not on which child to bestow her principal attention.
>
> The servant, who saw only that Miss Marianne was taken ill, had sense enough to call one of the maids, who, with Mrs. Dashwood's assistance, supported her into the other room. By that time Marianne was rather better, and her mother leaving her to the care of Margaret and the maid, returned to Elinor, who though still much disordered, had so far recovered the use of her reason and voice as to be just beginning an inquiry of Thomas as to the source of his information. Mrs. Dashwood immediately took all that trouble on herself.
>
> "Who told you that Mr. Ferrars was married, Thomas?"
>
> "I see Mr. Ferrars myself, ma'am, this morning in Exeter,"

and he gives an account of his meeting with Lucy Steele, in the course of which he did not really see Mr. Ferrars at all. Hence the heartbreak and confusion, which only the visits and explanation of Edward himself was to resolve into a happy ending.

Thomas is the only servant who is given more than a one-line part and even allowed a finger in the plot. The rest are at best only supers, at worst, little more than furniture. When Fanny welcomes William to Mansfield Park "the first minutes of exquisite feeling had no interruption and no witnesses, unless the servants chiefly occupied in opening the proper doors could be called such." We are indeed a long way from *Joseph Andrews* and *Humphrey Clinker*.

At Brambleton, at Branden, at Booby Hall, the servants were still "famuli," junior members of the family. In Jane Austen's time they had already become "servi," domestic workers who served the family but had no real part or lot in it. The mistress of the house no longer worked in her own kitchen at the head of her maids. When Mr. Collins asks Mrs. Bennet which of her daughters was responsible for the excellent dinner he had eaten—remember that he had not yet made his choice among them—she "assured him, with some asperity, that they were very well able to keep a good cook, and that her daughters had nothing to do with the kitchen"—involving him in an apology which lasted "about a quarter of an hour."

It would be hard to say to what exactly the change was due. Maybe, as I have already suggested, it was the emergence of a new class with a new form of snobbery. Maybe it was the beginning of class antagonism (as distinct from class consciousness) brought about by the French Revolution. Or maybe it was the first faint shadowing of nineteenth-century industrialism—the sketch, the adumbration of that Victorian machine-age, which was to sink the kitchen into the basement and make of domestic service a life "below stairs."

But it is certainly a fact that the attitude of employers and employed to one another changed at about this time and began to deteriorate. The deterioration has gone on till we have reached a point when if ever we see the old relations surviving we look upon them as we look on an ancient building—very pleasant and picturesque, but involving exhausting efforts in the way of upkeep. We for our part will return thankfully to the service flat and ring the bell for the waiter whose name we do not know.

CHAPTER XI

Walking-on Parts

I. SHEILA KAYE-SMITH

JANE AUSTEN'S novels being what they are—family novels, sociable novels, cosy novels—it is not surprising to find her stage closely packed with all sorts of characters besides the chief performers. She stands at the opposite extreme from such novelists as Emily Brontë, whose small caste is bounded by a wilderness. One would not expect the Earnshaws or the Heathcliffes to have friends and neighbours—their natures as well as their location are such as would keep most human beings at a distance. But it would be very surprising if the Bennets, the Woodhouses, the Elliots, and all the rest, living in their villages and playing their normal part in local life, did not have their circle of neighbouring families with whom they associate in varying degrees of intimacy.

Her stage bears no resemblance to that of the old-fashioned theatrical company, which would concentrate its talent on the chief parts and leave the rest to inferior and cheaper performers. Her genius brings all to life even with the smallest touch. To vary the simile, her plums are embedded in a rich paste, so that we are never tempted to emulate Jack Horner. We can eat the whole slice without putting in our thumbs, as even the greatest novelists have tempted us to do sometimes.

The ingredients of this paste vary in importance. In fact we had better change the simile again and call them a hierarchy. At the head, of course, are the minor characters who have speaking parts—Sir William Lucas, Mr. Allen, Mrs. Bates, Charles Hayter, Robert Ferrars, Dr. Grant, to mention only a few of these. Then follows our immediate concern—a large, indeed vast, cast of walking-on parts, varying in importance just as do the principal actors, but all—like Mrs. Bennet in a (for her) unique situation—"without uttering a syllable."

I can see these divided into three classes. First come those who though they have nothing to say, have nevertheless an important influence on the course of the story—for example, Admiral Crawford in *Mansfield Park* and Mr. and Mrs. Churchill in *Emma.* Next are those who, though the main stream of the novel could flow on without them, are responsible for certain incidents and situations. I mention Miss Bickerton in *Emma* and Dr. Shirley in *Persuasion.* Last comes a multitude of names, varying from those who are constantly on the lips of the speaking actors—such as Colonel and Mrs. Wallis, "My brother Mr. Suckling" and all the Maple Grove gang—to those who get no more than a mention or two, such as Mrs. Allen's friends the Skinners, Lady Catherine de Bourgh's "treasure," Miss Pope, the Lady Frasers, Lord Courtland, Mrs. Long, "my friend Sneyd" and hosts of others.

Admiral Crawford

Though he never speaks or appears, he is in a sense the origin of the whole story of *Mansfield Park,* for it was entirely owing to him that the Crawfords came to Mansfield Parsonage. If he had not behaved so outrageously when his wife died, choosing "instead of retaining his niece, to bring his mistress under his own roof," Mary would have almost certainly have settled down with him in London. Even in the circumstances she gave him "some months further trial" before seeking another home. She had no wish to leave London and live in the country.

One of the mysteries of *Mansfield Park*—and for me it has always been a sort of mystery novel—is the censure which Mary's reference to her uncle brings on her from Edmund and Fanny. Even assessing them both crudely and inaccurately as a precious pair of prigs, their condemnation seems excessive. We are told that Mrs. Crawford had "doted on the girl," and Admiral Crawford had treated his wife badly both before and after her death. Yet Mary is condemned for referring to him as "not the first favourite in the world." I can find no more violent expression than this in her account of the "improvements" at Twickenham. But "Edmund was sorry to hear Miss Crawford speak so freely of her uncle," and later on "felt grave" when she playfully announced "with an air of grandeur, 'we know very little of the inferior ranks . . . of various admirals I could tell you a great deal; of them and their flags and the gradation of their pay, and their bickerings and jealousies. . . . Certainly, my home at my uncle's brought me acquainted with a circle of admirals. Of *Rears* and *Vices*, I saw enough.' "

If Edmund had looked grave at the pun, he might be understood. But the cause of his gravity was the indecorum of her previous remarks.

> "Was there nothing in her conversation that struck you, Fanny, as not quite right?"
>
> "Oh, yes, she ought not to have spoken of her uncle as she did. I was quite astonished. . . ."
>
> "I thought you would be struck. It was very wrong—very indecorous."
>
> "And very ungrateful."

Really, Mr. Bertram and Miss Price, I am surprised at you, and you doubtless would be surprised at me because I can see nothing indecorous or ungrateful in Mary's remarks. A modern niece would not have expressed herself so mildly on an uncle like Admiral Crawford.

My own opinion of him is that he was a horrible old man, who ill-used his wife and abused her memory. Mary Crawford tells her brother "that if I could suppose the next Mrs. Crawford would have half the reason which my poor ill-used aunt had to abhor the very name, I would prevent the marriage if possible." Even Henry has nothing more definite to say in his uncle's favour than "he is a very good man and has been more than a father to me. Few fathers would have let me have my own way half so much." And while believing that "when Fanny is known to him he will dote upon her," he has to confess that "she is exactly the sort of woman he thinks does not exist in the world. She is the very impossibility he would describe—if indeed he has now delicacy of language enough to embody his own ideas." The Admiral, we have already been told "hated marriage, and thought it never pardonable in a young man of independent fortune."

It is true that he was the instrument of William Price's "making," but one is given to understand that this was owing to the persistence of a favourite nephew, for, says Mary "the admiral hates trouble and scorns asking favours." We may perhaps grant him the virtue of independence, and willingness to be of service at least to those he valued. No doubt Henry Crawford was a man after his own heart, largely because he himself had moulded him. I cannot see, however, that the ill-used Mrs. Crawford had done any better for her niece—indeed, of the brother and sister I find Henry much the more attractive. They were both alike in selfishness, insincerity, liveliness and charm. It is possible that they owed their failings no more than they owed their virtues to their uncle and aunt.

Mr. and Mrs. Churchill

Here we have another invisible source and fount from which a story springs. If Frank Churchill had lived at home with his father and met Jane Fairfax in the ordinary way there would have been none of the complex intrigue that makes the story of *Emma*. But, as we know, he was adopted as a very young child by the Churchills and brought up as their son, though with considerably less independence than a grown-up son usually enjoys. The easy, cheerful character inherited from his father would give him the pliancy normally associated with weakness. I never can be quite sure if he was really devoted to Mrs. Churchill—as devoted as his constant concern for and attendance on her would indicate—but there is no question but that she lavished on him the selfish, possessive love which spoils the mother and son relationship even where, as in this case, it does not naturally exist.

Mrs. Churchill is an enigmatic character. Because she uses her ill-health as a means of domination, everyone in Highbury (except of course Mr. Woodhouse) believes her not to be ill at all, or no more than ailing. It is her death that finally brings the conviction of her illness being something more than a string to hold her adopted son. Isabella Knightley is glad that she has no children of her own— "poor little creatures! how unhappy she would have made them." Mr. Weston compares her to the "dark gentleman," and though Emma and Mr. Knightley alternately argue that there must be something of choice in Frank Churchill's apparent subjection, that was before they knew the facts of the case. Most certainly she would not have tolerated his engagement to Jane Fairfax, or indeed, one surmises, to anybody else. She was the kind of woman who devours her young, and in this case is defeated only by the ingenuity of the young in question, reinforced by a marvellous stroke of luck. "Miss Woodhouse calls me the child of good fortune"—and his good fortune was Mrs. Churchill's death at exactly the right moment.

Mr. Churchill is the sort of man you would expect the husband of such a lady to be. Though he never emerges very clearly, we see his submission reflected in nearly every action of his wife's. The journeys, the changes, the invitations, the puttings-off, are all her doing. He follows her meekly, and unlike Frank has apparently never used the weapons of concealment and evasion. When she is dead he immediately, at his nephew's behest, allows what she would never have tolerated. Either his yielding to her was against his conscience and inclination, or he was a born yielder who would yield to anyone—or rather let us say, for Mr. Churchill appears to be an entirely estimable character, to anyone he loved and valued. One likes him enough to be pleased with the thought that his good offices towards Frank and Jane probably brought him comfort and peace in his last years, such as he can hardly have known as the husband of Mrs. Churchill.

Miss Bickerton

Here is an instance of a nonspeaking character who does not hold any main thread of the story, but is responsible for a single important incident. Miss Bickerton makes but one appearance, or rather disappearance, in the course of *Emma*. She, like Harriet Smith, was a parlour boarder at Mrs. Goddard's and accompanied her friend on that fateful walk which led to the episode of "Harriet and the gipsies." Miss Bickerton was not a lady of strong courage, and at the approach of nothing more alarming than a gipsy child "gave a great scream, ran up a steep bank, cleared a slight hedge at the top, and made the best of her way by a short cut back to Highbury." It is true that she called on Harriet to follow her, but when she was unable to do so Miss Bickerton did not go back or even wait for her. In her panic she was either unaware or did not care. She left her poor friend to be set upon by the main body of trampers and owe her deliverance to the timely appearance of Frank Churchill—with all the consequent misunderstandings and misrepresentations of "that dearest part of Emma, her fancy."

This is absolutely all we see or know of Miss Bickerton, except that she like Harriet had been at the ball—though unlike Harriet she does not appear to have suffered from cramp in consequence. She must have been a good runner, and let us hope she had plenty of wind, for it is a choice between her lungs and her heart. If she ran all the way home to Highbury without stopping she may never have known her friend was not following her, but if in a pause for breath she became aware of Harriet's absence and heard the sounds of her beleaguerment, then I have nothing to say for her and must join in Frank Churchill's indignation at her "abominable folly."

So Emma's plans for Harriet and Frank Churchill began to germinate— "there could be no harm in a scheme, a mere passive scheme. It was no more than a wish"—and were destroyed only in that dreadful interview with Harriet which showed how different Harriet's plans and schemes had been, and how she had encouraged them by "the blunders, the blindness of her own head and heart." It was through no wisdom of hers that Miss Bickerton was responsible only for a single incident in her story and not for its unhappy ending.

Dr. Shirley

Here we have no incident, even in fact no walking-on. Dr. Shirley is little more than a reference, an incentive to Henrietta Musgrove's matrimonial hopes and plans. But he interests me because he is one of Jane Austen's few really pleasant clergymen.

On the whole her clergy are not an attractive set. There is always Henry Tilney, of course, but he is so unlike a clergyman that except when he goes off to Woodston one forgets he is one; and Edmund Bertram, though obviously a favourite with his author, does little to recommend "the cloth" to her readers. Mr. Collins is no more than a figure of fun. If he had not been treated farcically we should have found him, as Elizabeth Bennet did, "a conceited, pompous, narrow-minded, silly man." Mr. Elton has nothing to recommend him personally but a "gentle" manner which disguises a great deal of pride and pretentiousness, and his deterioration after his marriage to a woman even deeper dyed in these than himself is exceedingly marked. Dr. Grant is "an indolent selfish *bon vivant* who must have his palate consulted in everything" and cannot get the better of "a disappointment about a green goose." Mr. Morland, it is true, is "a very respectable man," and Edward Ferrars is neither more nor less wooden after his shadowy ordination. But on the whole they are not an inspiring lot. One cannot see any one of them, even Edmund, becoming the father of his flock in the same way as Parson Adams or the Vicar of Wakefield.

But Dr. Shirley was evidently a faithful and beloved parish clergyman. For more than forty years he had been "zealously discharging the duties of his office" as Rector of Uppercross. He is thought of by the Musgroves and Hayters as "their dear Dr. Shirley" and "dear, good Dr. Shirley," and one of the advantages of Charles' becoming his curate is that he should "belong" to him. At the same time though there is not expected to be any difficulty, at his age, of "procuring a dispensation"—i.e. to retire to Lyme and appoint Charles Hayter to the curacy of Uppercross— Henrietta doubts "whether anything could persuade him to leave the parish. He is so very strict and scrupulous in his notions."

It was indeed unusual at that time for a clergyman to object to handing over his parish to a paid substitute. Nonresidence and plurality were common, and even Edmund Bertram, though he "had no thought" of the former, had not a soul above the latter. Dr. Shirley seems to have been exceptionally devoted to his cure of souls and Mrs. Shirley to have faithfully supported his labours— "Such excellent people," says Henrietta, "as Dr. and Mrs. Shirley, who have been doing good all their lives . . . Do not you think it is quite a mistaken point of conscience when a clergyman sacrifices his health for the sake of his duties, which may just as well be performed by another person?"—in fact, Charles Hayter.

After all this it is almost a disappointment to find that Henrietta's marriage had nothing to do with Charles' being appointed Dr. Shirley's curate, but was brought about by his being "applied to by a friend to hold a living for a youth who could not possibly claim it under many years"—another relic of bad custom which we feel would have outraged the good doctor's clerical conscience. But it is pleasant to think —and we hope it is true—that Dr. and Mrs. Shirley lived on, in consequence, for many years more in the place where they were so much loved. In spite of Henrietta's remarks I cannot believe that the duties of a Hanoverian clergyman were likely to bring him to the grave before his time.

Mrs. Younge

Mrs. Younge interests me because she is the only character in all the Jane Austen novels who may be said to belong to the underworld. Of course she does not start there—she makes a very good start as the governess and chaperone of Georgiana Darcy, "when an establishment was formed for her in London." But later on, at Ramsgate, the young woman's guardians, her brother and Colonel Fitzwilliam, soon found that in Mrs. Younge's character they "were most unhappily deceived," for she was nothing else but an old friend of George Wickham's, and gave her "connivance and aid" to his wicked designs on Miss Darcy. When these were discovered "Mrs. Younge was of course removed from her charge."

And serve her right, too. But though she is dropped for a time she does not fall out of the story. She reappears as the keeper of a low-class lodging house in Edward Street—I say "low class" because she was apparently willing to let rooms to couples without any fussy stipulations as to their being married. Wickham and Lydia went to her very naturally on their elopement, and it was only because all her rooms were let that she had to pass them on to another establishment. This sort of lodging house is more common in the novels of Fielding and Smollett and Richardson than in the novels of Miss Austen. In such a house poor Clarissa Harlowe anguished and was betrayed. Wickham and Lydia did not anguish at all —all the anguish was for Darcy, who had to extract from the despised and hated Mrs. Younge the fugitives' address. "It was two or three days before he could get from her what he wanted. She would not betray her trust, I suppose, without bribery and corruption." True Mrs. Gardiner writes to Elizabeth, and Elizabeth has the intelligence and feeling to realize how much it must have cost the proud Fitzwilliam Darcy to go hat in hand to beg and bribe a favour from the woman whom a short time ago he had sent away in disgrace.

Elizabeth's heart was already his, so I cannot give Mrs. Younge a place in the actual movement of the story. But it was the thought that he had stooped in supplication "to a woman whom he must abominate and despise" that helped her towards a faint hope that, in spite of other appearances, he still cared for her and might renew his addresses. It also added gratitude to an attachment from which it might otherwise have been lacking, and admiration for something more than his appearance and possessions— "For herself she was humbled; but she was proud of him—proud that in a cause of compassion and honour he had been able to get the better of himself."

All the Skinners

"And her kind compliments to all the Skinners." That is what Mrs. Allen would have liked to send by James Morland if only she had known he was going to Fullerton. Who were the Skinners? We know hardly anything about them except that they were the family whose presence in Bath would have made all the difference to Mrs. Allen, if only they had been there. "I wish we had a large acquaintance here," she says on that awkward, embarrassing occasion of Catherine's first visit to the Rooms. "I wish," says Catherine, ill at ease in the midst of strangers, "that we had *any*."

"Very true, my dear; and if we knew anybody we would join them directly. The Skinners were here last year. I wish they were here now."

On another occasion we hear that they had come on Dr. Skinner's account, and that is all we ever hear about them. Presumably Dr. Skinner was a clergyman, as the normal run of doctors in Jane Austen's day were not doctors of medicine but doctors of divinity. Presumably, too, he lived close to Fullerton, or Mrs. Allen would not have wished to send the family a message by James Morland. Perhaps he lived in Fullerton itself and was nonresident in his own parish. Or he may have retired altogether. We do not know. Nor do we know how many Skinners there were in "all." They exist on Mrs. Allen's lips only, and she is not much given to imparting reliable information. We can guess that they were an easy good-natured family, able at least to endure being on good terms with such a foolish lady—perhaps they were as foolish as she was, perhaps not. After all, Mr. Allen was a sensible man who put up with her very well, so perhaps the Skinners were sensible too. They may even have been intellectual, for Mrs. Allen had not even enough intelligence to feel uncomfortable with those who had very much more. It is Catherine, not she, who finds Henry Tilney "odd." To her, I think, all human beings are very much alike.

Aunt Norris' Guest

This is a character who deeply interests me, though she exists at two removes from reality—not in Jane Austen's imagination, but in the imagination of one of her characters. She—for though no name or sex is given I cannot conceive a "he" in this connection—is the guest for whom Mrs. Norris reserved her spare room at the White House, when she was expected to take charge of Fanny.

We know that she had firmly refused to have her at the start. After she had officiously arranged her arrival at Mansfield, it was not surprising that Lady Bertram should ask: "Where shall the child come to first, sister, to you or to us?" But, knowing our Mrs. Norris, we do not share Sir Thomas' surprise, when she claims "that it would be totally out of her power to take any personal charge of her . . . Poor Mr. Norris' indifferent state of health made it an impossibility: he could no more bear the noise of a child than he could fly."

But now Mr. Norris is no more, and Mrs. Norris has consoled herself for his loss by "considering that she could very well do without him." So it is natural that the family at the Park should expect her to be glad of Fanny's help and companionship in her new home. Everybody thinks so. Lady Bertram thinks so: "My sister always meant to take you when Mr. Norris died. But you must come and tack up my patterns all the same." Poor Fanny thinks so. "Something has happened and I do not like it at all. I am going to live entirely with my aunt Norris." Edmund thinks so. "Well, Fanny, and if the plan were not unpleasant to you, I should call it an excellent one."

But when Lady Bertram carelessly observes:

"I think, sister, we need not keep Miss Lee any longer, when Fanny goes to live with you."

Mrs. Norris almost started. "Live with me, dear Lady Bertram! What do you mean?"

She goes on to elaborate the subject:

"Here am I, a poor desolate widow, deprived of the best of husbands, my health gone in nursing him, my spirits still worse, all my peace in this world destroyed, with barely enough to support me in the rank of a gentlewoman . . . what possible comfort could I have in taking such a charge upon me as Fanny? If I could wish it for my own sake, I would not do so unjust a thing by the poor girl. She is in good hands and sure of doing well. I must struggle through my sorrows and difficulties as I can."

"Then you will not mind living by yourself quite alone?"

"Dear Lady Bertram, what am I fit for but solitude? Now and then I shall hope to have a friend in my little cottage (I shall always have a bed for a friend); but the most part of my future days will be spent in utter seclusion . . ."

This is the spare room's first appearance as a bulwark against invasion by Fanny, but its position is consolidated at the end of the conversation— " 'If Sir Thomas should ever speak again about my taking Fanny, you will be able to say that my health and spirits put it quite out of the question—besides that, I really should not have a bed to give her, for I must keep a spare room for a friend.' "

I wonder if anyone at Mansfield Park ever expected that friend to materialise. I do not think so. They would know that Mrs. Norris was not the sort of woman to have many friends, or to offer hospitality to them if she had. She was far too economical to entertain a visitor, because even if she brought them to all their meals at the Park, there would still be such expenses as fire and soap and candles.

Personally I imagine that Mrs. Norris had no friends in the strict sense of the word—only acquaintances formed during her long residence in the parish. Any of these that had left would quite naturally never want to see her again and would not have accepted her invitation even if she had given it. The others would still be close neighbours. She was not a woman without affections, of an enclosed, bitter sort, but these were all lavished on Sir Thomas' family as extensions of her own self-love. She was too busy, and spent too much time at the great house, ever to feel lonely, and a visitor would not only have been unnecessary but a terrible encumbrance.

Certainly we never hear of one coming or even being expected, and as soon as Mrs. Norris feels herself quite safe from Fanny, we hear nothing more about the spare room. The last mention is significant. Edmund has been vexed to find that Fanny has "the headache," as the result of dancing attendance on her aunts instead of taking her usual exercise on horseback (her horse having been given over to Mary Crawford's use). Mrs. Norris blames the headache on Fanny's labours in the rose garden, where she had been cutting the last of the season's roses. " 'Suppose,' " she says to Lady Bertram, " 'you let her have your aromatic vinegar. I always forget to have mine filled.' "

But Lady Bertram never lets her sister get away with quite all her nonsense, and tells her that "she has had it ever since she came from your house the second time."

"'What,'" cries Edmund . . . "'were these roses enough to oblige her to go twice?'"

"'No; but they were to be put into the spare room to dry; and unluckily Fanny forgot to lock the door of the room and bring away the key, so she was obliged to go again.'"

The spare room has become the storeroom and is kept safely under lock and key. And if ever a friend should wish to come—if "my poor dear sister Price" should long for an escape from family cares but feel afraid of the grandeurs of the Park—Mrs. Norris can now write and say that she has not got a spare room at all.

There is a story of St. Elizabeth of Hungary, who finding a little sick boy in the street brought him home and laid him in her own bed. Her unsympathetic husband demanded to see what she had brought in and hidden from him. Trembling and praying she opened the door of her room, dreading her husband's wrath and the casting out of the child. And there, in the middle of the bed, lay—a huge heap of roses. I hope my readers will not think me impious if I see an unworthy parallel in the story of Aunt Norris' Guest.

II. G. B. STERN

When we think of a character as a "nonspeaking" part, that is naturally not to say that they are dumb or even particularly shy or inhibited; simply that an author like Jane Austen, who creates a world of live people, must be limited in time and space to those whom she can actually follow round, pick up and reproduce with a minimum of effort the thoughts and acts and words of each one, that nothing may be lost; she has to select and discard; form and coherence suggest that some should be cast for leading rôles, and many more as supers, crowd parts, walking-on parts and one-liners.

Yet even these she presents so vividly and with such a happy touch, that we have only to remember, for instance, Mr. Robert Ferrars' friend, Lord Courtland, who (the former complacently relates) came to him the other day on purpose to ask his advice on building a cottage . . . when immediately our imaginations begin to play on the subject of Lord Courtland, who had never before appeared in *Sense and Sensibility* and does not appear again. What manner of lordling can this be who asks advice from Robert Ferrars, of all people? Can he be *compos mentis*? Always supposing that Robert Ferrars has not invented the whole episode, with Lord Courtland thrown in. But no; his mind is too enormously swollen with conceit to have room for the smallest inventive power. Therefore Lord Courtland *did* come to him and lay before him three different plans:

> I was to decide on the best of them. "My dear Courtland," said I, immediately throwing them all into the fire, "do not adopt either of them, but by all means build a cottage." And that, I fancy, will be the end of it.

A very young man, I dare say, might have been taken in by such dazzling self-confidence; a very young man and very silly, with far more money than was good for him. Nevertheless, I cannot think that even he could have been altogether pleased at seeing his expensive plans of Bonomi's go up in flames. After all, Bonomi was the best architect in London, and, dash it, the plans could not all three have been so utterly footling, so inexpert and unattractive as to deserve such high-handed treatment. Lord Courtland, timid of asserting himself, and accustomed to think highly of such a leader of fashion as Robert Ferrars—(a pair with Mr. John Thorpe in *Northanger Abbey*; both rattle on from an empty mind, both were overfull of their own praises)—would not have protested. "Oh, here, I say!" maybe, but nothing more. . . . I see him stroll away discontented, sucking his cane. Nevertheless he would not have gone again in a hurry to ask Robert Ferrars' advice: "All very well, but we are no further now than we were before; not so far, in fact, because I can't very well, can I, go back to Bonomi and tell them their plans have gone into the fire? All very well to say 'By all means build a cottage,' but deuce take it, I can't build it without a plan, can I?" And thus from a sense of injury, it might just begin to occur to his almost nonexistent mind that his elderly guardian had possibly been right in warning him that he could find a more sensible companion than an empty-headed coxcomb unable to have benefited by his education at Westminster nor at any other school, public or private.

. . . " 'And that, I fancy, will be the end of it,' " remarked Robert Ferrars.

Perhaps it was.

Mr. Wingfield

Mrs. John Knightley (Miss Isabella Woodhouse that was) put the greatest faith in her London apothecary, Mr. Wingfield. She had inherited a large share of her father's tendency to nervous hypochondria, and so she called in Mr. Wingfield pretty often to look at her family of four; Henry, John, Bella and little Emma (they are mentioned once as a family of five, but the fifth remains nameless, a little cipher of the nursery; we do not even know if it was a boy or a girl). In further likeness to her father, being of the same gentle, affectionate, and amiable disposition as he, her hypochondria also appeared rarely on her own behalf; for instance, she did not in the least fear (or said she did not fear) walking home after dining with the Westons through the snow in her evening slippers: "It is not the sort of thing that gives me cold"; for her one idea was not to be blocked up at Randalls while her children were at Hartfield. Fortunate for her that she had this same implicit trust in Mr. Wingfield as her father in Highbury's apothecary, Mr. Perry. Without these two professional supports, Mr. John Knightley and Emma must have been driven almost distracted in their attempts to allay the many fears of the two beings dependent on them for moral fortitude. But Isabella, before she married and removed from Hartfield, shared her father's complete confidence in Mr. Perry; so whenever she returned home to Brunswick Square from a visit to Hartfield, we surmise that Mr. Wingfield, immediately summoned, we may be sure, could not but notice in Mrs. Knightley many little stray anxieties that were not there before, tags and odds and ends of anonymous questions regarding the children's health. And not so anonymous neither: Mr. Wingfield would know well enough that it might be several weeks before Mr. Perry (or Mr. Perry mistranslated by Mr. Woodhouse) could be altogether worked out of his patient's system. He would have been very good about it, very tactful indeed; for had he been overbearing, or too roughly attempted to dispose of Mr. Perry as a mere country apothecary, Isabella would have taken fright at once.

"Mr. Wingfield, do you not think, perhaps, that you had better look at little Bella's throat without further delay?"

"Certainly, Mrs. Knightley. I am indeed sorry to hear that the air of Surrey has brought back her early weakness; she was so much better since we applied that embrocation. In fact, it had almost gone."

"Oh, but my dear Mr. Wingfield, you must not think . . . A most excellent embrocation, and she is not any worse for her visit, far from it. I have not heard her complain once of her throat. It is only—"

Mr. Wingfield waited with a grave air.

"It is only that my father, Mr. Woodhouse—"

"I trust," said Mr. Wingfield, "that Mr. Woodhouse himself is in good health?"

"Oh yes, I have rarely seen him better. Mr. Perry—you know our good Mr. Perry?—takes such care of him."

Mr. Wingfield still waited.

"My father," she faltered, "was a little afraid—the effects of the sea air at South End last autumn on little Bella's throat; particularly of the bathing; mud, you know."

The time had arrived for Mr. Wingfield's chivalry to help her out; expedience dictated that he should hide his annoyance: "But my dear Mrs. Knightley, I am ready to believe—I do believe that sea air could never have agreed with your father, as it does not with many people; or he could not have this, shall we say somewhat unreasonable prejudice. But for children, and particularly for your little girl, I should not have so strenuously recommended it had I had any doubts as to its efficacy. And look at the change that we have seen in her ever since. She needed bracing, and the air at South End is noted for its bracing qualities."

"I collect that Mr. Perry would have preferred Cromer. He holds it to be the best of all the sea bathing places. Mr. Perry told my father that it was fine open sea and very pure air."

"I have nothing against Cromer. I have not been there myself, but some of my own patients have benefited very considerably by Cromer. Nevertheless, the air at Cromer is in no way superior to the air at South End. And why travel a hundred and thirty miles when you can achieve equally good results by travelling only forty?"

"Yes, so my husband said. It is remarkable, how often Mr. John Knightley has said exactly that."

"My own brother and his family have stayed repeatedly at South End, and never found the least inconvenience from the mud."

"No, and I told my father— Only of course it is natural he should be a little— Perhaps I was foolish to mention it to him, but the cook we hired at South End—you remember I told you?—she could never be trusted to prepare us a basin of gruel—of nice smooth gruel, thin, but not too thin. I kept on ordering it, but I was never able to get anything even tolerable."

"We have no assurance," remarked Mr. Wingfield drily, concealing a desire to kick and scream and bellow with rage, "that a hired cook at Cromer would have understood the nature of gruel any better. Do I understand that you consulted Mr. Perry while you were at Hartfield?"

"Oh, no, no! There was no need at all; the children were perfectly healthy all the time. It is simply that my father always worries about us a little, living in London as we do. I continually assure him that you thought the vicinity of Brunswick Square so very airy, so different from almost all the rest; but you see he could not help noticing how pale with fatigue we all looked when we arrived."

"My dear Mrs. Knightley, I do not believe I have ever sent you off altogether in such good case."

"No, that is certainly true. I remember you said so; and if only I could have persuaded my husband to see you before he left home—"

"Has Mr. John Knightley been ill? Do you wish me to pay him a professional visit?"

Mr. Knightley's wife did not quite know whether to say yes or no; she certainly required reassurance, since her father had roused her alarms on the subject of her husband's appearance— ("Middling, my dear; I cannot compliment you. I think Mr. John Knightley very far from looking well")—but she knew also that the response to anything in the nature of coddling or overanxiety was likely to be more violent than polite. Mr. Woodhouse had pronounced with an air of omnipotence: "Nobody is healthy in London, nobody can be. . . ."

Her mind swung like a pendulum. She gazed helplessly at her own Mr. Wingfield. Was it her fancy, or was he looking a little grim?

Mr. Campbell

Jane Austen speaks of Mr. Campbell, the surgeon on the "Thrush," as "a very well behaved young man." She did not tell us more, but that can only have been because *Mansfield Park* was not, strictly speaking, a chronicle of the emotions which surged up in the breast of Mr. Campbell at his first and last sight of Fanny Price, just arrived in her father's home, when he came to call for his friend William.

He had, of course, heard much from William, since the latter was recently appointed the sloop's second lieutenant, of this favourite sister who had been brought up so far away from her small crowded shabby little home in Portsmouth: how beautiful she was, and how elegant and delicate; how she had profited by the amenities of Mansfield Park, her mind improved, her dancing beyond comparison, her riding —well, perhaps her riding was not quite to be mentioned in the same breath as her other accomplishments. And then she had such a pretty soft voice, and was knocked up so easily (could anything be more refined?), and in short, William was persuaded that his new friend had only to see Fanny—

Privately, Mr. Campbell had not the slightest desire to see Fanny; these die-away young ladies with extravagant notions of what was due to them from their uncle's position in the county, were not at all to his fancy; he preferred a gypsy complexion, and moreover a gypsy with spirit, who would not have minded coming to sea with him had he been mysteriously able to change his profession and be given a commission in a ship. Besides, though he could find nothing amiss with William, who was to be his companion in the "Thrush" when they sailed, William must be exceptional from what Mr. Campbell could see of the rest of the Price family at Portsmouth: Mr. Price, a retired marine without education, fortune or connections, appeared to him as a coarse fellow, a bore, a blusterer, dirty and gross, expecting you to laugh at his jokes when in good truth there was no laughter and no point in them beyond a general conviction that they should not have been made, especially in front of ladies. What a father-in-law! Mr. Campbell shuddered; then wondered why he should take an interest in Mr. Price in that capacity, for

William had asserted that his sister was not ever likely to be home except perhaps for a brief visit when she was the wife of one Henry Crawford of Everingham, a rich gentleman of leisure. Not that they were actually betrothed, laughed William; but Henry Crawford, to whose good offices he owed his commission, and with it his present happiness, was so in love with Fanny that he could not forbear telling Fanny's brother of his intentions, even though he had not yet spoken of them to Fanny herself.

Aloud, Mr. Campbell civilly wished them happy. Privately he did not suppose this unknown Henry Crawford would have much joy of his future relations-in-law; of Mr. Price with his oaths and drunken habits; of Mrs. Price, as bad a manager of a home as he had ever encountered; of all those ill-mannered, hallooing boys, and little Betsey, whining and spoilt. He congratulated William on his sister's prospects of being so respectably settled, and thought no more of the matter.

—Until now, when he beheld her, drooping a little from the journey, pale with fatigue, a creature from another world.

Neither Mr. nor Mrs. Price had seen fit to inform the young surgeon that after ten days' leave at Mansfield, William was bringing his sister back with him for a visit to Portsmouth. Perhaps they had forgotten. Had he been prepared, he might not have blushed so deep nor bowed so clumsily when she rose for her curtsey. Above all—oh fool! fool!—would he have badgered them over and over again, to be sure that William would be ready, absolutely ready to return with him immediately he called? Impressing on all of them the urgency of leaving at six, now that the "Thrush" had slipped her moorings and was out of harbour three days before they had even thought of it:

"And Mr. Campbell was here at four o'clock to ask for you; he has got one of the Thrush's boats, and is going off to her at six. . . ."

"Campbell has been here, quite in a worry about you."

"Sharp is the word, you see! By G— you are just in time! The doctor has been here enquiring for you; he has got one of the boats, and is to be off for Spithead by six, so you had better go with him."

Six? It was almost six now. Let the "Thrush" wait at Spithead for them, no matter if they had their orders to sail westward the very next day, or eastward to the Texel— Suddenly it occurred to Mr. Campbell that if only Captain Walsh were right in thinking they would cruise to the westward, he might contrive to see this beautiful girl again, for the prevailing wind would not allow them to sail.

However, all that now mattered was to extricate himself from the odious necessity of a hurried and immediate departure. There they were, bustling round with the tea things, fidgeting over William's uniform, only too anxious that Mr. Campbell should not be kept waiting, when all he asked was endlessly to wait and sit gazing at Fanny. With an effort at composure, he addressed himself to her particularly (disregarding Mr. Price's attempt to make him join in a lewd joke about unmarried daughters and what surprises were in store for them); in a low voice charged with emotion, he asked her whether she ever walked on the ramparts at Portsmouth?—or if he came ashore within the next few days, as of course he would at every single opportunity— Yes, of course William too, naturally; he and William ("as fine a lieutenant as we have ever had in the "Thrush," I do assure you, Miss Price") took all their walks on the ramparts, always did, always would; at least, there had not been much time in the last ten days—but certainly walking on the ramparts was his—was William's, was his—was their favourite recreation when on leave; and if Miss Price and her sister Miss Susan required an arm—if Miss Price required an arm—both or either—if he could have the honour of attending them, she could see Spithead from the ramparts; the air was generally said to be very fine up there.

"Do you," he enquired very earnestly, "do you care for sea-air?"

. . . Lingering was of no avail; they had to go. Mr. Price, Mrs. Price, William, Susan, Sam, Tom, Charles and Betsey all combined to remind him of his known determination to be off on the boat by six. They parted him from Fanny, they hustled him away, they formed a bodyguard round him. The three boys were determined to see their brother and Mr. Campbell to the sally-port. Not one moment alone with her; he could barely press her hand and look into her eyes.

It was not until they were in the boat that he remembered Henry Crawford; remembered that not an hour ago he had actually wished him happy in his suit.

Miss Nash

. . . The collecting and transcribing all the riddles of every sort that she could meet with into a thin quarto of hot-pressed paper, made up by her friend, and ornamented with ciphers and trophies . . . In this age of literature, such collections on a very grand scale are not uncommon. Miss Nash, head teacher at Mrs. Goddard's, had written out at least three hundred.

Miss Nash (head teacher at Mrs. Goddard's) actually only speaks once in her own person, as far as I can remember; hardly that, indeed; she is quoted by Harriet repeating school gossip about Mr. Elton, the new clergyman at Highbury. Yet scattered through the pages of *Emma,* we collect a good deal of interesting information about Miss Nash, and I am not sure that I altogether approve of Mrs. Goddard's choice. Can it be that I am right in summing up Miss Nash as rather a foolish woman, a snob and a sentimentalist, a lover of tittle-tattle? These are not accusations that can be made without solemnly going into the evidence. Let us listen first to Harriet Smith; revelations from an innocent mind like hers, with no thought of being ill-natured, are always the most valuable.

Harriet is babbling, of course, of Mr. Elton:

"I think Mrs. Goddard would be very much surprized if she knew what had happened. I am sure Miss Nash would; for Miss Nash thinks her own sister very well married, and it is only a linen-draper."

"One should be sorry to see greater pride or refinement in the teacher of a school, Harriet."

(Now what could Emma possibly mean by that? Really!)

"I dare say Miss Nash would envy you such an opportunity as this of being married. Even this conquest would appear valuable in her eyes. As to anything superior for you, I suppose she is quite in the dark."

Poor Miss Nash, and poor teachers of all schools at that period, so carelessly relegated to their proper and humble sphere, below that of a linen-draper's wife, and "even" Harriet's conquest of a mere farmer valuable in their eyes. We must deal gently with Miss Nash and her collection on a grand scale of at least three hundred riddles . . . and not even whisper a suggestion that she might have been wasting her time and setting an idiot example to her pupils of how Serious Literature should be pursued.

Anyhow, the real clue to Miss Nash does not lie in any riddle book; it lies in her estimate of Mr. Elton:

Miss Nash has put down all the texts he has ever preached from since he came to Highbury. Dear me! When I look back to the first time I saw him! How little did I think!

(And indeed, Harriet, how little!)

"The two Abbotts and I ran into the front room and peeped through the blind when we heard he was going by, and Miss Nash came and scolded us away, and stayed to look through herself; however, she called me back presently, and let me look too, which was very good-natured. And how beautiful we thought he looked."

Of what was Miss Nash thinking when she put down all those texts? Not, we may be sure, of the texts as she put them down. She called Harriet to peep at him through the blind of the school, because Harriet had lately been promoted a parlour boarder and as such had certain privileges, while the two little Abbotts were no such thing. Miss Nash, being only human, finds it more fun to peep and sigh together (where no definite rivalry is in question) than to peep and sigh alone:

"Is he not beautiful?"

"Yes, indeed. I vow I have never seen anyone so beautiful and such a gentleman. Everybody looks up to him. His company is so sought after that he need not eat a single meal by himself if he does not choose to. He has more invitations than there are days in the week."

"That does not surprise me. To be sure, everyone at Highbury would be glad."

"And such a mine of information as well as such elegant manners. You know, Miss Smith, that Elizabeth Martin's mother was so kind as to send Mrs. Goddard a very fine goose a little while back—"

"Oh yes, I know. It was I who brought it back to school after I was staying with Elizabeth for two months. They were very happy months." Harriet blushed at her memories of Abbey Mill Farm.

"—Mrs. Goddard had it dressed on a Sunday, and asked the three of us, Miss Prince and Miss Richardson and me, to sup with her. But young Mr. Martin, the son, cannot be compared with Mr. Elton."

"Oh no, he cannot be compared with Mr. Elton."

"Nobody can be compared with Mr. Elton."

"Oh no, nobody at all."

Miss Nash, we cannot doubt it, was painfully infatuated with Mr. Elton. His very furnishings had glamour ("There," said Harriet, walking along Vicarage Lane with Emma, "there are the yellow curtains that Miss Nash admires so much.") She cannot keep off the subject, and we collect from Harriet's innocent manner of presenting to Emma items of gossip about this prince among men, that Miss Nash somehow contrived that all Highbury with whom she came in contact should immediately, nobody knows how, abandon topics of ordinary interest and yield up the latest news of Mr. Elton: Mr. Perry went to Mrs. Goddard's to visit a sick pupil, and he himself told Miss Nash that he had met Mr. Elton the day before, returning from Clayton Park— And so on, through the whole bewitching anecdote (bewitching, that is, to Harriet, and vicariously so to Emma, the Matchmaker) of Mr. Elton's being on his way to London—

> the bearer of something exceedingly precious. Mr. Perry could not quite understand him, but he was very sure that there must be a *lady* in the case and he told him so; and Mr. Elton only looked very conscious and smiling, and rode off in great spirits. Miss Nash had told her all this, and had talked a great deal more about Mr. Elton, and said, looking so very significantly at her, "that she did not pretend to understand what his business might be, but she only knew that any woman whom Mr. Elton could prefer she should think the luckiest woman in the world; for, beyond a doubt, Mr. Elton had not his equal for beauty or agreeableness."

Was Miss Nash already jealous of Harriet, instinct warning her that all this fresh pink and gold might soon find its way from Mrs. Goddard's school to the Vicarage? Did she have to hurt herself by encouraging (unconscious assistant to Emma) this illusion in Harriet? We cannot tell, for I am afraid that after Mr. Elton marries his Augusta, we never hear of Miss Nash again.

Captain Brigden

"Brigden stares to see anybody with me but my wife."

Can it be that Captain Brigden has not got a very nice mind? Will he make a tale of it all over Bath, that he has seen Admiral Croft walking along Milsom Street arm in arm with a pretty young woman—"and not so very young neither, twenty-seven if she's a day; and he too wrapped up in her to stop and talk to me; just 'How d'ye do' as they passed. Wait, I remember; heard it from Admiral Brand's brother: Mrs. Croft is tied by the leg, with a large blister on one of her heels. Ha! here's a fine chance for him to spread a little more canvas and get away from her for once in his life. I've never known a man so dependent; the only woman on board most times; stayed with him on every foreign station; conversant with all his business; drives his gig whenever she can put her hand on the reins. And it doesn't do, y'know, it doesn't do. They kick over the traces. I wonder at it that this is the first time. A sad lack of complexion— I can't bear these weather-beaten ladies. In fifteen years of their marriage I do assure you she only let him leave her one winter at Deal; aye, Deal. Otherwise, we all remarked on it, it was Mrs. Croft here and Mrs. Croft there; crossing the Atlantic, the East Indies and back again, Bermuda, the Bahamas. A woman has no *right* on board a man-of-war but the Admiral was too afraid of her to put his foot down. Pitiful. Pitiful."

Mr. Hurst

Towards Mr. Hurst (who had married the elder Miss Bingley and came to stay with his brother-in-law at Netherfield at that vital moment when Darcy first meets Elizabeth) our chief emotion is profound sympathy for him as a visitor for whom nobody cares to put himself out. From the hour Elizabeth arrived at Netherfield to nurse her sister Jane through a putrid feverish cold, all interest was lifted away from his favourite subjects, and he suffered acute neglect:

> Miss Bingley was engrossed by Mr. Darcy, her sister scarcely less so; and as for Mr. Hurst, by whom Elizabeth sat, he was an indolent man, who lived only to eat, drink, and play at cards,—who, when he found her prefer a plain dish to a ragout, had nothing to say to her.

Surely Elizabeth might have dissembled a little? She was not usually lacking in invention: "Tell me, Mr. Hurst," she could have said, raising up her fine eyes admiringly towards him, "tell me of the different ragouts you have eaten, and where, and with what variety of flavourings? And I will do my utmost to remember what you say, that I may repeat it all to my mother when I return to Longbourn; for I do assure you that when it comes to cooking a ragout, our Mrs. Hunt is sadly inferior, and I cannot get my mother to pay the matter the attention she should. Venison Mrs. Hunt can roast to a turn, and her partridges, it must be acknowledged, are always remarkably well done, but ragout—no."

We are informed several times that Mr. Hurst in himself was not a striking personality, and needed drawing out: "His brother-in-law, Mr. Hurst, merely looked the gentleman," and on Elizabeth's appearance, after her three-mile walk across fields in dirty weather: "Mr. Darcy said very little, and Mr. Hurst nothing at all . . . The latter was thinking only of his breakfast." He and Elizabeth were decidedly not affinities on the subject of the cooking department; but worse was to come: On entering the drawing-room, she found the whole party at loo . . . Mr. Hurst looked at her with astonishment: "Do you prefer reading to cards?" said he; "that is rather singular."

Elizabeth's presence in the room proved a distraction from the card table. Mr. Bingley, his sisters and Mr. Darcy could not refrain, whilst they were playing, from talking about books; I almost said from chattering about books, but really that is a word not to be allied with any dialogue in which Darcy takes part. Via Miss Bingley's sycophantic enquiries, the conversation swung over to Darcy's sister Georgiana and her accomplishments in general; one might almost say that an evening that was to have been devoted to cards, had become a *Conversazione*—"when Mr. Hurst called them to order, with bitter complaints of their inattention to what was going forward."

My sympathies are entirely with Mr. Hurst. After all, talk is talk and cards are cards; why try to spoil both by mingling them? And for all the deference they paid to his tastes and preferences, he might have been enjoying ragouts and loo in London where (as we have already been told) "he was a man of more fashion than fortune." Elizabeth Bennet's intrusion into the Netherfield intimate circle was completely spoiling his visit, but who cared about that? Who had the politeness to remark: "But Mr. Hurst is not interested in libraries"? Or "Mr. Hurst cannot bear aimless discussion; he is a man of very few interests, and those are highly concentrated and should be awarded the consideration they deserve"?

And on the very next evening: "the loo table did not appear." Ominous sentence. We are certain that Mr. Hurst enjoyed loo more than piquet, yet Elizabeth entered and found him and Bingley at piquet, with Mrs. Hurst observing their game, and Miss Bingley sitting by Darcy to make comments as he wrote his letters. When these were finally written, accompanied by a deal of irrelevant argument in which all joined (except Mr. Hurst, who had more sense), Mr. Darcy asked for music. Mrs. Hurst sang and Miss Bingley played, and nobody questioned Mr. Hurst on whether *he* cared for music? Of which, as these were the only two performers, he had probably had a sufficiency in his own home. Really, I am at a loss to understand every person's total lack of manners where he in particular was concerned; nobody else suffered. Almost it amounted to persecution.

We now approach a crisis: on the next evening, when to Bingley's delight Jane Bennet is able to make her first appearance in the drawing-room after dinner: "Mr. Hurst also made her a slight bow, and said he was 'very glad'; but diffuseness and warmth remained for Bingley's salutation . . ."

However, nobody could expect Mr. Hurst to say more than that he was "very glad"; probably he had some apprehensions of what was still to come:

When tea was over, Mr. Hurst reminded his sister-in-law of the card table; but in vain. She had obtained private intelligence that Mr. Darcy did not wish for cards, and Mr. Hurst soon found even his open petition rejected. She assured him that no-one intended to play, and the silence of the whole party seemed to justify her. Mr. Hurst had, therefore, nothing to do but to stretch himself on one of the sofas and go to sleep.

You would think that criminal negligence could go no further, but you would be mistaken; there is always the final martyrdom:

"Do let us have a little music," cried Miss Bingley, tired of a conversation in which she had no share.— "Louisa, you will not mind my waking Mr. Hurst?"

Her sister made not the smallest objection.

(Again the italics are mine!)

CHAPTER XII

Personal Appearance

SHEILA KAYE-SMITH

I DO not know how it happened and I certainly do not know why. I only know that it did, though the memory now is like the memory of a dream which at each recall adds to itself a skin of waking thought. I was sitting by the fire reading *Northanger Abbey*. The room was not dark, but neither was it brightly lit, for I had switched off the tall standard lamps and kept alight only the small lamp on the wireless cabinet and the one on the bookcase beside me, that shone upon my book.

I had begun by listening to *Northanger Abbey* on the radio, but had switched off after about ten minutes and picked up the book instead. I am always shy of adaptations of Jane Austen's work, whether for the stage or the screen or the wireless. I have so often found them intimidating with archness and quaintness that I look out for those defects from the beginning and probably find them whether they are there or not. They generally are. What is there about Jane Austen that goads her admirers—for presumably none but an admirer would attempt the work—to "guy" her scenes and characters, often angling—sometimes with inserted dialogue—for laughs *at* rather than with the author?

I do not know and it does not concern us now, for I was reading—not listening—when I looked up and noticed something queer about the shadows. They seemed to be thickening on the low settee which stands between the two lamps and should therefore have been shadowless. I rubbed my eyes, thinking the fault must be in them, but the shadows were still there and seemed to be growing denser. Then I saw that there was colour in them—the colours of the room, as if these were reflected in a curious way. I put down my book and gazed. I had no feeling of alarm, only of surprise and interest. Then even these vanished as the colours acquired an outline. I saw the outline of a woman on the settee. She was flat, like a silhouette, and a little misty, so that it was possible dimly to see the cushions through her. Somehow I took for granted who it was, and watched with detached interest while the cloudiness thickened into opacity and the outline became stereoscopic. Jane Austen was sitting opposite me.

For some moments neither of us spoke. I did not even know that she *could* speak, and at first I was afraid she would vanish away before I had absorbed her appearance entirely. I was naturally curious to see how she looked and what she wore. But I soon realised that I was not going to learn much about her that way. Her face was exactly the face of the portrait in Emma Austen—Leigh's *Jane Austen and Steventon*—even the angle was the same—and the author herself had told me that the family had never considered it a good likeness. It was a pretty face, all the same. The hair curled prettily round it and the complexion was a warm rosy brown—such as I might have expected from descriptions I had read. Her clothes were equally disappointing to my curiosity, for to appear in them she had obviously been driven to make use of what was already in the room. The colours were the colours of walls and furniture—green and rust, with touches of cream and brown—while the material had a vague and makeshift look, as if she had searched in vain for the fine India muslin she would have considered proper wear for the occasion.

I thought it best to speak.

"I'm deeply honoured by this visit. I never expected such a thing."

It certainly was difficult to account for. Surely it could

not be the broadcast that had materialised her, for she had ignored *Emma* and *Pride and Prejudice* when they were on the program. Nor could it be the book that I was reading, for I had read it countless times before. Could it be possibly the book that I was writing? Did she know I was writing a book about her and come to help me, or even to stop me? But in that case why had she come like this when I was alone? It was not so long ago that G. B. Stern had been with me here and she could have tackled us both together, had she wished to tackle us.

Her voice broke suddenly into the futility of these questions.

"Good evening, ma'am. You seem very comfortable here. This is a charming room. I hope you like your book."

She spoke with the broad slow vowels of the older people in these parts, and I remembered that she was a south-country woman and had lived in the days when the local accent warmed the speech of all classes.

"I like it very much."

I held out the title page towards her: "*Northanger Abbey* by Jane Austen."

She looked at it and then at me.

"That is strange indeed—for I am the author."

I bowed my acknowledgements, and she immediately continued: "But I have never seen it printed, or I should not have allowed my name to appear. It should have been like the others 'by the author of *Pride and Prejudice*.' "

"It's too late now to object to your name being known."

"But I am surprised that my brother should have allowed it. For it must have been he who had it published. I myself had put it aside, finding it obsolete. It must be thirteen years at least since it was written and sold to Crosby. Had it been published then I should not have felt doubtful of it, but though it was advertised it did not appear, and he would not allow it to be sent elsewhere or return me the manuscript."

"And was his name Richard?"

"Richard Crosby. Are you acquainted with him?"

"No, I'm not. But here's a sentence from the first page of your book: 'Her father was a very respectable man, though his name was Richard.' Did that phrase creep in during revision?"

She smiled without answering, showing a very pretty dimple near her mouth—the first thing I saw about her which was not the reflection of something I knew. Then she said: "My brother most kindly purchased the copyright for me two or three years ago. I rewrote much of it, but could not make of it what I wished."

"You've made it what countless readers enjoy. I think we may all be glad you didn't rewrite it entirely."

"But Mrs. Radcliffe's novels are no longer read. Parts of it must seem forced and unnatural."

I was beginning to say that nothing was further from the case, when she interrupted me with:

"My eyes are not accustomed to this light. Your working candles must be of an amazingly fine quality."

I had noticed that she was shading her eyes with her hand, and immediately, without thinking, switched off the lamp nearest her. She looked startled.

"How did you that? Did you snuff them all?"

"I switched off the light. We don't use candles now."

Then realising that she had no conception whatever of the time between us, I added:

"Since you rewrote this book nearly a hundred and fifty years have gone by."

She seemed more pleased than surprised.

"Indeed. And it is still read? This is not the one I should have chosen for such a long life; nevertheless I am delighted."

"Excuse me, but *all* your books are read. And not only read, but turned into plays and films and broadcasts."

She looked puzzled.

"Films and broadcasts—what are those?"

I tried to explain.

"Reproductions similar to plays, but in another medium—one is seen and the other heard."

"How is that?"

It was my turn to look puzzled. I felt quite unequal to explaining the cinema and the radio to a visitor who had never seen a camera and probably knew nothing about electricity except that it was a certain curious property of amber. Then I remembered the broadcast of *Northanger Abbey*.

"I can't show you a film. But there's a broadcast of *Northanger Abbey* going on at this very moment."

I rose and crossed the room to the wireless set and switched it on. There was a faint whisper of music. Then the voice of Catherine Morland came on the air.

"I have only just learned to love a hyacinth."

And Henry Tilney asked:

"How might you learn? By accident or argument?"

The creator of them both looked surprised—even alarmed.

"What is that?—a musical box?"

"Well—er . . ." I hesitated. I had sometimes as a sort of private entertainment played with the idea of showing the wonders of our civilisation to Jane Austen, to picturing her amazement at the differences between the world in which her books were written and the world in which they are still being read. But now it had come to the point, I felt myself unequal both in words and knowledge to the task.

"I suppose," I evaded weakly—"you might call it that, though this isn't a musical box in quite the same way as you knew them in your time."

"Indeed, no, for never in my time did I hear of one that played the human voice. They played instrumental music only. Also never did I know one that gave so long a performance as this." I switched off. "That was very cleverly done. I am amazed to think how much your age must have added to the comforts and pleasures that I knew. Pray tell me what sort of carriage does a gentleman now keep? Towards the end of my day the lighter kind was coming more and more into use. But I dare say it was not a fashion that could last, for in a barouche or a curricle you have never enough room for a family."

Never again would I picture myself explaining the wonders of science. As far as I was concerned now, the car was a carriage, just as the wireless was a musical box.

"I suppose our carriages are more comfortable and better sprung than those you drove about in. But don't let us talk about carriages. I want to ask you about your novels."

"My novels! You seem to set greater store by them than readers in my own day. What can I tell you about my novels?"

"You can tell me which is your favourite. Everyone will want to know that."

She mused.

" 'Tis hard to say. I liked each one best as I wrote it."

"Then perhaps you can tell me which is your favourite heroine?"

She smiled.

"That is easier, but I doubt if I can point to one only. I dearly love Elizabeth Bennet and I also have a very warm regard for Emma Woodhouse."

"I think Elizabeth would be a popular choice today, but I doubt if many care as much for Emma."

"I am not surprised, for she is a young woman I expected no one to like but myself."

"Personally I like her best of all, but I think that many readers find her too headstrong and also too much of a snob."

"A snob! How can a young lady be a snob?"

I had forgotten the changes that the nineteenth century had brought into our language.

"With us a snob no longer means a shoemaker, but someone who's overanxious about social rank. Some readers think that Emma was a little too—too—exclusive and superior."

"Whereas I tried to show how she erred in allowing flattery to make her oblivious of rank. Evidently I have failed in that part of my endeavour. But it is something that I have succeeded where I expected to fail—in making at least one of my readers like her. Pray, tell me, ma'am, how do you like my Fanny? What does your public think of my Fanny, the heroine of *Mansfield Park*?"

"Well—er—"

"I love my little Fanny and had hoped to find others the same. I may not have been altogether successful in bringing her before the reader as I see her myself, but to me she is a sweet little thing—and not only sweet but good."

"To tell you the truth, we—this generation—find her a little *too* good."

"Too good! How can that be?"

"Too good, perhaps, for *us*."

"That is surprising. One would expect each age to increase in goodness, so that what is good in one becomes only tolerable in the next. For your age my Fanny should not have been good enough."

I felt unequal to pursuing this argument, so remarked instead:

"Some of our modern readers would put Anne Elliot first of all the heroines."

"Anne Elliot!— Now that is truly surprising, for I will confess that I found her a little too good for *me*. I did not know the book was published, but I dare say it was my brother's doing like the other. So Miss Anne is a favourite!—your readers do not think her too good—they think that only of my poor little Fanny. But, pray, ma'am, do they not think her rather too old to be a heroine?"

"Twenty-seven is not old by our reckoning. Many heroines in our present-day novels are over thirty."

"That certainly surprises me. It shows, however, that there is no longer any prejudice against second marriages. In my day a novel would not have been read if the heroine had ever contemplated a second marriage."

Whereas, I might have said, we would allow her even a

third. But I was determined to keep the conversation out of the present.

"Anne Elliot isn't as young as some of your heroines," I continued, "but she has a most engaging personality. And the way you tell her story—"

I stopped and looked at her. Dared I ask if there was a shadow of autobiography in that story? I myself did not believe that Jane Austen's romance was to be found in *Persuasion,* but here was a fine chance of clearing up the matter. Certainly if anyone were to hear about this interview I should never be forgiven if I had not asked the question. Yet there was something about her that held me off. Though I knew her novels almost by heart, she was still personally a stranger. So far there had been nothing intimate in our conversation. We were a lady and her visitor, and one does not ask a visitor paying her first call if she has ever been in love. I compromised by reaching out an arm and taking a book off the shelf.

"Here's a poem about you. It was written by Rudyard Kipling, one of our most famous poets. May I read it to you?"

She seemed almost artlessly gratified.

"Read it most certainly, ma'am, if you will. A poem—and about me . . . you have raised my curiosity."

And I hope, thought I, you will satisfy mine. I began to read:

> Jane went to Paradise
>   That was only fair.
> Good Sir Walter let her in
>   And armed her up the stair.

She interrupted me, and I noticed that she did not seem pleased.

"But that is wrong. It was *I* who let *him* in."

"I'm sorry. He must have muddled his dates. I hope that won't spoil your enjoyment of the poem as a whole. This is how it goes on. . . ." But as I read I saw the shadow of displeasure growing on her face. It had become a cloud by the time "Jane answered 'love'."

> In a private limbo
> Where none had thought to look
> Sat a Hampshire gentleman
> Reading of a book.
> It was called *Persuasion*
> And it told the plain
> Story of the love between
> Him and Jane.

Then once more she interrupted me, and this time she looked really angry.

"Pray read no more. Who is this Mr. Kipling?—and by whose leave does he call me *Jane*?"

I was speechless, for I had not expected her anger to spring from this source.

"Jane, indeed!"—and it might have been Frank Churchill rebuking Mrs. Elton. I blushed, and murmured something about poetic license.

"My name has certainly helped him to more than one rhyme. But you will excuse me, I hope, if I say there seems to be more license than poetry in all this. Who is this Mr. Kipling that he should write of me so impertinently? You observe that I allow myself no liberties with *his* name."

I noticed with concern that both her voice and outline had become blurred, as if her indignation were affecting the conditions of manifestation. I was terrified that she was going to leave me. I could not let her go while I knew no more about her than before she appeared.

"Please don't be offended," I begged her. "Please don't go." I remembered the interest I had checked at the beginning of our conversation— "Let me tell you more about these times."

"I had rather you told me more about this Mr. Kipling. Can he be one of your leading poets?"

"He has a reputation for rugged rather than polished verse, and this poem belongs to his latter period. When he died he was over seventy."

"Ah—" I noted with relief a ring of satisfaction in her voice—"he is no longer with you?"

"No, he died about twelve years ago."

"That is well, then. I myself can deal with him. Pray excuse me, ma'am."

And she was gone.

Where she had sat was only a vague prismatic outline, and in a moment that too had vanished. I stared in consternation. She had left me—she was gone—gone to deal with Rudyard Kipling—gone to teach him not to call her Jane . . .

"Miss Austen, please . . ."

But there was nothing I could do or say to call her back. Only on the air—or only perhaps in my ear—was a faint quiver of sound— "Jane, indeed!"

I had driven her away—through a vain itch to satisfy my curiosity and maintain decorum at the same time. I had done neither, because in observing my own ideas of decorum I had forgotten hers. And now she was gone. On the sofa was only an empty pool of light. She had left nothing to prove that she had ever made this personal appearance—no physical trace that might be preserved, no new piece of information that might be tested. No one would ever believe that I had seen Jane Austen. I was not even quite sure of it myself.

Towards a Jane Austen Calendar

PRIDE AND PREJUDICE

"It is a truth universally acknowledged, that a single man in possession of a good fortune must be in want of a wife."

"In nine cases out of ten, a woman had better show more affection than she feels."

"It is better to know as little as possible of the defects of the person with whom you are to pass your life."

"People themselves alter so much that there is something new to be observed in them for ever."

"I have often observed that resignation is never so perfect as when the blessing denied begins to lose somewhat of its value in our eyes."

"It makes me very nervous and poorly to be thwarted so in my own family, and to have neighbours who think of themselves before anybody else. However, your coming just at this time is the greatest of comforts, and I am very glad to hear what you tell us of long sleeves."

"What are men to rocks and mountains."

"Lady Catherine is far from requiring that elegance of dress in us which becomes herself and her daughter. I could advise you merely to put on whatever of your clothes is superior to the rest."

"Though this great lady was not on the commission of the peace for the county, she was a most active magistrate in her own parish, the minutest concerns of which were carried to her by Mr. Collins; and whenever any of the cottagers were disposed to be quarrelsome, discontented, or too poor, she sallied forth into the village to settle their differences, silence their complaints, and scold them into harmony and plenty."

"They were of course all intending to be surprised, but their astonishment was beyond their expectations."

"I have not a doubt of your doing very well together. Your tempers are by no means unlike. You are each of you so complying that nothing will ever be resolved on; so easy, that every servant will cheat you; and so generous that you will always exceed your income."

SENSE AND SENSIBILITY

"Many young men, who had chambers in the Temple, made a very good appearance in the first circles, and drove about town in very knowing gigs."

"A young man of eighteen is not in general so earnestly bent on being busy as to resist the solicitations of his friends to do nothing."

"To be together was, in his opinion, to be intimate."

"The pain of being parted from friends will be felt by everybody at times, whatever be their education or state. Know your own happiness."

"The business of self-command she settled very easily;—with strong affections it was impossible, with calm ones it would have no merit."

"His temper might perhaps be a little soured by finding, like many others of his sex, that through some unaccountable bias in favour of beauty, he was the husband of a very silly woman."

"Mr. Palmer is always going about the country canvassing against the election. . . . Poor fellow! it is very fatiguing to him; for he is forced to make everybody like him."

"Resigned herself to the idea of it with all the philosophy of a well-bred woman, contenting herself with merely giving her husband a gentle reprimand on the subject five or six times every day."

"A fond mother, though in pursuit of praise for her children the most rapacious of human beings, is likewise the most credulous; her demands are exorbitant; but she will swallow anything."

"Oh! dear! one never thinks of married men's being beaux—they have something else to do."

"Self-interest alone could induce a woman to keep a man to an engagement of which she seemed so thoroughly aware that he was weary."

"The due celebration of that festival which requires a more than ordinary share of private balls and large dinners to proclaim its importance."

"To a man whose prevailing anxiety was the dread of being alone, the acquisition of two to the number of inhabitants in London was something."

"She was not a woman of many words; for, unlike people in general, she proportioned them to the number of her ideas."

"No temper could be more cheerful than hers, or possess, in a greater degree, that sanguine expectation of happiness which is happiness itself."

"Eleanor agreed to it all, for she did not think he deserved the compliment of a rational opposition."

Northanger Abbey

"That little boys and girls should be tormented is what no one at all acquainted with human nature in a civilised state can deny."

"A taste for flowers is always desirable in your sex, as a means of getting you out of doors and tempting you to more frequent exercise than you would otherwise like."

"I am come, young ladies, in a very moralising strain, to observe that our pleasures in this world are always to be paid for, and that we often purchase them at a great disadvantage, giving ready-monied, actual happiness for a draft on the future that may not be honoured."

"Her youth, civil manners, and liberal pay, procured her all the attention that a traveller like herself could require."

"It is always good for young people to be put upon exhorting themselves."

"Wherever you are, you should always be contented, but especially at home, because there you must spend the most of your time."

"I consider a country-dance as an emblem of marriage. Fidelity and complaisance are the principle duties of both."

"Modesty, and all that, is very well in its way, but really a little common honesty is sometimes quite as becoming."

"Mrs. Allen was one of that numerous class of females, whose society can raise no other emotion than surprise at there being any man in the world who could like them well enough to marry them."

EMMA

"Till I have outlived all my affections, a post office, I think, must always have the power to draw me out."

"Young ladies are delicate plants. They should take care of their health and their complexion."

"With all the right of being principal talker, which a day spent anywhere from home confers."

"To be the favourite and intimate of a man who had so many intimates and confidants was not the very first distinction in the scale of vanity."

"General benevolence, but not general friendship, made a man what he ought to be."

"Those pleasantest feelings of our nature—eager curiosity, and warm prepossession."

"It is always incomprehensible to a man that a woman should ever refuse an offer of marriage."

"Real, thorough sweetness of temper and manner, a very humble opinion of herself, and a great readiness to be pleased with other people. I am very much mistaken if your sex in general would not think such beauty and such temper the highest claims a woman could possess."

"Vanity working on a weak head produces every sort of mischief. Nothing so easy as for a young lady to raise her expectations too high."

"It is poverty only which makes celibacy contemptible to a generous public."

"She . . . had no romantic expectations of extraordinary virtue from those for whom education had done so little."

Mansfield Park

"Their vanity was in such good order, that they seemed to be quite free from it, and gave themselves no airs."

"He has been ill ever since he did not eat any of the pheasant today. He fancied it tough, sent away his plate, and has been suffering ever since."

Persuasion

"Personal size and mental sorrow have certainly no necessary proportions. A large bulky figure has as good a right to be in deep affliction as the most graceful set of limbs in the world."

"An agreeable manner may set off handsome features, but can never alter plain ones."

"She was convinced of sailors having more worth and warmth than any other set of men in England; that they only knew how to live, and they only deserved to be respected and loved."

"She thought it was the misfortune of poetry to be seldom safely enjoyed by those who enjoyed it completely; and that the strong feelings which alone could estimate it truly were the very feelings which ought to taste it but sparingly."

"Nor could she help fearing . . . like many other great moralists and preachers, she had been eloquent on a point in which her own conduct would ill bear examination."

"As to the universal felicity and advantage of firmness of character . . . like all other qualities of the mind, it should have its proportions and limits. . . . A persuadable temper might sometimes be as much in favour of happiness as a very resolute character."

"Everybody has their taste in noises as well as in other matters; and sounds are quite innoxious or most distressing, by their sort rather than their quantity."

"The notions of a young man of one or two and twenty as to what is necessary in manners to make him quite the thing, are more absurd, I believe, than those of any other set of beings in the world. The folly of the means they often employ is only to be equalled by the folly of what they have in view."

"My idea of good company . . . is the company of clever, well-informed people, who have a great deal of conversation; that is what I call good company."

" 'You are mistaken . . . that is not good company; that is the best.' "

"That elasticity of mind, that disposition to be comforted, that power of turning readily from evil to good, and of finding employment which carried her out of herself, which was from nature alone. It was the choicest gift of Heaven."

"Everybody's heart is open, you know, when they have recently escaped from severe pain, or are recovering the blessing of health."

"She could so much more depend upon the sincerity of those who sometimes looked or said a careless or a hasty thing, than of those whose presence of mind never varied, whose tongue never slipped."

"The elegant stupidity of private parties."

"One does not love a place the less for having suffered in it."

"He is so very much occupied by the idea of *not* being in love with her, that I should not wonder if it were to end in his being so at last."

"One man's ways may be as good as another's, but we all like our own best."

(We are sure our readers will like to choose the other three hundred for themselves.)